WITHDRAWN

Interdisciplinary perspectives on modern history

Editors
Robert Fogel and Stephan Thernstrom

The congressman's Civil War

The congressman's Civil War

ALLAN G. BOGUE

University of Wisconsin

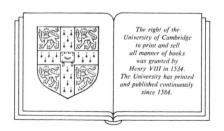

The right of the
University of Cambridge
to print and sell
all manner of books
was granted by
Henry VIII in 1534.
The University has printed
and published continuously
since 1584.

CAMBRIDGE UNIVERSITY PRESS

Cambridge
New York   New Rochelle   Melbourne   Sydney

Published by the Press Syndicate of the University of Cambridge
The Pitt Building, Trumpington Street, Cambridge CB2 1RP
32 East 57th Street, New York, NY 10022, USA
10 Stamford Road, Oakleigh, Melbourne 3166, Australia

© Cambridge University Press 1989

First published 1989

Printed in the United States of America

Library of Congress Cataloging-in-Publication Data
Bogue, Allan G.
The congressman's Civil War
Allan G. Bogue.
    p.   cm. – (Interdisciplinary perspectives on modern history)
Bibliography: p.
Includes index.
ISBN 0-521-35405-6.   ISBN 0-521-35705-5 (pbk.)
1. United States.   Congress.   House – History – 19th century.
2. United States – Politics and government – Civil War, 1861–1865.
I. Title.   II. Series.
JK1323 1861
328.73'09 – dc19   88–26001
                                                                              CIP

British Library Cataloging in Publication applied for

ISBN 0 521 35405 6 hard covers
ISBN 0 521 35705 5 paperback

TO THE SPECIALISTS IN AMERICAN HISTORY IN THE
DEPARTMENT OF HISTORY OF CORNELL UNIVERSITY
BOTH PAST AND PRESENT

historians who have been uniquely successful in
blending tradition and innovation

Contents

Acknowledgments

We never succeed in acknowledging our debts to all of those who have contributed to the making of a manuscript. But I must acknowledge the assistance of some. Had it not been for the decision of the specialists in American history at Cornell University to invite me to give the Becker Lectures there, I might never have undertaken this particular venture. Of that group of fine scholars, Joel H. Silbey particularly helped me to articulate the direction that the lecture series would take. I owe thanks to the National Endowment for the Humanities and to the Andrew W. Mellon Foundation for providing fellowships that enabled me to devote full time to this research during the academic year 1985–86, as well as to the Research Committee of the Graduate School and to the College of Letters and Sciences of the University of Wisconsin/Madison for helpful supplementary grants. This assistance enabled me to accept the kind invitation of the Center for Advanced Study in the Behavioral Sciences at Stanford University to spend the year in a truly facilitative and inspiring intellectual setting in the company of several other scholars who are deeply interested in the history of the United States Congress. Gardner Lindzey, Director of the Center, and Associate Director Robert A. Scott were unfailingly kind and supportive; one could have no better hosts.

Special thanks must go also to my immediate colleagues at the Center. More than anyone else, Nelson W. Polsby generated the idea of organizing a working group to study the federal legislative process in historical perspective, and once it was assembled, he graciously introduced the other members to Bay culture. He, David W. Brady, and Joel H. Silbey were provoking in the most constructive sense of the word. I thank as well all those who gathered on Thursday afternoons for the weekly seminar on the U.S. Congress and others who joined the midday walkers on the hills above the Stanford University campus under the indefatigable leadership of Lance E. Davis.

Perhaps the greatest privilege enjoyed by the American historians at the University of Wisconsin is the pleasure of doing research in the magnificent library research collections, and of these the crowning glory is the Library and Archives of the State Historical Society of Wisconsin. Of the many helpful staff members there, I owe particular thanks to Ellen Burke, Gerald R. Eggleston, John A. Peters, Wilma E. Thompson, and Lloyd F. Velicer. At different stages of this research, Rebecca S. Williams and Brian Q. Cannon served as my project assistants, and Monys Hagen and Kathleen M. Brown provided me with exemplary help at an early stage. As usual, I am deeply indebted to Margaret Beattie Bogue, who is always willing to discuss my research with me, although she is involved in an exhausting professional career of her own.

Introduction

After the initial gratification at being invited to present a lecture series honoring a distinguished historian has subsided, a difficult question usually remains. What should the topic be? While working on a study of the Republican senators of the Civil War period, I was recurrently surprised at the number of important questions about the role of the United States Congress in that great conflict that either gave promise of rewarding further research or, indeed, had not been answered at all. The legislative history of the House of Representatives appeared to be particularly unclear. This is not, of course, meant to diminish the worth of that substantial and often distinguished body of scholarly research that several generations of historians of the Civil War have accumulated. But the members of each generation of scholars bring a different sense of what is interesting and important to their tasks. Perhaps an effort to view the war through the eyes of the members of the House of Representatives would be rewarding? I decided to try to find out by devoting the Carl Becker Lectures at Cornell University in April 1986 to an exploration of several themes in the history of the U.S. Congress during the Civil War and the years immediately preceding it.

Most Americans know something about the history of the Civil War. Few social studies or history teachers in the public schools either can or wish to avoid treating so dramatic and fateful a struggle. Immigrants to this country must be prepared to answer questions about it during naturalization proceedings. College students are sure to encounter Abraham Lincoln, Ulysses S. Grant, and Robert E. Lee if they enroll in the United States History survey course. But the full story of the Civil War is a very involved one, because the great conflict influenced almost every aspect of the economic, social, and political processes of both the Union and the Confederacy and was, in turn, affected by the nature of the contrasting societies. And if we all know something of the Civil War, its duration, magnitude, and complexity

ensure that even the most learned of scholars will never know everything about it.

The war forced the governments and people of both the North and
the South to mount a mighty mobilization of armed forces on both
land and sea, to recruit men, mules, and horses, to buy and build
ships, to contract with brokers and manufacturers for great supplies
of clothing, ordnance, and food. The suppliers, in turn, mobilized
the labor, capital, and plant necessary if they were to meet their
commitments to the federal governments. Such activity could only
be successful if appropriate fiscal and monetary policies were developed. And once the armies and naval cadres were mustered in, and
properly armed, clothed, and provisioned, courageous and wise leaders had to be found to lead them to victory. No less courageous and
even wiser leaders had to emerge to direct the national governments
and lead the effort, on the one hand, to save and purify the Union
and, on the other, to assert successfully a rebellious section's claim
to national identity. Although such men of necessity found their major
challenge in evoking the patriotic energies of their countrymen, they
had on occasion to look outward as well; the neutrality, and preferably
sympathy and active support, of Great Britain and the nations of
continental Europe might be as great a prize as a strategic victory of
arms.

Our concern here is with the Union, the loyal states of the North
and the border regions. Although some, like ex-Governor Joseph A.
Wright of Indiana, urged that political party and factional animosity
be set aside for the duration of the war, this was not to be.[1] Ostensibly
eleven southern states had raised a new national standard because a
northern sectional party, united in its opposition to the further extension of slavery, had succeeded in electing Abraham Lincoln to the
presidency in 1860. The new president and the Republican party
assumed the responsibility of putting down the armies of the rebellious states, reestablishing the old boundaries of the Union, and bringing state and national political institutions into accord with the
enlightened conscience of the age. Lincoln's followers, however, were
by no means united in their views on public policy in general or the
national crisis in particular. The national political parties had been
undergoing realignment at least since 1854, when the remaining un-
organized regions of the Louisiana Purchase were in theory opened
to the possibility of slavery under the popular-sovereignty provisions
of the Kansas-Nebraska Act. Supporters of Lincoln's candidacy in
1860 had once been Whigs, or Free Soil Democrats, members of the
nativist American party, or supporters of assorted other state-level
transitional parties. Undoubtedly the seventeen planks in the national

Republican party platform of 1860 held different meanings for the many party supporters, and such differences would modify the behavior of both Republican legislators and officeholders after the new administration was organized and the representatives and senators met in the first session of the Thirty-seventh Congress on July 4, 1861.

The members of the Democratic party, on the other hand, were also divided in counsel as they, in effect, asked themselves, What are the appropriate policies and measures of a legitimate opposition party during a national crisis? The dilemma of the members of the congressional delegations from the border states was even more harrowing as they struggled to represent the best interests of their constituencies while rival armies recruited their sons and while old friends, brothers, and cousins from the Confederacy called upon them to forsake their allegiance and follow the Bonnie Blue Flag. The war crisis would test both the political beliefs and the mettle of every citizen of the Union from the president to the most humble of voters. Some historians argue that we should view the party realignment of the 1850s as continuing throughout the war, and there is much to be said for that point of view.

None understood the heterogeneous nature of the Republican party more clearly than did Abraham Lincoln, its titular leader. He was a master politician, and from the organization of his administration to his death, he used the massive political patronage under his control with calculating skill. By placing his most important rivals for the presidential nomination in the cabinet, Lincoln recognized major blocs within the party, and innumerable less notable appointees reflected the same principle of selection. Such skillful political maneuvering provided Lincoln with a sounding board of party constituency opinion, but the cabinet was never a harmonious instrument, and in this respect it truly reflected the Republican party both in Congress and in the national electorate. Throughout the war the Republicans remained divided in opinion and decidedly factious in behavior. Still, the members of the cabinet were all in their way able men – even the much criticized Simon Cameron – and it was mainly with their assistance that Lincoln used his executive powers to begin mobilization of the Union during the first several months of his administration. Before Congress assembled, Lincoln had on occasion suspended the writ of habeas corpus, proclaimed a blockade of the southern coastline, made the decision to supply Fort Sumter, called armed forces into the field, and through his secretaries of war and the navy begun a great effort to purchase or contract for the ordnance, army livestock, and vessels needed for a major war effort.

When Congress met in emergency session in early July 1861, a new phase of the civilian's war began. Now the legislative branch had to become involved, validate Lincoln's executive actions, and provide a legislative foundation for the war effort. The members of this first session of the Thirty-seventh Congress pledged themselves to consider only the measures necessary to sustain the war effort, and although the efforts of some to spur the army into immediate action and of others to investigate the loyalty of government employees revealed some flexibility of definition, by and large they honored their intent. After recessing on August 6, many of them hurried home to assist in the recruiting of volunteer regiments.

When Congress reassembled in early December 1861, the Republican members were free to apply their minds not only to the problems of the war and its legislative ramifications but also to the enactment of the free soil agenda contained in the national party platform of 1860 – the exclusion of slavery from the territories, the passage of a protective tariff, a homestead law, a Pacific railroad act, and other pledges. If the congressional Republicans could agree among themselves on appropriate measures, they had the necessary votes to send them to the president – about two-thirds of the sitting senators were Republicans, and a *New York Tribune-Almanac* count identified 106 Republican members of the House of Representatives, 42 Democrats, and 28 Unionists, mainly from the border states. The Unionists might be expected to vote with the Democrats on some issues. From this position of strength the Republicans were able to write their platform pledges into law in impressive fashion. But the opportunities the war provided for attacking southern institutions – particularly slavery – precipitated disagreement both within the legislature and between the legislative and executive branches. It was mostly in consideration of such matters that contemporaries defined Republicans as radical, moderate, or conservative – a distinction that clarifies much of the continuing disagreement between congressional colleagues and between Lincoln and members of the House and Senate.

Basically the war crisis provided two distinct foci for controversial congressional activity – first, the drafting and discussion of legislation that affected or would affect southern practice and social structure and, second, the exercise of congressional oversight over the direction of the army and other executive functions. In the first category during the last two sessions of the Thirty-seventh Congress fell, among others, the act providing for emancipation in the District of Columbia; the confiscation law of 1862 directing the seizure of the property of rebels and the freeing of their slaves; the 1862 Act amendatory to the Militia Act, containing provisions authorizing the enrollment (and consequent freeing) of black Americans in the armed forces; and the bill providing assistance for emancipation in Missouri. During the Thirty-eighth Congress, the Wade-Davis reconstruction bill, repeal of the fugitive slave acts, creation of the Freedmen's Bureau, and the resolution that would become the Thirteenth Amendment would be somewhat similar in nature and effect.

Issues of oversight might range from informal efforts of congressmen to effect changes in executive policy or staff by personal contact with the president, through simple requests on the floor for information, to the constitution of investigative committees – the most famous, of course, being the Joint Committee on the Conduct of the War. The formal constitution of a committee of inquiry was almost by definition indicative of dissatisfaction with some aspect of executive activity. Senatorial reservations about President Lincoln's decision to remove the flamboyant and careless John Charles Frémont from his western military command played a large part, for example, in the congressional decision to establish the Committee on the Conduct of the War. Meanwhile America's deadliest modern war ground on, and Lincoln's patient but frustrating effort to identify effective generals and to decide on the appropriate disposition of armed forces inspired congressional kibitzers both to question the abilities of the president and to press upon him the qualifications of their military protégés.

The congressional elections of 1862 provided the Republicans with little comfort. The Democrats regained seats in various northern states, particularly those of the Midwest. Although the final totals were less depressing than initially feared, the *New York Tribune-Almanac* recorded the election of no fewer than 75 Democrats in the House, 33 more than in the preceding Congress. The recruitment of 16 Republicans from the border states gave the Republicans 102 seats, but could such men be counted upon to stand firm beside the northern members of the party? Had Lincoln's preliminary Emancipation Proclamation of September 1862 been too mild a commitment to all-out war, as radicals within his party believed, or had it repelled a significant number of voters, as some moderates feared? The new political arithmetic accounts in part for legislative achievements in the second of the Civil War congresses that were more modest than those of the first, though redeemed in part by the great achievement of approving the Thirteenth Amendment. Involved in this result as well was the climax of the effort on the part of Republican radicals to discredit the Lincoln administration and to place a radical in the White House. Then as now, when president making became of major interest in Congress, legislative achievement diminished. When the second of the Civil War congresses ended and Lincoln died, complete agreement on the civil and political future of the South and its people was still unachieved.

Interpreting the Civil War has provided the ultimate challenge to American historians, and they have risen to that challenge by the legion – in numbers sufficient at times, some believe, to set the nation's historiography somewhat out of balance. As a multitude of historians during the last generation have developed the "new histories," such fears have become unjustified; perhaps, indeed, the balance has tipped a bit in the other direction. But one suspects that whatever era of historical writing we consider, some aspects of the Civil War have tended to receive more attention than others. Few have suffered utter neglect, but the generals, the president, and his cabinet secretaries appear to have won the war of words. The results seem somehow symbolized in a passage from Stephen Vincent Benét's epic poem of the Civil War, *John Brown's Body*, in which he reported that Fighting Joe Hooker once demanded, "Who ever saw a dead cavalryman?" but never, despite his sharp tongue, found it necessary to inquire, "Who ever saw a dead congressman?"[2] Politicians simply were not worth bothering about.

Of the hundreds of men who served in the House of Representatives or the Senate during the Civil War, only a handful appear typically in connection with that service in the indexes of college-level textbook accounts of the Civil War. And yet without a full understanding of the contributions of Congress we simply do not understand the history of the Union's war. The *Federalist* author wrote, "The great security against a gradual concentration of the several powers in the same department, consists in giving to those who administer each department the necessary constitutional means and personal motives to resist encroachments of the others. . . . Ambition must be made to counteract ambition."[3] And indeed, during the Civil War it did. There is more new light to be shed on the course and outcome of the Civil War in further study of Congress and its members than in perhaps any other aspect of the great struggle.

I can, of course, make no claim to being one of the forerunners in examining congressional events and the men who contributed to them during the Civil War. But there has been a tendency for historians to approach Congress along a small number of well-trodden paths. Some have looked up Pennsylvania Avenue from the White House. They have seen the congressmen largely through Lincoln's eyes or those of members of his cabinet. Political biographers have traced a few of the several hundred Civil War congressmen through their experiences in the wartime congresses, their eyes fixed primarily on their subjects and concerned with legislative processes only insofar as these involved them. Other historians have examined the development of particular wartime policies or laws, or categories of legislation. And during the last generation, still others have used quantitative techniques of roll call analysis to map the voting behavior of the members of the Senate and the House in ways that allow us to place the floor behavior of individuals in better perspective and to delineate accurately partisan and factional behavior. In sum, these efforts represent a considerable contribution to our knowledge of Congress during the Civil War.

Historians have shown less interest in putting the various approaches together and in developing broader conceptions of how the congressional machinery actually worked during the war years. Social scientists argue that most of a congressman's energy is devoted to activity off the floor; but historians have not, in general, paid much attention to such obligations during the Civil War, although there are some striking exceptions to this generalization. Nor have historians much considered the ways in which Civil War congressmen used, adapted, or altered the institutional machinery of Congress to fulfill personal, factional, and party agendas. So-called institutional approaches and history have not been popular for some time, but there is again a growing understanding that institutional imperatives and context play an important part in shaping political ambitions, plans, and outcomes. The chapters that follow are written from this perspective.

Chapter 1 uses the personal histories of the members of a special, yet typical group to examine the career lines of the politicians who served in Congress during the years 1844–65. These were the eighty-three representatives and senators who died while serving during this span of two decades and were therefore eulogized by their colleagues, who have provided us with a unique set of sources – analyses of the personalities and careers of congressmen prepared by their associates. Based in part on various bodies of quantitative data and in part on documentary and interpretive materials, this chapter surveys the personal and political training of federal representatives, notes the elements that seem to have contributed to successful careers, and provides a typology of electoral candidates. Finally it deals with the question of whether there were differences between the southern and northern political systems so crucial that they contributed materially to the outbreak of the Civil War.

Chapter 2 is an effort to reverse the usual view of Congress from the Executive Mansion and to consider what the congressman hoped to gain from his relations with the president patronage and executive intervention in the furtherance of personal objectives – and Abraham

Lincoln's methods of dealing with such desires on the part of his friends in Congress. We are concerned here also with the president's role as a legislative agenda setter and enunciator of ideology, as well as with the question of whether or not Lincoln followed Whig prescriptions on the appropriate relations between the executive and legislative branches.

In Chapter 3 we examine an important aspect of off-the-floor congressional activity during the Civil War, the investigative-oversight function. A number of scholars have studied the Joint Committee on the Conduct of the War, but historians have placed less emphasis on the fact that there was much other congressional investigative activity under way at the same time relating to disloyalty, contracting, and many other issues. Here I examine the inquiries developed during the Thirty-seventh Congress by one of the standing committees, Judiciary, and the efforts of its members to investigate press censorship, the Democratic congressman Benjamin Wood, and other subjects. Also considered are the investigative activities of an illustrative selection of special, or select, committees. I shall argue that the activity of such committees of inquiry, both select and standing, influenced the war effort, brought changes in the institutional structures of the government, and played an important role in the partisan and factional conflicts in Congress. In line with my emphasis on developing the perspectives of the individual congressman, I shall consider the opportunities that the committees of inquiry presented both for career advancement and for defending and repairing reputations.

Chapter 4 deals with the authority patterns in the House of Representatives during the Civil War. Our central question is simply, Who provided the internal leadership in the House of Representatives during the Civil War? I describe the selection of the Speakers of the House and assess their contributions, and I discuss the chairman of the Ways and Means Committee, Thaddeus Stevens, and evaluate his style and degree of success. Then the standing committees are examined and their chairmen and their changing membership. Turning from these formal structures of leadership, I search for evidence of leadership and the exercise of authority in the Republican Party Caucus. In conclusion I relate scaling evidence to the subject of Republican leadership in the House and argue that no one individual or faction was able to establish firm control of the congressional agendas during the Civil War.

This is by no means a definitive study. It is, instead, a reconnaissance, an effort to investigate the possibility that a somewhat different research perspective – a view from Capitol Hill rather than from the

White House – and an emphasis on the individual lawmaker, his personal objectives and institutional constraints, will contribute to a better understanding of the great national trauma of the 1860s. Within such a perspective, many other questions can appropriately be asked: What was the full range of relationships between the representative and his constituency, and how did the Civil War affect them? What did service on representative standing committees involve? How effective was Republican floor leadership, and how was the individual representative affected by it? Both the value systems and the party ideologies that the congressmen of the period brought to their work as representatives need further explication. How did the representative use and contribute to party ideology – to what degree was it motivating force and in what measure forensic weapon? To what extent did the influence of party define, constrain, or enhance the congressman's personal strategies of advancement? And so one could go on at length, describing an arena of research that I hope many scholars will help to develop still further in the future.

1   *The paths of power: congressional career lines and the coming of war*

During the 1850s, sectional stress fatally weakened the political structure that the Founding Fathers had so skillfully crafted some seven
decades before. One eminent historian has used the word "disruption" to describe the fate of the dominant political party of the 1850s;
another described the political leaders of that decade as a blundering
generation.[1] When Abraham Lincoln, the presidential candidate of
the Republican party, won election in 1860 despite the fact that he
obtained no electoral votes from below the Mason-Dixon line, most
southern states seceded from the Union and formed the Confederacy.
Efforts to compromise the sectional differences between North and
South failed, and four years of internecine warfare followed. Finally
the South capitulated; 620,000 soldiers had lost their lives; even more
carried physical or psychic scars to their graves; slavery, which had
been the major institutional distinction between the North and South,
was ended – a great accomplishment – although the realities of racial
distinction and discrimination would persist, even to today. The Civil
War was the greatest trauma the American nation has ever suffered,
and quite naturally historians have found the struggle and its political
prelude to be subjects of keen and continuing interest.

    The political history of the American middle period is complex, and
scholars in search of greater understanding may bring many different
perspectives to it. Political careers and the various institutional and
social roles that made up the individual career course challenge our
understanding. Colorful and exciting personalities abound. It was an
era also of clashing ideologies and arresting rhetoric. Stubbornly troublesome issues of public policy challenged the wisdom and conscience
of both politician and statesman. And within the framework of local,
state, and federal political institutions, personalities and values, careers and career roles, rhetoric and ideologies were all part of the
complicated processes of formulating, articulating, and approving legislative agendas and public policy. Although the possible approaches
are, therefore, many, historians throughout the course of their dis-

1

cipline's development have tended to emphasize personalities, divisive issues, and legislative and judicial landmarks. Some thirty years ago, however, some American political historians became particularly interested in the realignment of the common voters during the middle period and the party reorganization of which this shifting was part. At about the same time other scholars began to explore the ideologies or political cultures of the antebellum era. Historians have given less attention to Congress as a political institution and to the general characteristics and roles of congressmen during this recent era.[2]

Scholars investigating the middle period have usually treated the U.S. Congress as stage setting or even backdrop; they have seldom explored the challenges and opportunities it provided for its members or the demands it made on them, or tried to understand the shaping power of institutional elements in general upon the national government of this period. Perhaps it is now time to examine the congressional system more closely. Becoming and being a representative or senator must have created a unique perspective among those who served in these capacities. Here I wish to examine the career lines of congressmen of the middle period, identify some of the factors contributing to success, and speculate upon the question of why the congressional politicians of the late 1850s became the architects of civil war.

To declare one's intention to study congressmen and their world is to announce a difficult assignment. There were many, many congressmen; some 3,300 men served in the House of Representatives before 1860 and about 1,000 in the Senate, with some overlap. The more prominent of these men have been the subjects of biographies, biographical articles, or notes, but the literature is surprisingly selective. Of most congressmen we know very little beyond the brief sketches available to us in the *Biographical Directory of the American Congress.*[3] And if we wish to understand fully how the congressmen were educated, received their political training, found their way into Congress, and conducted themselves there, we must look both at the Clays and the Websters and at those whose names drifted into quiet insignificance after their terms of service.

In this chapter I shall focus on a particular group of federal lawmakers whose careers I believe to be broadly illustrative of the congressional experience in the middle period but that was also unique because its members died while serving. As a result, each of these men became the subject of a particular type of biographical reminiscence – the congressional eulogy. The eighty-three representatives and senators who died during 1844–65 (see Appendix) will provide our primary focus.[4] The obscure, or short-term, congressman received much less elaborate attention from his grieving fellows than did his more famous colleagues, but in each case lawmakers, in effect, turned historians and recounted the life of the deceased or chapters from it. Not only are we provided with an outline of the dead man's career, we also learn what his living colleagues believed was worth saying about him. Some of these statements were highly stylized funeral rhetoric abounding with platitudes and interspersed with exhortations to "be ye also ready," or funeral verse of which the moving passage from Ecclesiastes 12:1 "or ever the silver cord be loosed . . . " was a particular favorite. If congressmen ever spoke about politics in public with their guard down it was in these ceremonial observances.

The members of this group of eighty-three illustrate the kinds of background and training that the members of Congress possessed during the mid nineteenth century, the types of career patterns that brought them to Congress, and some of the personal and contextual factors that apparently were of importance. We can use their personal histories to explore, if not definitively answer, important questions about the congressmen and the congressional system of the late antebellum period. What did the typical career line of the representatives and senators of that era involve? How open was the federal political system of the time? What education and occupations best fitted men for service in the Congress of the United States? How did spatial mobility influence the recruitment of representatives and senators? How and to what degree had they learned the political arts? At what age could the ambitious politician realistically expect to appear on the Washington stage? How long was the run to be once he had been accepted in the cast? Were there differences in such matters between northern and southern politicians so significant that they might have been of some influence in contributing to the outbreak of war between the sections or that they may perhaps be viewed as somehow predictive of that struggle? If we find the contrasts to be less than striking, are there perhaps other aspects of these personal histories that should be assessed in relating the congressmen to the coming of the Civil War? How did the congressmen describe themselves? What clues do they give us of change in mind sets, of values, and of behavioral attributes that might have helped to exacerbate sectional tensions?

What were typical congressional career patterns of the 1840s and 1850s? Each member of our group of representatives and senators had his own special history. Some, like John C. Calhoun, John Quincy Adams, and Henry Clay, were highly distinguished. Others were much less well known, their names unrecognized by most outside their districts or states. Each pursued a particular path to Washington.

Let us examine a few of these special paths as an introduction to the antebellum world of the congressman.

William Rufus de Vane King was born in North Carolina, the son of William King, a gentleman of character and fortune who was active in the revolutionary cause and a member of the state ratification convention that approved the federal Constitution. Thereafter, he was repeatedly elected to the General Assembly of his state. "His situation in life," noted an observer, "enabled him to bestow on his children all the advantages of education, which our country at that time afforded." Among these fortunate offspring, young King was sent to the University of North Carolina, from which he emerged at the age of seventeen to read law with a distinguished jurist. After admission to the bar, he began practice in his native Sampson County and, in the following year, successfully stood for election to the state legislature. He was just twenty-one years of age. His colleagues elected him solicitor for the Wilmington judicial district, a post he held for two years. He then returned to the state legislature for a further two. As he approached twenty-five years of age he broadened his horizon and won election to the Twelfth Congress of the United States, the famous "War Congress" that approved the declaration of war against Great Britain in 1812. Here King's "bold and chivalric temper" led him to support Madison's war policy with "firm and fervid earnestness."

Young King remained in Congress during the War of 1812 and then went to Russia as secretary of legation. Returning after two years, he decided to seek his further fortune on the frontier, emigrating to Alabama Territory. There he was almost at once elected to the convention called to draft a constitution for the new state of Alabama. When the first legislature of the new government met, its members sent William King to the U.S. Senate; he took his seat in 1819. He remained in that body until the spring of 1844, when he resigned to become minister to France. Having skillfully ascertained that France would remain neutral if the United States annexed the Republic of Texas, he returned and was promptly reelected to the Senate.

Although a Democratic partisan and a states' rights man in the Calhoun tradition during his later years, King was both independent and judicious. He "possessed in an eminent degree, that quickness of perception, that promptness of decision, that familiarity with the now somewhat complicated rules of congressional proceedings, and that urbanity of manner . . . required in a presiding officer," as well as "the rare and highly important talent of controlling with impartiality, the storm of debate, and moderating between mighty spirits." As a result, his colleagues chose him president pro tempore of the

Senate on many occasions, and a succession of vice-presidents called upon him to preside over the chamber. In 1852, King was himself elected vice-president. But, enfeebled by tuberculosis, he journeyed to Cuba seeking a restoration of health. Although a special act of Congress allowed him to take the oath of office in Havana, he sensed the futility of his mission and returned to King's Bend, his plantation home on the banks of his beloved Alabama River. Here he soon died.[5]

Kinsley S. Bingham was born into a farm family of moderate circumstances in Onondaga County, New York, in 1808. Farm work in the summer and district school, later academy, in the winter shaped the seasonal routines of his youth. He interspersed periods of teaching primary school with four terms of attendance at various academies. After reading law near Syracuse, he migrated, at the age of twenty-four, to the territory of Michigan, where he turned to farming. Bingham became the first justice of the peace in his settlement, the first postmaster, and the first supervisor in his township. He won election to the first state legislature in Michigan and was five times reelected, serving in three of those terms as Speaker of the House. A Democrat "of the Jeffersonian and Jackson school," he stood successfully for Congress in 1846 and was reelected two years later. In Congress, Bingham supported the Wilmot Proviso, opposing both the annexation of Texas and the "extension of slavery over free territory." His fervent opposition to the compromise legislation of 1850 led his constituents to repudiate him in the district nominating convention. Phoenixlike, Bingham rose from the ashes of failure, successfully standing as the gubernatorial candidate of the new Republican party in 1854. Two years later, he was returned to office with a majority greater than that achieved by any other Michigan candidate for state office up to that time. He was particularly proud of the fact that the State College of Agriculture was established while he was governor. The Michigan legislators sent him to the U.S. Senate in 1859 "almost by acclamation."

While a legislator at the national level, said a eulogist, Bingham was "emphatically a working member" who "did not often mingle personally in debate, seldom made what is called a speech, did not attract crowds by his eloquence, nor move the mirth or applause of the galleries" but left an enduring legacy in his roll call votes. In the confusion and hysteria engendered by the decision of the southern states to leave the Union, Bingham stood firm. He would not compromise with slavery. In the committee room in which the Michigan delegation was holding its last caucus during the closing days of the special summer session of the Thirty-seventh Congress in 1861, he rose and said, "Gentlemen, I am going home, and you need not be surprised to see me return with a musket on my shoulder; I am ready when my country calls; gentlemen, I am ready *now*." But Bingham did not return. While actively assisting in the war mobilization of his state, he died of apoplexy on October 5, 1861.[6]

Others enjoyed less distinguished careers than William King and Kinsley Bingham. Few could boast more distinguished lineage than Henry Augustus Muhlenberg. His father had served in the U.S. House of Representatives from 1829 to 1838. An unsuccessful candidate for governor in Pennsylvania, the elder Muhlenberg declined both a seat in Martin Van Buren's cabinet and the ministry to Russia. He did, however, become minister to Austria in 1838 and was the Democratic candidate for governor in Pennsylvania when he died in 1844. A cousin of the ambassador also served briefly in the U.S. House of Representatives. The political record of the revolutionary generation of Muhlenbergs had been even more distinguished. A great-uncle of young Henry Augustus served in the Continental Congress and was Speaker of the U.S. House of Representatives in the First and Third congresses as well as filling many posts of honor in Pennsylvania. Another great-uncle served with distinction in the Continental Army, attaining the rank of major-general. Later, he held high political office in Pennsylvania and was both a U.S. representative and senator. Henry Augustus's maternal grandfather was governor of Pennsylvania.

Descendant, then, of a distinguished family, the young Muhlenberg graduated from Dickinson College, studied law, and won election to the Pennsylvania senate at the age of twenty-six, serving from 1849 to 1852. Now he successfully sought election to the U.S. House of Representatives. A colleague noted, "In point of ability [he] had very few superiors. In deportment he was extremely kind and gentlemanly, yet firm and unwavering in his attachment to the principles which governed his conduct in life." After sitting but a month in the first session of the Thirty-third Congress, this brilliant young man died of typhoid fever on January 9, 1854.[7]

Henry Nes was born in 1799, the son of a respected and influential citizen of York, Pennsylvania. As a youth he took an academic course and won entrance to Princeton University. After graduation he studied medicine and supported himself as a medical doctor. He apparently had no military connections and held no local or state political offices. In 1842, however, he ran for Congress as an independent and, remembering his faithful service to the community, the citizens of Pennsylvania's Fifteenth District elected him, as they would again in 1846 and 1848. His congressional career was unremarkable in every sense. In September of 1850, he died of a "painful and wasting disease."[8]

We could chart individual careers at length and gain considerable insight into the fortunes of particular legislators. At the other extreme of generalization, we know that fifty-two of our group served only in the House of Representatives, fifteen held seats in the Senate, and a further sixteen served in both houses. If we are to understand these careers most fully, however, we must examine the characteristics of these legislators that bear most directly upon the questions raised above.[9] First let us consider the openness of the federal system and those variables of education and occupation that apparently helped to place young men on the road to Congress, remaining alert through this and subsequent consideration to the possibility that there were interesting differences in the makeup of the northern and southern delegations.

About a quarter of the eighty-three apparently received no more education than could be had in the common schools of the new nation, fifteen (or 18 percent) had gone to academies or the equivalent, but some 57 percent were college alumni. The picture is one therefore of a political elite, demonstrating educational training far beyond the average for the general population. But it was also an elite that was permeable; the lack of impressive formal education had not barred a sizable minority from finding membership in the congressional fellowship. There was in this respect little difference between the northern and southern delegations.

In terms of occupation, lawyers dominated the group. Fifty-four (65 percent) of the group had trained in the law, although seven of these followed other vocations as well; the lawyer-planter was fairly common in the South. Nine of the total of eighty-three representatives and senators were members of other professions – clergymen, medical doctors, or teachers. Ten were agriculturists, mostly southern planters. Conversely, seven of the eight businessmen came from the North. These categories classify all but two of the eighty-three. The lawyer-politician was dominant both north and south, but agriculturists came primarily from southern states or constituencies, businessmen from northern.

What of the effect of spatial mobility on individual careers? In all, thirty-nine of our eighty-three lawmakers represented states different from those in which they had been born. Slightly fewer than half of the northern congressmen were migrants by this definition, and the prevailing direction of migration was indeed westward. But the western migration was less characteristic than might have been expected. A Vermont-born congressman represented a Pennsylvania district, individuals of Connecticut birth found constituencies in Massachusetts, New York, and Pennsylvania, and so on. Although many of the northern lawmakers had turned west to seek their fortunes, about a third of the migrants stayed within what became the northern metropolis.

As a whole the southerners were less mobile than the northerners. Sixteen of the thirty-eight southern legislators (42 percent) had migrated to the states they represented, and for the most part these men did move westward. The migrants seldom strayed far to the north or south of their points of origin; only three northerners established themselves in slave states, and but two southerners journeyed north across the latitude of the Mason-Dixon line or the Ohio River. If the new territories and states offered additional chances for political success, these were usually realized within the same setting of free or slave labor that the office seekers had known from birth.

How were the eighty-three legislators schooled in the tasks of governance? The careers of the congressmen who died in office in the middle period of American history show that holding of local political office was common but not part of the usual path to Congress. Fewer than one out of three members of the group began their political careers at the local level. But here there was a regional difference. Of those twenty-four whose biographical data reveal local officeholding, eight were from southern constituencies. Sixteen northern lawmakers, however, had held local office at various levels from village to county, ranging across most of the functions of local government; several had held more than one position. Local office did not, in general, appear to serve as a substitute for holding some kind of state office prior to winning a seat in Congress, but in four cases, two in the North and two in the South, that was apparently so.

The major legislative school of our congressmen was the state assembly. Fifty-two of the eighty-three lawmakers served in the lower house of their state legislatures. Of these, more than one in four (26.9 percent) also served in the state upper house; a somewhat smaller group (eleven) bypassed the assembly and received their only state-level legislative experience in the state senate or the equivalent body. Ten obtained state-level experience in other capacities. Twenty-two of the state legislators held other state office as well. The state constitutional convention was a far more important element in state politics then than now, and about one-fifth of our group (seventeen) served in one or more of these assemblies. Five used them as a substitute for service in the state legislature.

All told, sixty-eight of our federal lawmakers served in the state legislature or in a state constitutional convention. Another five held other state-level office. Ten of the eighty-three brought no state-level experience to Washington, but five of these had held local office or military rank. Just five members of our group succeeded in reaching Congress without having held either state electoral office or a military commission. This circumstance alerts us to another important characteristic of the system. Military rank was an important political asset in this period. More than a quarter (28.9 percent) of the legislators boasted such credentials in their records, service almost invariably having been at the commissioned level.

The state legislative experience of our group of eighty-three was apparently somewhat greater than the institutional norm of the period, but not strikingly so. Seventy-six percent of the lawmakers had served in state legislatures or upper houses. The equivalent percentage in the House of the first Civil War Congress, the Thirty-seventh, for example, was but 54. When we examine the subregional totals, however, we discover that the discrepancy is mainly due to the characteristics of the delegation from the Middle Atlantic states. Only 26 percent of those representatives had experience in their state legislatures. But for New England, the Middle West, and the border states, the respective percentages were 73, 68, and 65. Thus the pattern of prior legislative experience among our eighty-three was quite typical for much of the North and South at the outbreak of the Civil War.

We can consider prior experience from another perspective by examining the number of other political positions held by the congressmen. The fifty-two men who died while serving in the House of Representatives had on the average held two to three other public posts, the southerners (2.75 offices) being a bit better prepared in this respect than the northerners (2.0 offices). Sixteen men served in both the House and the Senate, and (if we count their House service) as senators they brought the greatest variety of experience to their work. Here the northerners displayed somewhat more training (3.1 positions in comparison to 2.6). Fifteen of the thirty-one senators in our group never served in the House of Representatives. They did not come to the Senate completely ill prepared, however. Although they had enjoyed a less varied experience than those who graduated to the Senate from the House, the members of the group had in general served in three other public capacities. Most had sat in a state assembly, and eight had displayed their talents in constitutional conventions. Seven had held other state-level civil posts, including that of governor. The great exception in this group was Senator Ashley of Arkansas, who established a statewide political reputation by promoting the Democratic slate while running for the honorific office of presidential elector. The group of senators who did not serve in the House of Representatives does provide a sharp contrast between northern and southern practices. Almost all of them (eleven) came from southern states. Clearly the southern man of political ambition had more viable ways open to the Senate than did the aspiring northerner.

Assuming that the data represent approximations, we can also compare the relative length of time that the members of our group of representatives and senators spent in political preparation for service in Washington and the length of their careers there. On the average those who served in the House of Representatives had held state or local office for only seven years; the northern figure was a bit under six and the southern was nine. Northerners who served as senators had logged about the same amount of time in local and state office as had the northerners whose careers terminated in the House. In the southern case, the senators had served in local and state office for almost ten years; the representatives had equivalent experience of just over nine years.

The age of the median lawmaker in our group was forty-three at the time of his entrance into Congress. The northern median member was a year older and the southern a year younger than the group median. The median age at the time of exit from Congress for the last time (discontinuous service was common) was fifty in the case of both southern and northern members. The fifty-two members of the House who saw no service in the Senate enjoyed a mean term of only 3.3 years. As is usual in such calculations, the northern House members served less long than did their southern colleagues – 2.5 years in comparison to 3.3. The southern senators remained in the chamber for 8.2 years and northerners for only 5.7 – the overall average was seven years. The median term of service among the representatives was three years – two in the north and four among southern members. Median service in the Senate was seven years – a span that also represents the northern median for the Senate. The southern median term of service in the Senate was somewhat less, standing at five. The southern advantage in the mean figure reflected the fact that four southern senators occupied Senate seats for extended periods, varying from fourteen to twenty-eight years. The three northerners who enjoyed comparable confidence in their states served sixteen, eighteen, and twenty-two years.

Scholars have described southern society as one in which patriarchy, family pride, the code of honor, and prescriptive values prevailed to a greater degree than in the remainder of the United States.[10] In such a setting the political dynasty based on family ties should be more evident than elsewhere. The biographical sketches of our group of representatives and senators do indeed accord with such a view, showing that 29 percent of the southerners and only 18 percent of the northerners had relatives, usually fathers, sons, or cousins, who also served in the U.S. Congress. Such societies have also tended to emphasize military achievement, and in our group of eighty-three some 42 percent of the southerners had military connections, in contrast to only 18 percent of the northern members.

The stark outlines of the political careers of those members of Congress who died while serving during the 1840s, 1850s, and early 1860s show considerable variety. A relatively small proportion of these men spent most of their adult lives in public service, primarily at the federal level – John Quincy Adams, Henry Clay, John C. Calhoun, John M. Clayton, William R. King, Charles G. Atherton, and Stephen A. Douglas. They were truly "public men" and, with others of more than average service, presumably provided an important core of continuous leadership and institutional memory. At the other extreme were those who served only a few months or did not even live to appear in Washington and take their seats. Overall, whether one examines the mean or the median, the representatives served for only about three years. Although the proportion in our group was higher, only about one in eighteen of the middle period representatives extended his federal service by winning a Senate seat.

The modern congressional career is much longer than that in the nineteenth century, and the current generation of political scientists argue that a great deal of the behavior of congressmen can be explained in terms of their desires and efforts to be reelected. No doubt many mid nineteenth-century congressmen also wished to return to Washington and worked vigorously to that end. They had the illustrious careers and long service of the great public men of the middle period to inspire them and to plant the seeds of hope. But in these same years the Jacksonian doctrine of rotation was widely espoused, and seats involving strong opposition may have been more common than in some later eras. Various measures of length of service in the House of Representatives reached their lowest level for the nineteenth century during the 1840s and 1850s. We can speculate, therefore, that sober judgment must have convinced many of the nineteenth-century politicians who stood for election to Congress or for reelection to their seats that they were trying to enhance their careers in general as public men or professional advocates rather than to build long careers in the House. For them, candidacy was the road to enhanced local eminence and to judgeships or other patronage places, and was a means of cultivating the broader circle of acquaintance that lawyers, as so many of these men were, found useful in their business.[11]

Examination of congressional career lines allows us to see the various steps that politicians took in rising to serve in Congress. Only by inference does it tell us about the social and personal context in which some men succeeded in joining the most prestigious political elite in the country and others were relegated to peripheral obscurity. Nor does career-line analysis emphasize the elements in the political system that impressed those who participated in it. In these respects the congressional eulogists can help us. What did they see in themselves and their fellows that may help us to understand them and their achievements a bit better?

The eulogists were fond of emphasizing that their deceased colleagues owed their success to their own efforts. Senator David C. Broderick, said Congressman Burlingame, "was the child of the people; born to that great American heritage, the right to labor and to enjoy the fruits thereof." And in life Broderick emphasized his humble origins, pointing to the fluted columns of the Senate chamber upon which his stonemason father had labored. Senator Foot referred to Senator Upham as the "artificer of his own fortunes" and believed him to be "another and beautiful illustration of the operation of the genius of our institutions, in that they open the pathway to station and honor alike to all." And returning to the same theme in saying farewell to Congressman Meacham, Foot described him as "cast, an orphan child, upon the chances and accidents of life, thrown upon his own resources" but successful under a government "which invites to seats of honor within the inner temple of fame the meritorious and well-deserving from among the humblest, as well as from among the highest and the proudest of the sons of men." General Brinkerhoff, noted Potter of Ohio, "was truly 'a self-made man.' "[12]

Despite these proclamations of an open system, almost 60 percent of the members of our group were college alumni, as we have seen. Still, some of the degrees were fragile reeds and others went unmatched by family station or influence. Clues in the obituaries suggest how bright young men of meager schooling in the West sought to remedy their deficiencies. Senator Benton described "a circle of young lawyers and students at law [in Nashville], who had the world before them, and nothing but their exertions to depend upon. . . . It was the custom of all that belonged to it to spend their leisure hours in the delightful occupation of reading. History, poetry, elocution, biography, the ennobling speeches of the living and the dead, were our social recreation." Congressman Arnold of Illinois told of a "remarkable combination of men," all comparatively young, who practiced law in Springfield, Illinois, in the 1830s. These men enjoyed "writing verses for the amusement of each other and their friends" while on circuit. Sometimes, Senator Browning recalled, they declaimed moving passages from popular authors to each other while riding to the next site of the court. Self-improvement was the order of the day in this era, and sometimes it led to Congress.[13]

But we can also file a reservation about these matters. Granted that intelligence and the will to improve against odds had to be present, some of the eulogists disregarded circumstances that qualified the rags-to-riches theme. Young Alexander Porter, later to be a judge and senator from Louisiana, left Ireland in 1801 as an orphan and an exile, his clergyman father dead as a rebel on an English scaffold. But a family member was waiting in Nashville to shelter him and to give him a position as a store clerk. Although Congressman Amos E. Wood of Ohio "commenced life without a fortune, and without a liberal education," he spent two years in his teens in the household of a near relative, a man of sufficient ability and station to become governor of Ohio.[14] The helping hands of extended family along the way often assisted the poor youth of promise on his early path toward Congress.

Other members of our group were more clearly children of privilege, quite apart from their schooling. In Congressman Muhlenberg's constituency his name might have served as the passport to Congress of men much less prepared to bear it proudly than that unfortunate young man. Paying his last respects to George C. Dromgoole, Richard K. Meade of Virginia described the love, affection, and confidence in which his parishioners and friends had held the congressman's clergyman father. When the son sought a congressional seat at a very early age "the virtues of the father stood as a guarantee for the promises of the son, until his own great abilities changed doubt into assurance." Of Judge Bayly of Virginia, who had a distinguished career in the House, a eulogist remarked, "He was not, as were many of the statesmen of America, reared amid privation and difficulty." The "confidence of his constituents . . . was strengthened by a sort of ancestral claim," for his maternal grandfather, General John Cropper, had distinguished himself in the Continental Army and his father, Colonel Thomas M. Bayly, had held public office for nearly forty years, including service in the U.S. House of Representatives. Senator Mason noted that public men from Bayly's section were "seldom changed from caprice, or other insufficient cause . . . society assumes there more of the character of a patriarchal state, than in the recurring collisions of life which attend more dense populations."[15]

The memorialists noted the spatial mobility of their colleagues almost as a matter of course. Although some whom they eulogized had moved as children with their families, the migration of many resembled that of one of Senator Bingham's eulogists. He was trained in the law in the old settlements but journeyed to the undersettled regions of Ohio as soon as he had a lawyer's certificate to put in his carpetbag.[16] Ambitious young men saw the opportunity to seek their fortunes out of state, and many did. There they might compete for political preferment with others who were richer in goods or real estate but would not have to oppose men like a young Muhlenberg, Dromgoole, or Bayly, whose families' community contributions in past generations ensured an instant and sympathetic recognition of their talents.

Although mobility spelled opportunity, that opportunity could be enhanced. Young William S. Fulton served as General Jackson's military secretary when Old Hickory and his troops rampaged across the international boundary into Florida in 1819. With both loyalty and foresight, he served the general well, and ultimately Jackson, ever mindful of faithful friends, made him secretary of Arkansas Territory. There he performed ably and served as acting governor for a time. When Arkansas entered the Union, Fulton became one of the new state's senators, his selection testifying to the skill with which he had both solicited and dispensed patronage.[17] Several others of our eighty-three also used personal or political contacts to obtain federal posts in the western territories and in turn used those positions as stepping stones to national political success.

The aspiring politico of this period could also enhance his political chances by his choice of profession. In this era, the preponderance of lawyers in Congress reached its highest point. They constituted about two-thirds of all members of the House. Why exactly this should be we do not know. The eulogists remarked upon it, however. "To a gentleman of finished legal education," remarked Chandler of Pennsylvania, "of easy fortune, and public spirit, the path of political preferment seems naturally open." In eulogizing Henry Grider of Kentucky in the Senate, Garrett Davis noted that "in Kentucky every lawyer of any ability is also a politician."[18] And indeed, border state delegations boasted the largest proportion of lawyers in their ranks; the profession was least represented among the members from the Middle Atlantic states. We can merely speculate on the reasons why lawyers appeared in Washington in such numbers. Attorneys moved through large districts on circuit, developing wide acquaintance among both politicians and voters. At this time lawyers tended to have general practices and reputations; the age of specialization still lay ahead. Partners at home could usually handle general activity easily while the congressman served. Once elected to legislative office, attorneys were comfortable and knowledgeable in drafting new laws and in revising old legislative formulas, as well as in discussing legislation in political campaigns. The Supreme Court sat in the national capital and provided provincial lawyers with opportunity for learning, for making contacts, and even for arguing cases. As a countrywide assemblage of lawyers, Congress provided the lawyer-lawmaker with a far-flung network of legal contacts that he might use in the future. And, in an era of highly partisan politics, the lawyer who wished to attain a seat on the bench moved several steps closer to his objective if he had served his party in some responsible position, such as in the U.S. Congress.[19]

Senator Fulton was by no means the only man in our group in whom we find the link between military experience and congressional service documented. Fame won in the Texan army helped send Texans Thomas J. Rusk and James P. Henderson to the Senate and David S. Kaufman to the House. The Mexican War added luster to the public record of many aspiring young politicians. Twenty-four of our group had military connections, and since the congressional obituaries sometimes referred to military honors unmentioned in the *Biographical Directory of the American Congress*, the estimate may well be an undercount. These were the days, noted Preston S. Brooks in his eulogy on Henry Clay, "when mere civil qualifications for high public place – when long civil training and practical statesmanship – [were] held subordinate."[20]

The eulogists noted other factors or relationships that contributed to the political success of particular members of our sample. One finds among them the man whose constituents had unique interests and believed him to be specially qualified for the task of representing them. Such a man was George Scranton. A Pennsylvania coal and iron tycoon, founder of Scranton, Pennsylvania, he was willingly recruited to work for tariff protection of the industries that had brought him fame and a growing fortune. Also from Pennsylvania, John Schwartz spoke in both name and voice as a Pennsylvania German from a constituency of that ethnic composition. Pierre Evariste John Baptiste Bossier had a name that could only be a political asset in the region of Louisiana he represented. Occasionally eulogists mentioned oratorical talents or, as in the case of Senator Lewis of Alabama, "the more than usual proportions that distinguished him physically." In other words, he looked like a senator, an attribute later shared by Senator Warren Harding of Ohio.[21] Wit, if the right kind, could endear as well. When Enoch Lincoln of Maine, speaking in Congress in behalf of Revolutionary War pensions, shouted, "Soldiers of the Revolution! Live forever!" Henry Clay interrupted to ask if nine hundred and ninety-nine years might not be just as acceptable to the congressman.[22]

If we can detect elements of training, experience, and special aptitude that undoubtedly smoothed the road to Washington, it is also true that these men had to come to terms with the political system of the times. An Illinois governor and congressman from frontier Illinois explained how, in the early days of statehood, men simply obtained the endorsement of a few friends and proclaimed their candidacy. But the rapid elaboration of party institutions and practices during the late 1820s and 1830s required most members of Congress to obtain formal party endorsements and to involve themselves in party activities unmentioned in the records of formal officeholding, not alluded to by the eulogists, and not found in the *Biographical Directory of the American Congress*.[23] Party leaders and convention faithful sifted, winnowed, and stood as gatekeepers to the world of political office. In the two decades before the Civil War, the sanctions of party continued to be important, regardless of the level of political office attained. "Few men . . . attain political distinction in a country like ours without party attachments and party feelings," remarked one of William R. King's eulogists.[24] And this was the era in our political history when the use of patronage was most partisan and unbridled. Faithfulness to party was the major criterion used to evaluate the individual's eligibility for sharing in the distribution of offices. Amid the disintegration and rebuilding of parties during the 1850s, party discipline continued to rule in much of the roll call voting in Congress.

On the other hand, the fact that the 1850s were years of party realignment shows that men sometimes did reject party discipline, whether for reasons of high principle or for crass party or personal advantage. None would break ranks more dramatically than Democratic Senator Stephen A. Douglas, one of our group of eighty-three. But although he rejected the leadership of a Democratic president, Douglas tried to reshape the guiding principles of the Democratic party to fit new realities. Others renounced old party allegiances completely and affirmed different loyalties. When Kinsley S. Bingham was a colleague of the Whig congressman from Illinois Abraham Lincoln in the Thirtieth Congress, the Michigan man was a Democrat. By 1860 both were Republicans. Meanwhile James A. Pearce of Maryland, a Whig senator during the same Congress, transferred his loyalty to the Democratic party. Pearce died in 1862 still, however, believing that office should seek the man and still exhibiting a "delicate sense of propriety" that "would not have permitted him to accept office, except in obedience to the unsought requisition of his fellow-citizens that his time and talents should be devoted to the public service."[25] Doubtless John Quincy Adams would have made the same point.

Among the eulogized representatives there were some amateurs who reached Congress without having held formal office. Such a man was Thomas Cooper, who was elected to represent Lehigh and Bucks counties in Pennsylvania in 1860. A member of the Masonic Order and a physician who "for seventeen years . . . rode by night and by day, whenever and wherever called, to visit and relieve the sufferings of the sick and afflicted," Cooper obtained his seat in part because of a rotation agreement between the Democratic managers of the two counties. One of his eulogists noted that for most U.S. congressmen "a seat in Congress was . . . the end of a long political struggle, the result of management or toil. Usually, the Congress of the United States is the highest attainment of political effort, and he is thought entirely successful in his political aspirations, who has climbed this dizzy height." But Cooper "came into the Thirty-Seventh Congress without effort or solicitation on his part."[26]

A slightly different category of lawmaker was the local notable sent to Congress to reward extended local party service and to cap a career of community or regional leadership. Such a man was Cyrus Spink of Wooster, Ohio, who had grown up with the country and who, in the eyes of Congressman Samuel R. Curtis, was the very model of a solid western merchant. These men, he said, "suppl[ied] their neighbors with all kinds of merchandise, and bec[a]me familiar and friendly with all the surrounding classes of men. They [were] the leaders of society, the deacons of the church, the founders of schools, the directors of banks and railroads, and the arbiters of accounts and controversies among their confiding friends." During long years while the Democrats dominated his district, Spink labored for the Whigs, and his reward for helping to organize the Republicans was nomination to Congress. The distinction was "the summit of his political ambition." Had not death interrupted his course, he would probably have been satisfied with one term of service. In part Spink was the beneficiary of political upheaval. The Thirty-sixth Congress included a number of local notables whose reputations seem to have attracted party managers under these circumstances. But some of them were, in Senator Sumner's words concerning John Schwartz, "protest" candidates rather than faithful partisans like Spink.[27]

Of his deceased colleague William Taylor of Virginia, Senator Pennybacker remarked:

> A purer man never lived. . . . He was remarkable for his modesty
> and courtesy; and no one excelled him in sensibility and honor. A
> lawyer, he stood very well at the bar; a member of Congress, he
> discharged his duties; a husband, a neighbor, and a friend – noth-
> ing was wanting. He was respectably connected in all branches of
> his family. A *gentleman* in every sense of the word, *he was an orna-*
> *ment to human nature itself.*
>
> In his life there was no striking incident. Like a placid stream, it
> flowed smoothly on until it was lost in the ocean of eternity.[28]

Allowing for some exaggeration in this case, we can believe that some
individuals seemed to reach Congress with little effort because their
talents coincided well with the apparent needs of the people and
parties in their constituencies at the time. The times found their man.
But such cases were rare.

Unless the eulogies mislead us, many politicians of the middle
period enhanced their careers by performing successfully in unusual
circumstances, by making the most of opportunities for outstanding
achievement, or by sensing possibilities where others had failed to
observe them. Indeed such challenge or opportunity was apparently
an essential requisite of success. Henry Clay and John C. Calhoun
laid the foundation for careers that established them as true national
figures by their performance in the famous "War Congress" of 1812.
The early Texan delegations were dominated by men who had distinguished themselves in the field, in the council chamber, and in
diplomatic maneuver during the Texan struggle for independence.
As governor of Maine when that state's boundary with the British
possessions was at issue and war seemed a possibility, John Fairfield
"displayed a decision and firmness of character" that "fixed upon
him the attention of the whole country." Silas Burroughs of New York
left his party rather than oppose the bill in the state legislature that
would provide $9 million to enlarge the Erie Canal system and greatly
benefit his constituents. As part of his reward, his fellow citizens sent
Burroughs to Congress.[29]

Until then a pastor, temperance advocate, and author of a historical
sketch of Fall River, Orin Fowler used his talents as a historian to
research the location of the border between Massachusetts and Rhode
Island in his county and to oppose the findings of the state boundary
commissioners. His articles and pamphlet on the subject "so impressed the public mind as to bring him prominently before the people," who "elected him to the Senate of the Commonwealth." There
his continuing labors on the boundary question and work on the
Education Committee and on a commission to consider building an

additional insane asylum further enhanced his reputation and contributed to his election to the Congress of the United States.

Luther Hanchett made his mark as a man of particular talent by
his leadership in revising the Wisconsin Code while serving as the
chairman of the Senate Judiciary Committee of the Badger State.
Thomas H. Bayly of Virginia was born on the family estate, Mount
Curtis, the son of a congressman. Elected to the state legislature in
his first year of eligibility, he rose to the rank of general and served
also as a judge during part of his career. Apparently he enjoyed all
of the family and social advantages that were so helpful in realizing
political success in the older southern states. He certainly enhanced
his career when, as a state legislator, he mobilized the Virginia legislature against the actions of the New York governor, William Seward, who had refused to surrender several sailors charged with
complicity in the escape of a slave so that they could be brought to
trial in the Old Dominion.

Less striking an achievement than those recounted, perhaps, a considerable number of our group had served as Speaker of the state
assembly or president of the upper house. Such honors marked the
individual as one who was already demonstrating exceptional qualities of leadership. Had such men failed to meet the demands of those
offices, their careers might well have terminated at that level of
service.[30]

Others found an opportunity to show their capacities in the numerous constitutional conventions that met in the various states during this period. John R. Thomson, a retired China merchant of New
Jersey, threw himself wholeheartedly into the efforts in the early 1840s
to replace the state's obsolete constitution, dating from the Revolutionary era. His was an important voice in the convention called to
revise this organic law in 1844. Thanks to his exertions there and his
connection to the powerful Stockton family, he entered the U.S. Senate with no formal political experience other than service in the convention and an unsuccessful gubernatorial candidacy.[31] Although the
constitutional convention may have been less important in their careers than in Thomson's case, others among our congressmen enhanced their political chances considerably by serving in territorial or
state constitutional conventions.

In our discussion of the paths to power and the men who walked
them, we have recurrently noted differences in the northern and
southern patterns. The New Englander was more likely to hold local
political office than the southerner. Businessmen were more common
in the northern delegations, and large-scale agriculturists appeared

most frequently among the southern congressional contingents. Southerners were more likely to have held high military rank than northern representatives or senators. A higher proportion of southerners were also likely to have fathers, sons, or other relatives who were also federal lawmakers than had northerners. Southerners tended to begin their congressional careers somewhat earlier in life than northerners, serve slightly longer, and skip service in the House of Representatives more frequently when on the road to the Senate.

The comments of the eulogists touch upon some of the institutional differences between the northern and southern delegations that were revealed in our quantitative collective biography, particularly concerning length of service, family ties, and military service. But we can perhaps make too much of such matters. I have for example sorted out all of the representatives and senators who served for at least three terms in the House or eight years in the Senate, a group of some 969 federal lawmakers from the approximately 4,000 who were elected to Congress between 1788 and 1860 (see Table 1). These were the men of long service, the leaders, the elite of the congressional elite of that time. When the total proportion of such men serving from each state is compared with the total number of House and Senate slots allocated to each state, it becomes clear that most of the contrast between the North and the South is attributable to the history of federal representation in a few states. If long-serving lawmakers had appeared from the various states in exact accord with the federal apportionment ratios, 9 percent of them would have come from Virginia. The figure was actually 10.2 percent. Among the other states, deviations, plus or minus, from the federal apportionment were minor except in New York, Pennsylvania, and Massachusetts; these differ from the predicted percentages by 4.5, 1.7, and 1.4 percent, respectively. This is a very different picture from the one suggested by casual references to the longer service of southern politicians and suggests that additional study of the antebellum political systems of New York, Pennsylvania, Massachusetts, and Virginia might be particularly rewarding.

Several years ago, Bogue, Clubb, and Traugott examined the various elements in the career lines of the members of the House of Representatives on a regional basis, decade by decade. The data showed persistent regional differences across time in the various biographical attributes of the congressmen during the antebellum period. In one sense, therefore, these findings reinforce the suggestion of regional differences found in analysis of the congressional decedents of the middle period. The more comprehensive study of regional contrasts among House members did not, however, show that regional differences became increasingly obvious as the mid-century

Table 1. *Long-serving representatives and senators, 1789–1865*
(N = 969)

State	Percentage of federal apportionment	Percentage of long servers	Advantage or disadvantage
Alabama	1.8	1.4	−
Arkansas	1	0.5	−
California	0.4	0.2	−
Connecticut	3	2.8	−
Delaware	0.9	1.3	+
Florida	0.2	0.4	+
Georgia	3.1	2.3	−
Illinois	2	2.7	+
Indiana	2.5	3.2	+
Iowa	0.5	0.8	+
Kansas	0.06	0.1	+
Kentucky	4.5	4.7	+
Louisiana	1.2	0.8	−
Maine	2.6	1.8	−
Maryland	4	4.5	+
Massachusetts	6.4	7.8	+
Michigan	0.8	1.2	+
Minnesota	0.2	0.2	None
Mississippi	1.2	1.2	None
Missouri	1.4	1.1	−
Nevada	0.02	0.2	+
New Hampshire	2.5	3	+
New Jersey	3	2.8	−
New York	13.6	9.1	−
North Carolina	5.3	6.0	+
Ohio	6	5.2	−
Oregon	0.2	0.1	−
Pennsylvania	11	9.3	−
Rhode Island	1.3	1.9	+
South Carolina	3.8	4.4	+
Tennessee	3.9	4	+
Texas	0.3	0.2	−
Vermont	2.2	3	+
Virginia	9	10.2	+
Wisconsin	0.6	0.8	+

Note: Long service is defined as involving at least six years in the House of Representatives or eight in the Senate.

mark neared. The contrast in regional means appeared to diminish in some cases; in others it became somewhat more evident.[32] But the comparisons hardly appeared to reflect political systems so different in practice and objectives that spontaneous combustion could be expected at any time. Still, they might have been straws in the wind, to some degree indicators of deeper systemic differences.

In the past, some historians have gone so far as to argue for the existence of different cultures in the northern and southern states. But comparison of such fundamental documents as the federal Constitution and the organic instrument of the Confederacy reveals the exaggeration involved in maintaining that there were distinct northern and southern political cultures, so similar are the two documents in reference to everything but the vital subject of slavery. It is surely best to categorize the northern and southern political systems as subcultural variants of a shared republican system, firmly based in English precedent and subjected to much environmental nurture. Central to a cultural approach is the concept of values. Growing divergence in, or increased regional commitment to, particular values might be far more important in explaining political behavior than minor institutional differences.

What does our group biography tell us, explicitly or implicitly, about regional values and the politician? Less than one would like, certainly, but enough perhaps to be suggestive.

Scholars have agreed that the American middle period was a romantic era, when the better read reveled in the tales and poetry of Sir Walter Scott and other romantic authors. Southerners, it has been suggested, particularly accepted Scott as their guide to a romanticized and fictional Middle Ages and as a mentor of life-style and values. Not only did southerners name their plantations after the sites found in his pages, but they accepted his more admirable characters as role models. Many of them saw the prototype of the plantation master in the medieval baron or highland chief, surrounded by his retainers. But would such fanciful stuff influence the representative or senator from a southern constituency or state? Listen to Thomas S. Bocock of Virginia and speaker-to-be of the Congress of the Confederacy eulogizing Senator Evans of South Carolina. The young Evans, he said, had been placed "in a society where the constant cultivation of high sentiments of honor, of lineage, and greatness have created a nation of cavaliers, with all the lofty spirit and chivalrous feeling of the days of Charlemagne." Then Bocock traced the career of Evans through his various trials and tests until he became the mature man of wisdom and virtue whom his colleagues mourned.[33]

The Normans set the pace of English chivalry in the pages of Scott.

In commemorating General Thomas Jefferson Rusk of Texas, Representative Laurence Massillon Keitt proclaimed that "the progress of society is southward, and thither our Anglo-Norman population is moving with the firm tread of a Roman legion," neatly equating the South, its chivalrous people, and the future. Speaking of William R. King, Phillips of Alabama affirmed that "the Republic never produced a man of more exalted integrity, or of a higher chivalry of character." When the fire-eater and advocate of Cuban annexation John A. Quitman died, Sydenhow Moore of Alabama extolled his sense of honor, his lack of ostentation despite wealth, and his bravery, and asked, "Yet who, in his daily intercourse with others, could have shown more of amiability and true knightly courtesy?" Quitman's friends enshrined the concept of chivalry in the congressional memorial resolutions. One of them ran: "In the death of General Quitman [note the use of military rank in commemorating the holder of a civil office] the country has lost a citizen eminent for his public and private virtues, a soldier of the highest chivalry of character, a statesman of the purest patriotism." Only a few years earlier, a Maryland representative had noted that Henry Clay, universally hailed as one of the last links with a bygone age, had died gracefully as a Christian in contrast to him who sought to meet his end as a "chivalric gentleman."[34]

If many southern lawmakers took knightly standards as their model, what was their attitude toward northerners who in their opinion transgressed their code? Would the response be a recourse to knightly forbearance, or would the southerner exercise the patriarchal right to punish transgression? When Charles Sumner became unpleasantly personal in his criticism of Senator Andrew P. Butler, the aged senator from South Carolina, his nephew and a member of our sample, Colonel Preston Brooks, caned the Bay State senator at his desk as he might have whipped a slave or a delinquent member of his family. The move to expel Brooks from Congress failed, but he resigned anyway, sought vindication from his district, and was triumphantly returned after having been presented by admiring constituents with innumerable canes to replace the one shattered across Sumner's back and head.[35]

The Sumner-Brooks incident has been emphasized in descriptions of the series of events that led to the Civil War. A less celebrated clash of values occurred when the resolutions commemorating Senator David C. Broderick of California reached the floors of the congressional chambers. This incident is more sharply indicative of sectional divergence than the Sumner-Brooks affair because of its impersonal nature. Broderick died in a duel rooted in the personal and political antagonisms of frontier California. In the House, his old friend Representative Haskin of New York explained that he would not "refer to the unfortunate affair which was the immediate cause of [Broderick's] 'taking off,' in language of harsh invective, because of the sectional dividing line which exists between northern law and civilization and southern custom and 'chivalry,' in relation to the duello. My friend believed in the 'field of honor' – mistakenly so-called, in my judgment – and sacrificed a life upon it that belonged to his state and his country." None of the representatives dissented from the memorial resolutions when they were put to the vote.[36]

But in the Senate the Broderick resolutions provoked an unprecedented response. Senator Lafayette Foster of Connecticut rose to note that under the common law "life taken in a duel" was murder. The practice of dueling was forbidden by law in all of the states. When a participant was slain or mortally wounded in a duel in the District of Columbia, all of the participants were guilty of a felony, to be punished by hard labor in prison for a term of up to ten years. "Giving or accepting a challenge to fight, or being the bearer of such challenge or acceptance" was a high crime and misdemeanor, subject to incarceration for as long as five years. Foster believed that dueling was directly contrary to the laws of God, a "proposition which will hardly be denied." He himself refused to "recognize the 'code of honor' as a 'higher law' than the laws of man and the laws of God." He had therefore to vote against the resolutions, an act unheard of in the congressional annals of this period. Foster was, in effect, speaking ill of the dead and, by implication, of those who shared his views. Foot of Vermont read a seconding speech prepared by an Ohio senator, Ben Wade, who was no admirer of southern institutions but who had provided a statement ending with an affirmation: Broderick "was the very soul of honor, without fear and without reproach." To this sentiment Foot expressed "entire and cordial concurrence." Then Robert Toombs of Georgia gave the southern retort to Foster: "I had not intended even to say this much but for the dissent which has been manifested to our proceedings in honor of his memory. He fell in honorable combat, under a code which he fully recognized. While I lament his sad fate, I have no word of censure for him or his adversary. I think no man under any circumstances can have a more honorable death than to fall in the vindication of honor. He has gone beyond censure or praise."[37]

We find also in various of the memorial addresses of the late 1840s and 1850s expressions of commitment to state and section that are in keeping with statements of knightly or chivalric values. "He did not love the Union less because he loved Alabama more," affirmed Milton

S. Latham of William R. King. Although in ill health, Senator Henderson of Texas returned to Washington, the representatives learned, to protect his section in the Kansas-Nebraska crisis and "fell a martyr . . . to the State of his love and the institutions of his section." Senator Butler, said a eulogist, "loved the gallant state which he represented with the devotion of filial piety [but] loved the union of the Constitution only less than South Carolina." When Representative Black of South Carolina lay dying in Washington, he said, "This is indeed a great trial, but I will try and meet it as becomes a Carolinian!" Later he made one request: "Let my bones rest in the soil of my native land!" – that is, South Carolina. On the other hand, New Englanders, said Clark of New York in eulogizing Republican Thomas L. Harris of Illinois, carry "principles of human conduct . . . engraven upon their hearts, in whatever spot upon the earth's surface their lot may be cast." And the hope that Congressman Winthrop of Massachusetts expressed in saying farewell to John C. Calhoun was to be short-lived. "Let us resolve," he said, "that, so far as in us lies, the day shall never come, when New England men may not speak of the great names of the South, whether among the dead or among the living, as of Americans and fellow-countrymen."[38]

But why was Winthrop's plea rejected? Changes in values are hard to document precisely, and yet some congressmen believed that they had occurred. Congressmen Roger A. Pryor explained that in 1832 the Virginia legislature (in the wake of the Nat Turner slave uprising) had thoroughly explored the question of introducing a system of emancipation. In one of those career-enhancing junctures I mentioned earlier, William O. Goode moved that the committee considering various emancipation schemes be discharged and carried his colleagues after a "speech of surpassing power." But the occasion had been provided for the lawmakers to explore the slave system to "its foundations." In so doing they discovered, said Pryor, that slavery was "an institution which exists in virtue of the most essential human interests, and the highest sanctions of the moral law. From that day," he argued, "the slaveholder stood on surer and more solid ground. . . . his conscience being clear, and his judgment convinced, he renounced the expedients of apology and extenuation, and planted himself on the impregnable basis of reason and right." The nature of slavery, southerners believed, did not need defense.[39]

The members of generations do not change beliefs and values easily. It was surely the rising generation of southern politicians who accepted the message of the Virginia example most fully. Wright of Tennessee recounted a conversation with General Quitman, whose penchant for befriending and assisting young men was well known.

Wright and a friend suggested that the country was facing a crisis that required the "mature wisdom of age and experience" to bring it safely through. "With an earnestness of manner peculiar to himself," Quitman responded,

> No sir; their opinions are formed, their habits of thought and principles settled. You are mistaken in your reliance upon the antiquated politicians of the country. I rely for the future . . . upon the rising generation of statesmen. It has been among the most pleasing duties of my life to endeavor to instill proper principles of government into the minds of the young men of the country, and I am happy to believe that my labors have not been entirely fruitless.[40]

In fact, the lessons of the Virginia slavery debates of the early 1830s, the sense of beleaguered unity that external criticism brought, John C. Calhoun's states' rights doctrines, the less sophisticated but highly active men like Quitman, and the view of the South as a uniquely chivalrous society all contributed to a fever of southern nationalism. So, apparently, did the example of the free Republic of Texas in winning its independence, the processes of constitutional revision through convention that were very much a part of this era, and the arresting outbursts of romantic nationalism in continental Europe, so strikingly reflected in American adulation of the Hungarian patriot Louis Kossuth and in southern participation in the Young America movement.

Such forces and examples played upon the generation that came into Congress during the 1840s and 1850s. And these processes of political education began even before the hopeful young politicians of North and South took their first steps in the adult world of politics. In an autobiographical fragment, Henry Winter Davis wrote of his experiences at Kenyon College in the early 1830s. Here the student body was divided into two student academic societies; one of these was composed of northern lads, the other of southern. When Davis continued his education at the University of Virginia he found that the basic text on constitutional principles was *The Federalist Papers,* but the instructor interpreted this document almost solely in terms of states' rights principles. As it happened, Davis, from the border state of Maryland, fought off the indoctrination to become an eloquent defender of Republican radical doctrines during the Civil War; many others accepted it as the training of the Civil War generation proceeded. The other side of this coin is found in Josiah B. Grinnell's autobiography, in which he recounts his experiences at the Oneida Institute, where northern youth were encouraged to debate the issues of social reform and were drilled in the evils of the institution of slavery. Here the reforming thrust of northern evangelical Protestantism found free rein.[41]

The point has on occasion been made that the congressional guard was changing in the early 1850s; an older generation was passing away. The last great contributions of Clay, Webster, and Calhoun came in connection with the compromise legislation of 1850. None can deny the importance of these figures or their influence during almost thirty years of shaping congressional policy, but the extent of the transformation has perhaps not been sufficiently stressed. King of Alabama, Clayton of Delaware, and Benton of Missouri all left the stage during the early 1850s after long and influential careers. In the South Carolina delegation the changes were not restricted to Calhoun; his successor, Senator Franklin H. Elmore, soon died, and the latter's successor, Senator Josiah J. Evans, passed away in turn during 1858. Senator Butler disappeared before the end of the decade. Various other federal lawmakers of substantial if not extremely long service left the national government as a result of death or other causes during the 1850s.

A short term of service in the congressional rank and file was much more common than a long term; the median number of years served in the House of Representatives as a whole was under three in the 1840s and 1850s. Thus the views of a generation with different values could gain full sway in short order. Nor was a clean sweep necessary. Legislators may be classified in various ways: aristocrats, managers, populists, and moralists, for example.[42] Such a mixture of types need only change so that members of different categories exercise significantly more power for outcomes to change materially. Moralists presumably gained in influence within the sectional delegations during the 1850s – my study of senatorial delegations during this era strongly suggests that this was indeed the case. With this possibility in mind, we should perhaps qualify James G. Randall's description of the congressmen of the 1850s as members of a blundering generation. If some sectional spokesmen showed increasing intransigence in the Congress, test by test, from the Kansas-Nebraska debates of 1854 onward, if southern and northern politicians refused to accept the suggested compromises that might have reunited the nation without resort to war, they did so, perhaps, because their training and political socialization led them to value the fruits of compromise much less highly than had Henry Clay and Daniel Webster. The emerging national legislators of the 1850s and 1860s were members of a generation inadvertently programmed for war. The principles and values of General Quitman and others like him were applied to the ultimate on the bloody fields of Antietam, Shiloh, the Wilderness, and dozens of other places. A generation of politicians purged their land with blood because it was dominated by men whose credo and whose reading of political context did not allow them to adopt other solutions.[43]

2 Lincoln and the "disorderly schoolboys": a chapter in executive-legislative relations

No American president has so caught the interest of historians as has Abraham Lincoln; the great Illinoian towers above the other political figures and the great soldiers in the scholarly literature of the Civil War. That he merits careful attention none can deny, and such an emphasis is all the more pleasing when the subject has so many admirable qualities – courage, honesty, forbearance, wide-ranging skills, humor, a marvelous command of the language, and, in the end, a martyr's death after victory had been achieved in the field. To sit with Lincoln at the White House, or follow him in his sauntering walks to read dispatches at the War Department, is to be in the very cockpit of the war. In his person the manifold threads of arms and policy come together.[1] Within the checks and balances of the American government, Lincoln was chief executive, head of the executive branch. But east and south down Pennsylvania Avenue the Capitol glistened, and there men had their own ideas of how the war should be fought, different in significant respects from those Lincoln stubbornly maintained. Many of the lawmakers were little trained in the legislative arts, as we have seen, and were undisciplined – "disorderly schoolboys," as a friend of one Speaker of the House put it.[2]

The fractiousness of the members also reflected the fact that the Civil War was an untidy conflict. It was a brothers' war, a struggle between once friendly neighbors and business associates, as well as between one-time rivals and protagonists of widely differing lifestyles, values, and conceptions of government. The war took place in a country characterized by complex interactive social, economic, and political institutions. Given this background, the Civil War had to be personal, perplexing, and evocative of outraged feelings. Lawmaking and execution of policy proceeded in an environment of recurrent crisis. Americans of this era were not unused to war, but they were ignorant of the challenges and stresses that a civil war would present to them.

In seeking understanding we can proceed furthest if we do not pick favorites, if we do not place our money on Abraham Lincoln, or on the Republican radicals, or on the moderate or conservative politicians who disagreed with them, but rather on recurring themes of interaction. Legislation did not emerge during the Civil War because Lincoln single-handedly conceived and guided it through Congress, nor did the radical Republicans of that body chart the course of war policy unhindered. Within Congress the interplay of radical, moderate, and conservative politicians shaped public measures. Lincoln, a moderate himself, had also assembled a microcosm of party opinion in his cabinet, and the counsel that its members provided ranged across the spectrum of Republican opinion.

Scholars have depicted many different Lincolns: There is James G. Randall's liberal statesman, Norman Graebner's conservative statesman, Jacques Barzun's philosopher Lincoln, and so on, even to the positive-negative Lincoln, developed in recent years by our friends in political science.[3] The Lincoln we shall examine here is the congressman's Lincoln. What did the individual congressman see in Lincoln? What did Lincoln do for the congressman? These are the basic concerns of this chapter; the final chapter will bear on them to some degree as well.

Clinton Rossiter's view of the presidency no longer dominates the scholarship of that subject, but his little book on that office still contains useful typologies and arresting insights. In approaching Lincoln's relations with the members of Congress, we can use Rossiter's argument that the president plays nine major roles. Lincoln was (1) chief of state, the ceremonial head of the government; (2) the principal executive, in whose hands the ultimate power of appointment and removal rested; (3) commander in chief of the armed forces; (4) senior diplomat; (5) chief legislator; (6) party head; (7) voice of the people; (8) protector of the peace; and (9) world leader. Some of these executive responsibilities were derived directly from constitutional mandate, others rested on the foundations of institutional development and tradition.[4]

Abraham Lincoln filled these various roles when the stakes were greater than at any time under the federal Constitution, when the future of the republican experiment hung in the balance and the exigencies and crises of a major war might well demand redefinition and reordering of presidential obligations. And Lincoln confronted these times of crisis with a supporting staff that was minute: his able personal secretaries John G. Nicolay and John Hay, the Land Office patent clerk, and some occasional clerical help. There were none of the specialized personnel who are today employed to give the occupant of the White House the clout that knowledge and expertise

provide. Instead Lincoln had to depend on his own immediate resources and the departments, also understaffed by our standards.
Given this situation, Lincoln developed priorities. He devoted much
of his attention to the duties of chief executive, commander in chief,
and party leader. The importance of his role as principal legislator is
less certain, as we shall see. In practice, of course, the varied functions
of the presidency were intermingled. The appointments he approved
as party head and chief executive might influence legislative outcomes, and presidential messages to Congress could reflect both public opinion and the strategies of the chief legislator. On occasion
diplomatic communications created tempests in the congressional tea-
pot. Although the Republican Civil War congressman might have
agreed with Clinton Rossiter's typology of presidential roles, he
would have rephrased some of them for closer accord with his own
perspectives. Lincoln was his party leader and chief executive, but
this relationship translated most powerfully for the congressman into
Lincoln's being the giver of office or patronage. To the congressman,
the president was also what we may term intervenor of last resort.
And Lincoln was a legislative agenda setter and a source of party
ideology that could perhaps be converted to the congressman's own
needs. Let us examine Lincoln's activities from these perspectives.

Lincoln later described himself as "rich with honorable and fat offices"
when he arrived in Washington, and with the outbreak of the Civil
War a political system already lubricated essentially by patronage was
required to distribute thousands of new offices.[5] The Civil War provided a patronage bonanza unparalleled in the history of the Republic.
Most obvious initially were military commissions of both large and
small degree. But the war effort also required the appointment of
many new civil officers – clerks, auditors, assistant secretaries, as-
sessors, revenue collectors, treasury agents, and assorted commissioners. A slate of political offices had to be filled for each of the
growing number of territories. The congressmen were prepared to
meet the challenge of distribution, and their performance had both
short- and long-run effects on individual and congressional careers,
as well as on the consolidation of political power that the Republican
party managed to effect. Here we shall focus on Lincoln's role in these
matters and on the practices and expectations of the congressmen
who descended on Washington in 1861 to obtain a share of the patronage pie for their districts, their friends, and themselves.
     In a political universe where career enhancement was a major mo-
tivating factor, rules of the patronage game were firmly in place by
the time of the Civil War.[6] Majority party members expected that their

recommendations for local federal offices in their districts would be honored. But the jurisdiction of many federal offices overlapped congressional districts, and the views of more than one member of a state delegation had then to be considered. In addition there were territorial and diplomatic posts that were not the patronage prerogatives of any particular congressman, senator, or state delegation. In the hands of Lincoln and his cabinet officers there rested the obligation to see that a "fair" distribution of offices was achieved. Congressmen sought of course to establish traditions that would strengthen their hands; westerners apparently believed that they had a special stake in the offices of adjacent new territories.

Recommendations came to cabinet officers and Lincoln from the aspirants themselves, from interested members of the House of Representatives and the Senate, from governors, and from party elders. Lists or files were kept at the departmental level for the different categories of office. Many requests came directly to Lincoln, and he referred them to the appropriate cabinet officer with a short endorsement written on the envelope or wrapper enclosing the various documents involved. When the time came for specific nominations to go to the Senate for approval, the cabinet officer brought or sent the appropriate papers to Lincoln for signature and transmittal. Sometimes Lincoln called in cabinet officers to go over particular lists of nominees with him. Although the chief executive's overriding authority was recognized, he did allow the heads of departments some freedom in selecting their close associates and clerks. In persuading Senator William P. Fessenden to enter the cabinet as secretary of the treasury in 1864, he prepared a memorandum of their discussion that ran in part: "I have to-day said . . . that I will keep no person in office in his department, against his express will . . . and he has said to me, that in filling vacancies he will strive to give his willing consent to my wishes in cases when I may let him know that I have such wishes."[7]

There were general assumptions shared by Lincoln and the departmental secretaries as to the kinds of experience in party service required to qualify for particular types of position. Although the process was an intensely political one, ability and personal qualities were not ignored, nor were the arts utterly disregarded. Middling or minor diplomatic or consular positions abroad were believed appropriate for men of letters or artists with political patrons of the right kind. Ministerial posts in the capitals of major foreign powers were reserved for eminent political figures, and ranking territorial officers almost invariably had served in Congress. George P. Marsh, ex-congressman from Vermont, scribbled out one of the classics of the conservation movement, *Man and Nature,* while representing the United States in northern Italy during the Civil War. The system of appointments was also flexible, allowing Lincoln to replace his secretary of war without great loss of face to the incumbent. Recognizing that appointments were vital both to the nation and to the party, Lincoln gave careful attention to them.

The members of congressional delegations tried to reduce competition among themselves by holding meetings and endeavoring to agree on a unified slate in the case of overlapping offices, and Lincoln was grateful for such efforts. On March 12, 1861, for example, Isaac N. Arnold, congressman from the First District of Illinois, reported the recommendations of the Republican members of the state delegation for marshal of the Northern District of Illinois, the U.S. attorney for this district, the equivalent offices for the Southern District in Illinois, the chief justice of Nebraska, the governor of Dakota, and the surveyor general of Utah, and also listed names for the "secretaryship in a Territory" and a territorial judgeship. There also appear in the Lincoln papers of that time various lists of nominees for federal offices in Philadelphia submitted by interested Republicans – that of collector, surveyor, naval officer, mint director, navy agent, postmaster, attorney, and marshal. Although the Philadelphia lists overlapped, there were also differences; these Lincoln and his advisors had to resolve while endeavoring to keep the goodwill of those who did not receive what they requested.[8]

George H. Yeaman asserted in a letter to Lincoln in early 1862,

> The business of office seeking has been reduced to a science, a science I do not understand and would scorn to study. Indeed sir, I don't want any *office,* but I *do* want the comforts and salary of a good office[.] I need these, and, I *deserve* them. And sir thats honest, more so than most of the applications you are bothered with. . . . to come honestly to the point I am qualified for *anything* from Brig Genl or District Judge *down* to anything except a clerkship. . . . There is but one material difference (the difference between the *Ins* and *Outs*) in our history. You were born in Hardin County, and so was I. You made rails and so did I. You studied law and – so did I. You are president, and I *expect to be.*[9]

Poor Yeaman had to settle for the House of Representatives when the incumbent died in 1862, but followed his defeat during the Thirty-eighth Congress with five years as minister to Denmark. Yeaman understood the system better than he admitted.

Few applicants were as arresting as Yeaman, although the plea of a self-proclaimed descendant of John Randolph's brightened the presidential offices and was embellished with the notation "a direct descendant of one who never was a father."[10] The two gambits par excellence of placemen seeking to interest Lincoln directly in their cause were, first, the effort to play upon some personal tie with Lincoln and, second, obtaining intercession from congressmen or senators. A surprising number of Lincoln's contacts during his single congressional term in Washington emerged to lay claims upon his generosity, including his former landlady. But a direct supplication, accompanied if possible by one's member of Congress, or the presentation of one's papers by a friendly representative or senator, was the more usual course. Lincoln's basic procedure in such cases was to scrawl a supportive endorsement on the letter or document binder for transmittal to the appropriate department. These statements typically carried both the explicit message and an implicit one understood by the cabinet officers familiar with Lincoln's style and procedures. One can arrange illustrative notations in ascending order of the urgency Lincoln apparently discerned in them:

"I wish this paper called to my attention, when, if ever, the vacancy mentioned occurs."

"I know James A. Briggs, and believe him to be an excellent man."

"Let it be fairly considered."

"As the appointment of a consul is desired by Mr. Hickman, who is much of a man, and does not trouble us much, I wish it to be made if it is within reasonable possibility."

"I would like for these gentlemen to be obliged as soon as it can consistently be done."

"I desire that [Congressman _____] be obliged."

"I shall be personally obliged if you will make the appointment."

"I would like for [Mr. Nixon] to be obliged."

"Oblige [Mr. Rollins] if you consistently can" – consistent, that is, with propriety and the requests of others.

"If consistent, let the appointment be made."

"If at all consistent, let it be done."

"Mr. Rice must be obliged in this."

"Let the appointment be made" and "Let it be done."[11]

When read or shown to the congressman or job applicant, such endorsements assured these worthies of the president's good intentions. But only in the last three cases did the president commit himself to action in the supplicant's behalf.

In their patronage presentations the lawmakers stressed party service, loyalty, and ability in the case of civilians, field experience and bravery on the part of military nominees. When Senator Doolittle sought to have William H. Upham appointed as a cadet to West Point, he noted the details of the wound the young man had suffered at

Bull Run, "the ball entering less than an inch from the left collar-bone and jugular, and coming out at his back[,] the two scars being five inches apart."[12] Upham began his studies at the Academy in July 1862.

Lincoln worried lest he be accused of favoring relatives or his state. "Deal with a man in Illinois, as you would if he were in any other state," he instructed Secretary Seward. Equitable division within the congressional community was also highly important. In addition to being "much of a man," Mr. Hickman "does not trouble us much," nor did Thad Stevens, factors that weighed in their favor when they requested patronage. Disappointed expectations also should be salved. When Representative Samuel S. Blair failed to obtain the consular appointment that he "had reason to expect" for one of his political friends, Lincoln instructed Seward to "show him what remains" in that category and "if there is anything that he will accept . . . let him have it." His old Illinois friend William Kellogg, Lincoln sadly noted, "has had more favors than any other Illinois member, not excepting, I think, Judge Trumbull," the senior Republican senator from the state.[13]

When sharp rivalries developed in state delegations, Lincoln's problems were exacerbated. He instructed the young governor of Rhode Island, William Sprague, on the rules of the game as they applied to his state. Although your "wishes in this respect . . . received the highest consideration, there [was] a difficulty." Both the senators, the two "old Representatives," and one of the new representatives recommended another man. "In these cases the Executive is obliged to be greatly dependent upon members of Congress; and while under peculiar circumstances, a single member or two, may be occasionally over-ruled, I believe as strong a combination as the present never has been."[14] Other cases were more troublesome. Connecticut was a particular source of annoyance. Both Connecticut senators were moderates, but James Dixon, Lincoln's colleague in the Thirtieth House, particularly irritated his radical constituents. When the positions of assessor and collector opened under the Internal Revenue Act of 1862, Dixon telegraphed the president that his "humiliation and disgrace" would be "complete" if his nominees were not approved. But Lincoln bowed to other pressures and sent forward the name of the Hartford radical Mark Howard for collector. Dixon opposed the confirmation in the Senate, and his colleagues, bowing to the conventions of senatorial courtesy, rejected the nomination. Lincoln then nominated a man more acceptable to Dixon, frustrating the Connecticut radicals.[15]

During the next year Lincoln wrote to the Connecticut senators to tell them that the vacant marshal's position in their state was giving him trouble. "Of the Sec. of the Navy [a Connecticut man], Gov. of the State, two Senators, and three Representatives in Congress . . . two are for Mr. Nichols, two for Mr. Hammond, two for Mr. Barnum, and one for Mr. Phelps." Lincoln explained that he was resolving the issue in favor of Mr. Hammond, who had been denied both of the internal revenue positions of the previous year despite strong recommendations. Again Dixon had triumphed.[16] Nor was Connecticut alone in providing such problems. After Lincoln had refused to see Senator Pomeroy, then squabbling with Senator Lane about federal offices in Kansas, Lincoln dropped Pomeroy a note wishing that "you and Lane would make a sincere effort to get out of the mood you are in. I[t] does neither of you any good – it gives you the means of tormenting my life out of me, and nothing else."[17] In this instance Pomeroy and the governor of Kansas were aligned against Senator Lane and the state's representative in the House.

In dispensing patronage, Lincoln tried to conduct himself, as he said, so that he would not "willingly plant a thorn in any man's bosom." When he could not accede to the wishes of senators or representatives, he might drop a note of condolence to them. He expressed "great regret, on your account" to Senator Wilkinson when he nominated Judge Edgerton to be governor of Montana Territory. "I could not do otherwise without much greater difficulty to myself," he wrote, "and I beg you to be assured that it is a great pain to me to know that it is disagreeable to you. Do not, for a moment suppose that this note is intended to constrain you to support the nomination." Lincoln understood the importance of touching base beforehand when the proposal for a particular appointment originated with him. "May I have your approval?" he wrote to Senator Ten Eyck as he contemplated appointing a provost marshal in New Jersey.[18] Sometimes also Lincoln turned away the individual member by requesting that he find additional support for his nominee in the state delegation.

Of course, the president's various executive roles at times overlapped or interlocked. Lincoln argued that in making military appointments he took ability where he found it, irrespective of party affiliation. But he well understood that his management of these appointments had political implications. He regretted that the officers' list involved in the addition to the regular army of June 1861 was "drawn from the different States in such unequal proportions." When the First and Third regiments of Rhode Island cavalry were so reduced in numbers that consolidation was appropriate, he decided to recruit for both: Uniting them "throws out one set of officers, and which ever set it may be, it offends either the Governor or a U.S. Senator. We cannot afford to offend either, while we can avoid it." He carefully monitored the progression in rank of Franz Sigel, Carl Schurz, and Julius Stahel because he realized that these men were not only soldiers but symbols of German American support of the war effort and of the fact that the administration recognized and appreciated the qualities of Teutonic leaders. He also understood the importance of the religious element in politics and penned an illuminating letter explaining why he accepted the Methodist recommendation for the position of governor of Washington Territory.[19]

Importunities tried Lincoln's patience. Major-generalships in the regular army, he wrote to western friends, "are not as plenty as blackberries." And a former senator learned that "you can never know until you have the trial how difficult it is to find a *place* for an officer [General Schurz], when there is no place seeking *him*." Lincoln accepted the patronage responsibilities of party leadership, agonized over the difficult decisions, and fully understood the coercive implications of the system. He appreciated the fervor with which members of Congress tried to reward the *"true men"* in eastern Pennsylvania and their counterparts elsewhere. Years before, he had been in their shoes.

But the callousness of the system also repelled him. Senator Baker died in his country's service at Ball's Bluff and his nominees stood unprotected. Lincoln wrote to Seward, "It pains me some that this tilt for the place of Col. Baker's friend [U.S. commissioner in Honolulu] grows so fierce, now the Col. is no longer alive to defend him. I presume, however, we shall have no rest from it."[20] Rascals and ungrateful appointees who went over to the political enemy had to expect short shrift, but Lincoln opposed any general overturning. He was not in favor, he told a correspondent, of turning out party members who had proven themselves to be faithful and effective officers.[21]

The houses of the Thirty-seventh Congress adjourned for the last time on March 3, 1863. A defeated congressman from Ohio, Samuel Shellabarger, wrote to Lincoln on February 27 inquiring whether it would be "worth while to present an application on my own behalf for Judge of Court of Claims or for any other important position under your administration at home or abroad." Harrison Gray Otis Blake, from the same state and in similar circumstances, did not apply to Lincoln for some "good paying position" until March 4. Campaign expenses and business failure had rendered him "poor," he said; he turned to Lincoln for help.[22] Blake had served briefly in the Thirty-sixth Congress, having succeeded to a seat left vacant by his predecessor's death, and had won reelection to the next Congress. In Ohio he had served in both the state assembly and senate and could claim to be a party wheelhorse with some rights at the patronage mill. We do not know how seriously he pressed his claims, or how vigorously the Lincoln administration tried to provide for him. Blake had various options and entered the army as a colonel in 1864. Subsequently he was offered the gubernatorial chair in Idaho, which he declined. Blake and Shellabarger were typical in that their thoughts turned imme-diately to appointive office once they had lost their elective positions. Like his colleague, Shellabarger failed to obtain a patronage place, but, regrouping his political forces, he won election to the Thirty-ninth Congress. Both men had good prospects, were strong in mind and body, and hardly boasted party service to the degree that they had to be aided at all costs.

But if the system of patronage and party is to work, there must be ample proof that faithful party service earns its just rewards. This Lincoln well understood. During early 1863 the Washington political environment was alive with the sound of lame ducks fluttering to friendly roosts on the federal payroll. In ill health and rejected by a hostile Democratic state assembly, Senator Wilmot reconciled himself to the loss of his seat by indicating his desire for a seat on the U.S. Court of Claims rather than on the district court, since the first position paid a thousand dollars per year more and he had "not many years . . . to make provision for the family I must leave behind." Lincoln honored his wishes and also noted in a memorandum of December 1862 his desire to appoint Wilmot's son to West Point "before I leave here."[23] Although some were not aided, many other casualties of the Thirty-seventh Congress attained the federal payroll – not always, however, to their satisfaction. Lincoln refused to read the letter of protest from his old friend William Kellogg, who had been offered the position of consul in Valparaiso. "At one time," the latter wrote, "I was indiscreet enough to indicate to your Excellency a desire for an appointment to an office, for which, I was vain enough to believe I was qualified but from the position now offered, I am forced to conclude, that your Excellency had a decidedly different opinion from my own on that subject, or that my political status was such that the administration would suffer by my appointment to an office of the grade of those held by Peck, Wilmot, Olin, Fisher, Swett, Gurley, and Cart[t]er and many other recent appointees."[24] Of those on Kellogg's list, two had attained seats on the Court of Claims, three had joined the U.S. court in the District of Columbia, one had become governor of Arizona, and one had been made commissioner of pension claims. Five on Kellogg's list were former congressmen.

When the vice-president, Hannibal Hamlin, was shunted aside for Andrew Johnson in 1864, an appropriate office obviously had to be found for the Old Carthaginian. To the consternation of the incumbent, the members of the Massachusetts delegation agreed that the position of collector of the Port of Boston should be freed for him, and this arrangement was effected.[25] We err, however, if we conclude that reward or payoff was the only consideration in such transactions. Another of the lame ducks of 1863, John A. Bingham, was recognized as a man of outstanding abilities, and his federal appointment reflected that fact. The system of political recruitment as patronage worked perhaps in part because political office was good training for many of the positions filled. The rapid turnover of congressmen suggested, however, that they were not always well qualified to make recommendations. And the system was burdensome for the lawmakers and vulnerable to corruption.

Lincoln brought an intensely personal approach to his position as party chief and arbiter of patronage. His system of scrawled endorsements appears offhand at best, and we suspect that some transactions were even more informal, made in the course of casual conversations with congressmen at presidential levees or in accidental encounters in the departments, on the street, or even at the theater. We find Senator Sumner writing to Montgomery Blair, the postmaster general, that the president had no recollection of a post office appointment that the senator had discussed with him earlier. But with mind refreshed, wrote Sumner, the president would now accept the nomination papers if Blair sent them along. When New York Senator Preston King and House Speaker Galusha A. Grow both pressed nominees on the president for the same office, they raised the possibility of an "unpleasantness, not to say a difficulty, or rupture" with these gentlemen. Lincoln passed along Grow's recipe for compromise to Salmon P. Chase: an auditorship for each. Chase responded, "Neither of the places . . . can be fairly considered as open. One is promised with your sanction to [Ezra B. French]. For the other you have named several gentlemen." In November of 1862, Lincoln explained to Chase, "If I have signed a commission superceding [Mr. Masten] I have done it inadvertently. . . . I do not wish to revoke such an appointment without a sufficient reason. . . . I wish him to have the office."[26]

Lincoln's use of patronage was highly skillful and contributed to relations with the members of Congress that were, on a personal level, usually amicable. The representatives seem in general to have complained little about Lincoln's role as patronage dispenser. He successfully weathered the efforts of Salmon P. Chase, his secretary of the treasury, to turn the office-dispensing power to his own uses, and the success of Lincoln's friends in organizing friendly state delegations to the Baltimore convention bespoke effective use of patronage. And he could be firm in opposing the demands of political enemies. John Hay noted that Senator Pomeroy, the author of an anti-Lincoln circular in support of the Chase candidacy, had tried to arrange an audience with the president "for the purpose of getting some offices. He is getting starved out during the last few months of dignified hostility." Hay concluded, "He did not get any."[27] There was so much patronage available in these years, of course, that the pangs of deprivation might not be fatal. And Lincoln managed to convey an impression of interest, good intentions, and solicitude that usually averted the hostility of members. Sometimes he did so by diverting irritation to cabinet members of, notably Stanton, but this too may well be categorized as skillful management.

Although the representatives and senators spent many mornings touring the executive departments on behalf of their constituents, they well understood that troublesome or urgent matters might be resolved more easily if they rallied the president to their aid, or if he could be induced to intervene. In particular, much congressional effort involved attempts to have Lincoln exercise his power to pardon. Lincoln spent much time in the mid and later phases of the war in pondering requests for stays of execution, remissions of sentence, discharges from the service on compassionate grounds, and pardons. And the general policy of pardon that Lincoln proclaimed in connection with his reconstruction plan of December 8, 1863, greatly increased the flow of such cases. Even then, the congressmen were frequently involved. Military courts-martial often recommended the death penalty in proceedings against deserters. Lincoln, in revulsion, and often prodded by members of Congress, tried to mitigate such sentences, particularly in the case of youthful soldiers.[28]

Border state congressmen were much interested in the issues of sentence remission and pardoning, given the divided loyalties of their districts and the ease with which the sentiments of constituents might have been misunderstood or misreported. Frequently they argued that youthful indiscretion had been followed by sincere repentance and that the disillusioned prisoner of war should be allowed to take the oath of allegiance and return to his family. Late in the war, General Grant protested the freedom with which prisoners of war were being pardoned, and Lincoln explained that he was acting on the recommendations of congressmen or senators in whom he had confidence. When challenged in one case by the secretary of war, Lincoln responded that Senator Garrett Davis of Kentucky was "of the highest moral character, and I still wish these prisoners discharged, because he asks it." Davis had been a Whig congressional stalwart of the 1840s and was so irritating a gadfly in the Civil War Senate that Sumner once attempted to have him expelled.[29]

Lincoln did not always yield to congressional pressure in such matters. When the Sioux uprising of 1862 had run its course in northern Iowa and western Minnesota, 300 tribesmen were held captive in Minnesota, condemned to death by military court for the massacre of several dozen western settlers. Senator Wilkinson and Representative Aldrich mirrored constituency sentiment when they demanded speedy execution of all the convicted prisoners. Well aware of the exaggeration and hysteria that attended Indian wars, Lincoln reviewed the record and revised the sentences of some 260 Indians, substituting jail terms for execution in the case of those who had not been specifically identified as violators of women, murderers, or leaders in the uprising.[30]

There developed in the border states a policy of imposing levies on known Confederate sympathizers to provide relief for loyalists whose property had been destroyed by rebel action. Here too, border state congressmen found it necessary to seek Lincoln's intervention on behalf of constituents whom they believed to be wrongfully included among rebel sympathizers.[31] Mingled with more serious cases were requests from distraught wives to visit their prisoner-of-war husbands or to go through the lines to nurse sick relatives who were supporters of the Confederacy. Tantalizing scraps of information remain in the Lincoln papers about two ladies stranded in Memphis who wished to return to Arkansas; the "Canada lady's case" about which Representative Portus Baxter was "so anxious"; the inventor of a new type of gunpowder who had been promised support for his research and then, according to his congressman, most unfairly abandoned.[32]

Governors sought Lincoln's assistance in modifying military policies. Oliver P. Morton of Indiana was sure that his state would be lost to the Copperheads if the maximum number of Indiana soldiers could not be given leave so that they could return home to vote in 1864. Governor Reuben E. Fenton of New York believed that the application of the war draft was unduly penalizing the Empire State. He was, thought Lincoln, probably "more than half right."[33] Others wished to change the local military commanders in their states or districts. And the congressmen interpreted and reinforced the complaints of the state executive officers. Sometimes groups of congressmen banded together in presenting constituency pleas, as when William D. Kelley and several other Philadelphia congressmen tried to have the application of the draft deferred in their city. When Lincoln referred the matter to Secretary Stanton, the latter responded, "I am respectfully constrained to advise most earnestly against your interference." He believed that such action would compromise the whole draft. Kelley and his colleagues, he suggested, were trying to gain political advantage for themselves by taking the popular but irresponsible side of an important public issue. Secretary Gideon Welles was annoyed with Lincoln when members of the Massachusetts delegation attempted to move to a regular tribunal in Boston the trial of two Boston merchant brothers arraigned by the Navy Department for fraudulent contracting, rather than allow the case to proceed in a naval court in Washington. Welles recorded that "political and party considerations had been artfully introduced," three congressional districts ostensibly hanging in the balance, so that Lincoln suggested that the trial should be at least transferred to Boston, thus conceding "something." Ultimately the president overturned the verdict of guilty handed down in the case.[34]

Lincoln was too adept to put himself at risk in some matters brought to him by the congressmen. "Could not" Mr. Fessenden and "the others of the Maine delegation fortyfy [sic] me a little stronger?" he inquired in a note to the senator from Maine. And again, "If Hon. Thaddeus Stevens will say in writing, on this papers [sic], that he wishes this man discharged, I will discharge him." When members of the Massachusetts delegation besought commutation of the sentence for a man convicted of outfitting a ship for the slave trade, Lincoln similarly required that the request be put on paper.[35]

Personal intervention in local politics at the behest of representatives was quite different from the uses of executive power discussed above. But on occasion Lincoln allowed himself to become involved. Both Isaac N. Arnold of Chicago and William Kelley of Philadelphia believed that the local postmaster, controlling substantial numbers of patronage positions, was marshaling forces against them in their campaign for party endorsement in the election of 1864. In both cases Lincoln instructed the postmasters that they must not take sides. John L. Scripps in Chicago was impudent, but his counterpart in Philadelphia sullenly announced that his employees were free to choose their own preference among the potential Union candidates. A request for support from Roscoe Conkling's friends in New York produced a peculiarly worded endorsement from the president. "I do not mean to say that there [are] not others as good as he in the District; but I think I know him to be at least good enough." And Henry Winter Davis obtained a statement of appropriate policy that he vowed to use to bring a balky candidate into line in Maryland. Interestingly, these were Republican radicals who sought such assistance. Comparable instances of aid to moderates are not found in Lincoln's correspondence.[36]

During the late stages of the war, the potential profits in extracting cotton from the southern states attracted many. Congressmen vouched for the loyalty of individuals intent on engaging in this trade, and former Congressmen Samuel L. Casey of Kentucky and Philip B. Fouke and William Kellogg of Illinois rose to the bait as well. Casey obtained various letters of safe passage from Lincoln, although his venture apparently failed after considerable amounts of cotton had been acquired.[37] An old friend of Lincoln's, Kellogg was one of the more importunate of those who badgered the president for an office subsequent to defeat in 1862. While in the Thirty-seventh Congress, he scandalized Stanton by seeking to have his son reappointed to West Point after the lad had resigned to escape dismissal. Lincoln intervened, explaining that Kellogg was a "personal friend of more than twenty years standing, and of whom I had many personal kindnesses. This matter touches him very deeply – the feelings of a father for a child – as he thinks, all the future of his child. I can not be the instrument to crush his heart." And so young Kellogg was reappointed. "It needs not," noted Lincoln, "to become a precedent." As we have seen, Kellogg found the original office provided by Lincoln to be unsatisfactory. By June of 1863 he was involved in a scheme that entailed having an associate sell "ordinary articles of commerce at Helena, Arkansas – not 'contraband of war' and to buy of loyal men cotton & other productions." Trade in the southern regions was under the oversight of the secretary of the treasury, and Lincoln sent Kellogg to him with an endorsement: "I wish him obliged so far as you can consistently do it." Chase read the note, listened to the proposition, and responded, "It cannot be done Sir," and Kellogg reported, "An iceburg [sic] would be as a furnace compared to your Sec of the Treasury." And so Kellogg dangled until Lincoln made him chief justice of Nebraska Territory in 1865.[38]

Sometimes congressmen's reasons for seeking Lincoln's intervention were intensely personal. James E. Kerrigan, New York congressman and colonel of the Twenty-fifth Regiment of New York Volunteer Infantry, wrote to Lincoln on February 27, 1862, noting that he was on parole since his arrest (for drunkenness) five weeks before and asking the president to see that justice was done in his case. A well-known Democrat from southern Illinois, William J. Allen, won the seat left vacant in the Thirty-seventh Congress by John A. Logan's resignation for army service. Since he openly advocated the division of Illinois so that the southern region might secede to join the Confederacy, Allen was arrested and held prisoner at Cairo and later in Old Capitol Prison in Washington. Seeking Lincoln's intervention, Allen was successful in winning his support for discharge and served, to the annoyance of many Republicans, during both of the Civil War Congresses.[39]

In his role of intervenor we see a Lincoln who was loyal to friends, as when he allowed the readmission of William Kellogg's son to West Point, and generous in his use of the pardoning power but also keenly aware of the political implications of his acts.

In an influential essay, "Abraham Lincoln: Whig in the White House," David Donald noted that "the presidency of Abraham Lincoln poses a peculiar paradox to students of the American government." Although he exercised sweeping powers on occasion, Lincoln seemingly exerted little influence over Congress. Lincoln, Donald argued, had "remarkably little connection with the legislation passed during the Civil War" and "singularly little impact either upon Congress or upon his own administrative aides," noting Lincoln's wry comment of late 1864 that he hoped he could exercise some influence on the incoming administration. Donald, however, was able to resolve the paradox. "Both in strongly asserting his war powers and in weakly deferring to Congress, [Lincoln] was following the Whig creed in which he was raised." Further elaborating the Whig view of appropriate executive behavior, a more recent author has written, "Whigs tended to think of the President as a glorified clerk who should follow the will of Congress, administer the laws, and not interfere with the legislative power."[40]

Specifically, how did Lincoln view his duties as he whistle-stopped his way to Washington during the late winter of 1861, speaking to supportive gatherings along the way? Lincoln had already taken action that showed his keen interest in congressional matters, writing to Senator Lyman Trumbull and to William Kellogg in the House to explain what he believed congressional policy toward the seceding states should be during the last months of the Thirty-sixth Congress. Hold the line, he instructed, and don't allow any commitments to be made to the idea of popular sovereignty.[41] In both his actual remarks at Pittsburgh on February 15 and in a preliminary draft of that statement, Lincoln enunciated his views on Republican legislative responsibilities. Speaking of the tariff, he commented, "The Chicago platform contains a plank upon this subject, which I think should be regarded as law for the incoming administration. In fact, this question, as well as all other subjects embodied in that platform, should not be varied from what we gave the people to understand would be our policy when we obtained their votes." In a working draft of his inaugural address, Lincoln returned to this theme, noting that "the more modern custom of electing a Chief Magistrate upon a previously declared platform of principles, supercedes [sic], in a great measure, the necessity of repeating those principles in an inaugural address. Upon the plainest grounds of good faith, one so elected is not at liberty to shift his position." He carried this idea forward into the inaugural address of March 4, 1861.[42] Lincoln, therefore, believed that enactment of the party's legislative agenda, as enunciated in the national party platform, was the responsibility of both the president and Congress. It was unnecessary for him to include a laundry list of desired legislation in his first regular message to that body.

In a trial draft prepared for Lincoln's remarks in Pittsburgh, there is also a more general statement of his view of the appropriate relations between the executive and Congress. Scholars have quoted it widely:

> By the constitution, the executive may recommend measures which he may think proper; and he may veto those he thinks improper; and it is supposed he may add to these, certain indirect influences to affect the action of congress. My political education strongly inclines me against a very free use of any of these means, by the Executive, to control the legislation of the country. As a rule, I think it better that congress should originate, as well as perfect its measures, without external bias.[43]

Certainly Lincoln's Whig predecessors, as well as some of the Democratic presidents, could have accepted this bland recipe as appropriate campaign gospel. But once in office and facing the national crisis of 1850, President Taylor tried to exercise strong executive leadership. How would Lincoln's pledges fare in a war for the Union?

Before the Thirty-seventh Congress had assembled in its emergency session of July 1861, Lincoln had exercised his powers as commander in chief to call out the militia, expand the regular army, authorize agents to purchase ships and military and naval ordnance, and suspend the writ of habeas corpus in certain districts. In performing these actions, Lincoln could look in justification to the "war power," a constitutional element that was, thought Democratic Senator David Turpie, more elastic than India rubber and more malleable or ductile than gold or silver.[44] Seldom emphasized is the fact that in taking these actions Lincoln provided Congress with part of its initial war agenda. Somehow for the sake of both the war effort and harmony between legislative and executive, Congress had to recognize Lincoln's actions. The credit of the country had to be maintained in support of Lincoln's efforts to build the armed forces; members of the executive branch had to be protected against the possibility of legal action by the passage of an indemnity law; and legislative prerogatives relating to habeas corpus procedures should be clarified by statute.

The representatives and senators devoted considerable thought and effort to these matters and experienced more than a little exasperation before all were satisfactorily arranged. Indemnification and habeas corpus proved highly troublesome.[45]

Lincoln regarded the Republican party platform of 1860 as a legislative agenda to which both he and his congressional colleagues were committed. But the southerners had challenged both the Republicans and the members of the opposition to recast the congressional order of business. Lincoln began that task when he affirmed by word and act that preserving the Union was to be the government's first priority. During the short special session in July 1861, the representatives and senators agreed that they would focus solely on issues relating to the military emergency; other matters, if introduced, were simply to be referred to the appropriate committees and held until the regular session of Congress began in December.[46] Despite the occasional disingenuous maneuver on the part of individual lawmakers, the congressmen observed Representative William S. Holman's resolution to this effect. When the second session began in December, however, the floor was clear for the inclusion of additional items in the second or supplementary legislative agenda. And the development of that legislative program opened a myriad of opportunities for questioning the appropriate relationship between the executive and legislative branches.

Although Lincoln did not present vast new legislative programs in his various messages, he was not a passive observer of proceedings at the Capitol. Scattered through his messages are a significant number of passages in which legislation is recommended. Sometimes, as in his messages relative to banking and currency, the recommendations bore particularly upon the problems of the war in the civil sector. In other cases he ranged further afield, as in his call for reconstruction of the government's Indian policies. Lincoln, it has been argued, gave Chase and Seward free rein to run their departments as they saw fit. Qualifications are in order. The reconstruction of the banking system was Chase's greatest claim to fame as an executive officer. But, according to John Hay, the president once remarked that the National Banking Act "was the principal financial measure of Mr. Chase in which he [Lincoln] had taken an especial interest. Mr. C. had frequently consulted him in regard to it. He had generally delegated to Mr. C. exclusive control of those matters falling within the purview of his dept. This matter [they] had shared to some extent."[47] And if Seward believed initially that he was the dominant force in the Lincoln administration, he was soon disabused. In the summer of 1863 Hay wrote to Nicolay, "He is managing the war, the draft, foreign relations, and planning a reconstruction of the Union, all at once. I never knew with what tyrannous authority, he rules the Cabinet, till now." After long observation, Secretary Welles wrote disapprovingly that the president "takes upon himself questions that properly belong to the Departments."[48]

Aside from the great tasks of raising and supporting armies, the second, or wartime, agenda of the Republicans focused on a number of major subjects relating to the South, matters of great long-run social and political importance. These were emancipation, punishment of southerners, and the formulas of reunification. They were interrelated, and each subsumed a considerable number of legislative initiatives – bills, resolutions, and ultimately law. Both Lincoln and the congressmen correctly sensed that these areas of policy were fatefully important. In developing such legislation Lincoln and Congress were in constant interaction, often fruitful in historical retrospect, but sometimes frustrating, even infuriating, to those on both east and west Pennsylvania Avenue. Neither Lincoln nor any particular group in Congress ever achieved their objectives in full, and Lincoln died with the issue of restoration unresolved.

While Congress was considering the bill to emancipate the slaves in the District of Columbia in March 1862, the president wrote to Horace Greeley noting some uneasiness on the grounds that he preferred one or more of the border states to take the lead in enacting an emancipation measure. If that was impossible, he hoped that the District of Columbia bill would "have three main features – gradual – compensation [to owners] – and vote of the people. I do not talk to members of congress on the subject," he continued, "except when they ask me." But of course his views were known in Congress, and Senator Wright brought them to the specific attention of his colleagues on the Senate floor. In suggesting minor legislation supplementary to the act as passed, Lincoln noted that he did not doubt the constitutional authority of Congress to abolish slavery in the District and had always wished to "see the national capital freed from the institution in some satisfactory way." His reservations had to do with expediency, and "if there" were "matters within and about this act, which might have taken a course or shape, more satisfactory to my judgment, I do not attempt to specify them." He was pleased, he affirmed, that both compensation and colonization were included in the act.[49] Only one of the three basic desiderata that Lincoln mentioned to Greeley appeared in the law, but radical congressmen deplored both its compensation and colonization features.

The issue of emancipation, with its military, social, economic, and political ramifications, was by all odds the most troublesome legislative problem of the war. Lincoln developed his own program and asked Congress to accept it. On March 6, 1862, he sent a draft joint resolution to the two chambers that, if passed, would commit the United States government to cooperation with "any state which may adopt gradual abolishment of slavery, giving to such state pecuniary aid" to ease the transition to a free labor system. Moved by Representative Roscoe Conkling, J.R. 48 had passed through both houses by early April 1862. Thirty-six representatives opposed the resolution in the House, including most of those from the border states. Subsequently the House approved the appointment of a select committee to consider the issue of federally assisted emancipation in those states. On July 12, Lincoln called the border state congressmen together to urge them "at the least" to commend his plan of federally assisted emancipation "to the consideration of your states and people." Two days later a majority of the group responded, refusing to support his proposal on the grounds that it would be excessively costly, would adversely affect the loyalty of slaveholders in the border states, and would not quiet the agitation for "unconstitutional" emancipation of the slaves in the rebel states. A minority of eight representatives and senators subsequently pledged support for the president's plan. Despite the unsatisfactory response from the majority of the Unionist group, Lincoln sent Congress a draft of a bill "to compensate any State which may abolish slavery within it's [sic] limits," recommending its passage, "respectfully, and earnestly."[50]

When Lincoln sent his annual message to Congress at the beginning of the third session of the Thirty-seventh Congress on December 1, 1862, he recommended three amendments to the Constitution that dealt with the emancipation problem. The first of these promised federal aid to those states abolishing slavery before January 1, 1900. The second confirmed the status of all slaves freed during the course of the war, but promised compensation to loyal owners who lost laborers by this provision. The third provided that Congress might appropriate money or proffer other assistance to help free blacks who wished to colonize in places outside the boundaries of the United States. Lincoln defended the propriety and wisdom of these proposed amendments at considerable length. But "notwithstanding," he wrote, "the recommendation that Congress provide by law for compensating any State which may adopt emancipation, before this plan shall have been acted upon, is hereby earnestly renewed."[51]

Lincoln's emancipation program for the border states came closest to success in Missouri. Both the senators and representatives considered bills to that end during the third session of this Congress. In early January 1863 Lincoln was sanguine about the chances of success, and both chambers approved the House bill. But the differences in the two versions were never reconciled. For all practical purposes, Lincoln's efforts to obtain federally compensated emancipation for the border states now ended. He continued, however, to urge action at the state level, and a draft joint resolution that he prepared, dated February 5, 1865, but never sent to Congress, empowered the president to expend up to $400 million to assist the sixteen slave states, including those that had remained loyal, in effecting emancipation, provided that no part was to be paid unless all resistance to the Union government was ended by April 1, 1865.[52]

We know that Lincoln's legislative program for compensated emancipation in the border states failed. But its outlines are incongruent with the view of a Lincoln who remained aloof from congressional activity.[53] Meanwhile the war power was used to justify Lincoln's emancipation proclamations of September 1862 and January 1863 and the enlistment of blacks under the provisions of laws that guaranteed the black slave recruit his freedom. But this policy raised questions of constitutionality in Lincoln's mind, as did the piecemeal efforts that members of the next Congress made to expunge from the statute books all legislation recognizing slavery. The action that would end all doubts about the wartime executive initiatives and legislation on the subject of slavery was passage of a constitutional amendment forbidding the institution. But ratification might prove difficult, since three-quarters of the states had to give their assent. Charles A. Dana, then in the War Department, later told of being delegated by Lincoln to bring three wavering congressmen into line behind the Nevada Admission Act by promising them whatever patronage was necessary. His mission was successful. Lincoln also continued to urge passage of the measure that became the Thirteenth Amendment after it had failed to win approval in the House during the first session of the Thirty-eighth Congress and took steps to see that it was endorsed in the national Republican platform of 1864. He was in close touch with the efforts in early 1865 to line up the two-thirds majority required for passage in the popular chamber. Cooperation from Democrats was essential to this end, and Lincoln conferred with some members of that group who might perhaps be persuaded to change their earlier votes from nay to yea or to abstain from voting. He counseled the resolution's floor manager, James M. Ashley, in his efforts to muster a majority. Various Democrats did switch their original votes to aye or abstained, and the House exploded in jubilation on January 31, 1865, when the amendment passed. Rumors of quid pro quo spread: Were patronage posts promised? Did presidential pardons go to the repentant southern relatives of congressmen? Was assurance given that the measure designed to eliminate the special privileges of the Camden and Amboy Railroad in New Jersey would be quashed? The specific details will always remain unclear. Certainly, however, Lincoln had not been a passive spectator. Nor did he stand uncommitted when less important legislation was under consideration.[54] In a letter to General Sherman, he noted that he had favored the act that allowed northern states to recruit blacks in the South to help in filling the northern state draft quotas.[55]

Clearly, however, Congress behaved otherwise concerning emancipation than Lincoln would have preferred. Perhaps his experience with this issue inclined him to pursue a different strategy in his efforts to restore the erring sisters to their proper places in the Union during the years 1863–65. Rather than provide a specific design for Congress to follow on reconstruction, complete with resolutions, proffered model bills, and constitutional amendments, Lincoln found justification for developing his own plan of national restoration in his powers as commander in chief and in the constitutional power to grant reprieves and pardons. In his proclamation of amnesty and reconstruction of December 8, 1863 – the 10 percent plan – the president carefully noted that admission to seats in Congress was the prerogative of those bodies alone and that "while the mode presented is the best the Executive can suggest . . . it must not be understood that no other possible mode would be acceptable."[56] Perhaps by promulgating his own plan and setting it in motion, he was trying to preempt the field, fully aware of the harshness that might be expected in a congressional solution. But whatever the reality, he was in fact again setting the congressional agenda by providing a model that would be used as the basis for congressional discussion.

In evaluating Lincoln's involvement and skill in legislative matters, we must also remember that Lincoln was dependent on the Senate to approve his major political and military appointments. The military nominations on occasion were particularly sensitive. Severe differences of opinion in this arena could seriously affect the progress of legislation, destroy military morale, or sour public opinion. Lincoln did not hesitate to marshal support for his recommendations in Congress if necessary. By late 1863, for example, he had decided that reaction to General John M. Schofield's civil policies in Missouri dictated his removal as the commanding officer in that department. Lincoln explained his strategy to Stanton:

> Now for the mode. Senator Henderson, his friend, thinks he can be induced to ask to be relieved, if he shall understand he will be generously treated; and, on this latter point, Gratz Brown will help his nomination as a Major General, through the Senate. In

no other way can he be confirmed; and upon his rejection alone, it would be difficult for me to sustain him as Commander of the Department. Besides, his being relieved from command of the Department, and at the same time confirmed as a Major General, will be the means of Henderson and Brown leading off together as friends, and will go far to heal the Missouri difficulty.

But the scheme was even more complex. In the reorganization attendant on Schofield's resignation, General Rosecrans was to take over in St. Louis and General Curtis to be given the command over territory to the west, both moves designed to please other individuals or groups. John Hay recorded his labors in lining up Senators Sherman, Wilson, Harris, and Doolittle in support of the arrangement, noting as well that Senator Foot had "agreed to do all he could to put the matter properly through." Despite some opposition from radical senators, the plan succeeded.[57]

If there was no firmly organized phalanx of Lincolnites in the chambers, there were men sympathetic to his views – men like the senators just mentioned or like the House member who desired "to be useful in any manner . . . which you may point out" or like the one who asked a favor and trusted "that you will appreciate my course during the last session."[58] Committee chairmen asked his opinion and sometimes accepted his legislative suggestions. Lincoln's control over a myriad of offices and his active role in dispensing them must have been sufficient to lead some congressmen into that course – along with the fact that some entertained policy views similar to those he held. Sometimes he even championed the pet measures of members in messages to Congress, as in the case of Arnold's much desired northwest ship canal and Representative Maynard's eastern Tennessee railroad. Such action did not ensure passage, however.

Lincoln was keenly aware of the jealousy with which the congressmen guarded their turf. He rejected the idea of placing a military governor over the District of Columbia on the ground that objections would come "from indignant members of Congress who will perceive in it an attempt of mine to set a guardian over them." To friendly advice suggesting in 1864 that he send a message to Congress urging passage of a constitutional amendment abolishing slavery, Lincoln responded, "Our own friends have this under consideration now, and will do as much without a Message as with it." Far from believing that Lincoln ignored them, some congressmen believed that he was too interested. In mid December 1862, Representative Cutler complained, "He has urged in his message a most impracticable scheme of compensated emancipation Nobody likes – Nobody will give it a cordial support & yet he has loaded his friends down with its odium."

When he sent a message to Congress suggesting that the system of currency was still in need of attention, the *Springfield Republican* reported grumbling because members believed that Lincoln "intermeddles" too much. Although Pendleton was a Democrat, his proposal to the Thirty-eighth Congress to bring cabinet officers officially onto the floor during two days of the week had bipartisan support, and its discussion reflected concern about the power of the executive branch to affect legislative outcomes. That power, believed Pendleton, was now "overgrown and . . . abnormal."[59]

In support of his contention that Lincoln had little impact on the legislative process, Donald noted that Lincoln vetoed only two measures and pocket-vetoed two others, three of the measures dealing with relatively unimportant matters. Actually the total number was seven, a record little different from the average of eight recorded by his two immediate Democratic predecessors, who presumably did not espouse Whig principles. Only three presidents up to 1860 vetoed more public measures than did Lincoln.[60]

Several of Lincoln's vetoes dealt with unimportant issues, but others were more important, particularly his pocket veto of the Wade-Davis reconstruction bill. That measure bore upon one of the great policy issues of the war. In this case, Lincoln shocked the congressmen still more by publishing a proclamation in which he explained his reasons for refusing to sign the bill. This statement is sometimes interpreted as indicating that the president believed reconstruction to be an executive rather than a legislative responsibility, and on this subject David Donald wrote, "Within the area of what he considered legitimate congressional power Lincoln was careful not to interfere." That interpretation is strained. In his message, Lincoln noted that progress already made in reestablishing loyal civil government in several states would be wiped out by the Wade-Davis bill. The constitutional issue he raised did not relate to the bill's major objective but, rather, to the power of Congress to abolish slavery, an issue the amendment process would presumably put to rest. He was, he affirmed blandly in the veto message, "fully satisfied with the system for restoration contained in the Bill, as one very proper plan for the loyal people of any State choosing to adopt it." Thus Lincoln justified his veto on the basis of expediency – the fact that it would nullify progress already made – rather than on the constitutional location of the power to effect reconstruction.[61]

Other incidents also show us a Lincoln who was quite prepared to be firm with his co-workers in the legislative branch. The Confiscation Act of 1862 held the attention of Congress as did no other measure of that session. Lincoln did not veto the bill in its final form, but his specific threat to do so forced the passage of a modifying resolution. Like the Wade-Davis bill in the next Congress, the Confiscation Act of 1862 came to Lincoln with but hours remaining during the session. On July 15, 1862, Lincoln requested the Speaker of the House and the president of the Senate to postpone adjournment for a day beyond the date then set. The House acceded, but Senator Foot, as president pro tempore of the Senate, reported that it would be "exceedingly difficult, if not impossible, to postpone the adjournment, unless some Senator can say *it is necessary.* To this end several Senators desire me to ask that you will state the ground or reason of such necessity."[62]

Lincoln responded on the same day, "I am sorry Senators could not so far trust me as to believe I had some real cause for wishing them to remain. I am considering a bill which came to me only late in the day yesterday, and the subject of which has perplexed Congress for more than half a year. I may return it with objections; and if I should, I wish Congress to have the opportunity of obviating the objections, or of passing it into a law notwithstanding them." Lincoln was given his postponement and signed both the bill and an explanatory resolution that he had demanded on July 17. The latter measure ensured that confiscatory action was to be based on future acts of rebellion, that taking an oath of loyalty to the Confederacy was to be an essential element in the indictment of some categories of southerners, and that any forfeitures of real estate must not extend beyond the offender's natural life. Despite the congressional concessions and his decision to sign the bill, Lincoln sent to Congress the veto message he had prepared "before I was informed of the passage of the Resolution." He noted his belief that the bill as originally approved would have deprived rebels of their property by methods that were unconstitutional.[63]

There is also in the Lincoln papers an exchange of views with the members of the cabinet on the constitutionality of the West Virginia Act, establishing the new state from the western counties of the Old Dominion. Although his cabinet officers were split on this matter, Lincoln convinced himself that this bold legislative departure was acceptable. Congressional action, he noted, showed that the measure was expedient. His own review convinced him that it was constitutional. But here again Lincoln had apparently been prepared to wield the veto if he thought it necessary.[64]

Nor was Lincoln afraid to set Congress straight in other ways when he believed it appropriate. On April 30, 1862, the House of Representatives approved a resolution censuring former Secretary of War Simon Cameron for the contracting policies the War Department had followed under his direction during the early days of the war. Lincoln prepared a long explanation, stressing the need for emergency measures at the time. He concluded by noting that "the proceedings . . . were not moved nor suggested by himself, and that not only the President but all the other heads of departments were at least equally responsible with him for whatever error, wrong or fault was committed in the premises."[65] He refused to allow Cameron to serve as scapegoat.

When the members of Congress decided to exclude the votes of states reconstructed under Lincoln's plan in the counting of the presidential ballots in the 1864 election, Lincoln signed the "Joint Resolution declaring certain States not entitled to representation in the Electoral College," but sent a message to Congress noting his view that the houses had complete power under the Constitution "to exclude from counting all electoral votes deemed by them to be illegal." It was not, therefore, "competent for the executive to defeat or obstruct that power by a veto, as would be the case if his action were at all essential in the matter." He disclaimed, he wrote, "all right of the Executive to interfere in . . . canvassing or counting electoral votes," but also denied that by signing the resolution he had "expressed any opinion on the recitals of the preamble or any judgment of his own upon the subject of the Resolution."[66] His signature, he was telling members of Congress, in no way expressed agreement with their course of action.

On the other hand, mere expediency, politics, or friendship was insufficient reason for nullifying the wishes of Congress. Ward H. Lamon, old friend, U.S. marshal of the District of Columbia, and sometime court minstrel, pleaded the case for veto when Congress approved a bill concerning the fees of U.S. legal officers and incorporated an amendment from Senator Grimes that materially reduced the fees of the marshal's office. It was one act in a small drama that began during the Thirty-seventh Congress when Lamon refused Grimes of the Senate Committee on the District of Columbia free access to the Old Capitol Prison. "I regret this," responded Lincoln, "but I can not veto a Bill of this character."[67] Grimes's amendment was a petulant slap at one of Lincoln's faithful retainers, but the act was technically proper; it had therefore to stand.

Although there was on occasion friction between the executive and legislative branches, Lincoln understood his obligations as both chief legislator and party leader. In those capacities Lincoln was committed to a Republican or Union majority in Congress. His use of patronage was designed to that end, as were his border state policies. And when it was feared that Colonel Emerson Etheridge, clerk of the Thirty-seventh House, might disallow a sufficient number of Republican credentials to permit the Democrats and Unionists to organize the House at the beginning of the Thirty-eighth Congress, Lincoln took the initiative in warning the members of threatened delegations to bring credentials in the form that he prescribed.[68] Here, as in other aspects of his relations with Congress, Lincoln was neither disinterested nor passive.

The evidence developed in this chapter makes it clear that the use of Lincoln's Whig past as dowser's wand is misleading. Although the Whigs called for a weak executive, even to the point of some proposing to abolish the presidential veto, the only Whig president with significant tenure in office, Zachary Taylor, tried to force his policy views on Congress during the crisis of 1850. Lincoln perhaps also pondered Polk's successes and failures in dealing with the congressmen of the Mexican War years, including a gangling representative from Illinois. But Lincoln had no insider's seat from which to assess the inner workings of either the Polk or the Taylor administration. Lincoln's observations in these cases were merely elements in the past experience of a thoughtful, subtle – even crafty – and wise man, who steadfastly, if sometimes sadly, grasped the levers of power and struggled pragmatically, as best he could, to preserve the Union. At times he might have preferred to ignore Congress, but in general he worked willingly with its members. He was also willing to provide leadership for the men on Capitol Hill, sometimes subtly or implicitly, at other times with forceful directness. Important issues of the wartime agenda – as distinguished from the party platform agenda – resulted in victory neither for the congressmen nor for the president; their outcomes reflected continuing interaction between the legislative and executive branches of the government.

In identifying a presidential role that he defined as serving as voice of the people, Rossiter was picking up the Jacksonian theme of the executive who spoke and acted for the whole people, in contrast to the lawmakers, who were bound by the constraints of more narrowly defined constituencies. That Lincoln saw himself to some degree in this light we cannot doubt. But he also grasped the fact that he had to speak not only for the people but to the people, that he had to provide an ideological, constitutional, and philosophical rationale for both the war and the policies that had been developed to wage it. This Lincoln did magnificently.

If a people are to wage a war of great sacrifice, they must have a strong sense of why they are fighting, and the objective must be a worthy one. We of our generation would regard the elimination of slavery as a worthy aim. Lincoln acknowledged that this institution was probably the root cause of the war, its presence providing the only aspect in which southern institutions differed radically from northern. But he was too astute to defend the war as one to end slavery in a constituency that included slaveholding states vital to the cause of the Union and where anti-Negro sentiment was widely prevalent. Rather, Lincoln emphasized what must be defended, retained, and preserved. In his first inaugural address he extolled the Constitution as the preeminent guide to action, lauded the Union perpetual, and emphasized the fact that within it the people determined the fate of politicians and their political creations. These themes he intermingled with reasoned arguments noting the unconstitutional nature of southern actions, the economic arguments against secession, and a commitment to change through the constitutionally authorized system of amendment.

By the time the special session of Congress convened on July 4, 1861, Lincoln had had more time to ponder the situation. In his message he presented his understanding of the outbreak of warfare and subsequent events along with a powerful analysis of the illegitimacy of secession. He extolled a United States that afforded to "all, an unfettered start, and a fair chance, in the race of life." In addition he affirmed the wisdom and understanding of "the plain people," and proclaimed the objective of "teaching men that what they cannot take by an election, neither can they take . . . by a war." Article IV, section 4, of the Constitution obligates the United States to "guarantee to every state . . . a republican form of government," and Lincoln invoked this pledge as a means of justifying the restoration of federal control over the southern states. In a later message he returned to this clause, and congressmen would look to it as the rationale for their plan of reconstruction. In December 1861 he was again to emphasize that the Union government had as its first principle the rights of the people, and it was here too that he developed his famous contrast in the relationship between capital and labor in North and South.[69] All such ideas Lincoln expressed in plain but forcefully felicitous language. And what Lincoln did in these formal statements he did through other channels as well, letters to editors or other important private citizens, addresses at sanitary fairs, and words of commendation to regiments passing through Washington on completion of their tours of duty.

Ostensibly Lincoln laid these ideas before the congressmen as arguments that they could themselves use in their dealings with their constituents. But if Lincoln hoped that his rhetoric would rally the members of Congress behind him, he was less than successful. These men were more inclined to use a harsher rhetoric of traitorous conspiracy and apocalyptic revenge. But taken with Lincoln's humanity, his stubbornness, his courage, and the other elements of a unique personal style, his ideas and arguments apparently won the confidence of a sufficient number in the Union public so that state-level politicians, skillfully recruited and marshaled by his friends and supporters, were able to procure for him the second-term nomination that a majority of the congressmen probably would have preferred to go elsewhere.

So, in conclusion, what did the congressmen see in Lincoln in practical terms? Of most interest to them was the fact that Lincoln was the chief patronage dispenser in the American political system. Amid the exigencies of a great domestic war, Lincoln was also commander in chief of a mighty army whose operations extended into every loyal state and congressional district. In this role also Lincoln was a patronage dispenser, since the officers of the Union forces were commissioned by Lincoln with the traditional advice and consent of the Senate. But the impact of Lincoln's military role was far greater than this; it involved calls for enlisted men, quota systems, military arrests, the suppression of newspapers, the disciplining of district or departmental commanding officers, and much more – all possible sources of challenge, problem, or opportunity to representatives. And across the whole range of federal activity, Lincoln was a kind of court of last resort to whom congressmen could appeal lower-level decisions or whom they might use to manipulate the federal system to their particular advantage.

How did Lincoln, on the other hand, view the Republican members of Congress? He and they were both elements of a new political party, dedicated to a free soil agenda and pledged, Lincoln made clear, to writing their national platform of 1860 into federal law. And the congressional Republicans were strikingly successful in realizing the major objectives enunciated in their national platform. But achievement that in a peacetime administration would have qualified as amazing success was obscured by the issues stemming from the national emergency. On many of the crisis issues there was no agreed party position; the solutions involved conflicting views and objectives on which the party members had not worked out a common position, as in the planks of a national party platform. Rather, such solutions had to be achieved by Congress and the executive working in concert as the problems gained salience. Lincoln enunciated his formula for working with Congress on his way to Washington, and it is probably correct to regard it as being a Whig formula, given its nature and Lincoln's origins. But in practice he did not take it seriously. There is little to suggest that he consciously tried, however, to build an administration team in Congress. With unrivaled amounts of patronage at hand, perhaps he could have done so. John Hay and other close associates bemoaned his tendency to ignore past betrayals and to proclaim his preference for a short statute of limitations in politics.[70] If representatives and senators longed to replace him with someone they believed to have more backbone, Lincoln did not waste his time with that kind of daydreaming; he had to do what he could with what the people sent him.

But to Lincoln the congressmen were much more than just legislators. They were his observers, not just manning the party listening posts in political constituencies but reporting on public opinion, morale, and the impact of war policies. Lincoln used the Illinois representative Elihu B. Washburne as an emissary in 1861 to evaluate allegations that General John C. Frémont's administration of military affairs in Missouri was both incompetent and corrupt, and other congressmen were prepared to inform the president of vital if less dramatic developments in dozens of other constituencies. In Kentucky during the early months of the war, Lincoln even designated some congressmen to oversee the distribution of arms to loyal residents. Throughout the North, many congressmen were, in effect, recruiting agents for Commander in Chief Lincoln. Although the president and his departmental secretaries occupied the apex of the patronage pyramid, they could never have prepared their appointment lists to maximum effectiveness and political advantage if the representatives and senators had not assisted in the essential task of screening the aspirants for public office. And the congressmen kept the chief executive and his secretaries in close touch with reality through the advice they gave and the complaints and requests for information they made to the executive branch – some informally in the executive offices or at social gatherings, others formally via resolutions of inquiry tendered on the floors of the congressional chambers.

Despite Lincoln's control of patronage, his legislative ideas and philosophy, and the common bonds of party and purpose, the congressmen failed Lincoln in a most important respect, that of providing support for his particular policies on the two most important civil issues relating to the South – elimination of slavery and formulation of a plan to set the rebellious sister states once more within the political and social fabric of the nation. Why so? Unfortunately this question can never be answered with certainty.

Granted that Lincoln's ideological commitments hardly matched those of others in his party, the outcome might have been different if Lincoln had carried the prestige of a Washington into the White

House. But Lincoln's curriculum vitae was scanty, even for an era when extended government service was exceptional: four years of tenure in the Illinois Assembly, but never a term as Speaker, no service in the state senate or in a constitutional convention, a single term in the House of Representatives, and twice failure in seeking a seat in the U.S. Senate. Such denigrated statesmen as Franklin Pierce and James Buchanan had more on their slates than this, as had that symbol of mediocrity New York's Millard Fillmore. Little wonder then that Republican senators questioned Lincoln's abilities and that representatives laughed at his jokes and stories but considered his track record little more impressive than their own. They did not initially understand the growth of character and wisdom that Lincoln had undergone during the prairie lawyer years. As unsuccessful general replaced unsuccessful general, as the seamy side of Civil War contracting was revealed, as both his colleagues and the Democrats continued their party warfare, representatives and senators still had reason to doubt. Despite the pronouncements on the relation of the executive and legislative branches that Lincoln made during the early weeks of 1861, his first major actions as president – the famous executive orders issued to mobilize the armed forces and to suppress disloyalty – placed a question squarely before the members of Congress: Where does congressional authority end and executive implementation begin? Whether he intended it or not, Lincoln's initial executive strategy worked to place the members of Congress on the institutional defensive.

There was also the problem of the second legislative agenda. In the midst of crisis, wartime policy had to be perfected across a wide spectrum of issues. Now the zealot and the ideologue could introduce proposals far more extreme than any peacetime national convention would have considered to be acceptable planks, enhancing the opportunities for conflict within the chambers and between the executive and legislative branches. Lincoln's failures suggest that his weapons were inadequate to shatter the ideological spectrum and policy alignment that prevailed in Congress. But perhaps there were institutional elements in Congress that helped significantly to shape results as well. In Chapter 4 we shall consider these possibilities further.

3 An "inquiring disposition": the investigative process in the House of Representatives

As a member of the Thirty-sixth Congress, rough-hewn Representative John Covode (R.,* Pa.) became a national celebrity in 1860 when he chaired a highly political investigation of President Buchanan's earlier relations with Congress and his efforts, or those of members of his administration, to subvert "the execution of any law now upon the statute book." Shortly after the publication of the committee report, Covode embarked upon a campaign swing through New Hampshire in company with Charles H. Van Wyck (R., N.Y.), a young politician who was considered to be a better speaker than the Pennsylvanian. But the voters of the Granite State proved to be much more interested in the findings of Covode's committee than in listening to Van Wyck's oratory. So impressed by this circumstance was Van Wyck, said Covode later, that "no sooner was [the Thirty-seventh Congress] organized than he had an investigating committee appointed, of which he was chairman." Covode continued: "While I run the investigating machine *over my enemies*, Van Wyck has run it *over his friends*." The Pennsylvanian's accusation emphasized an important aspect of congressional activity during the Civil War; Van Wyck had not been alone in his desire to investigate. "The last Congress," noted the *New York Herald* in 1863, "will be memorable for its inquiring disposition."[1] Both in this Congress and the next, investigation influenced the form of legislation, partisan and factional activity, and the behavior and careers of individual congressmen, as well as those of other public servants and ordinary citizens.

Beneath most bills or joint resolutions passed by Congress lies a foundation of information that was assembled by the drafters of such measures. The congressional power of inquiry or investigation flows from need for such information. So strongly based on British and colonial precedent was this prerogative that neither the architects of the federal Constitution nor the congressmen of the 1790s believed it

*Abbreviations of party affiliations appear in a list at the beginning of the endnotes.

60

necessary to discuss it at any length. Nor, as the practices of legislative investigation developed over the years in Congress, did the relationship between the information sought and future legislation need to be a close one. Historians customarily point to the select committee of the House charged with inquiring "into the cause of the failure of the late expedition under Major General St. Clair" in 1791 as the first of hundreds of congressional committees of investigation.[2]

Marshall Dimock, who made the first comprehensive study of congressional investigating committees, attempted to identify their essential characteristics. Such groups, he argues, were either select or standing legislative committees; were created by resolution of the sponsoring chamber; were directed to perform a circumscribed inquiry; had as their principal task that of investigating and reporting; presented reports that might be adopted and referred to a standing committee for action; and might or might not be given power to send for persons or papers. The objects of inquiry of such committees, Dimock also argued, could be divided into three categories: particular members of the chamber; subjects directly related to lawmaking; and the performance of members of the executive branch – the famed "oversight function," as it came to be called after World War II.[3]

Some years ago, the political scientist Roger H. Davidson discussed the functions of modern committees of investigation. Although they served the purpose of providing information, he suggested, they also allowed representatives of interested groups to state their positions on particular issues. To lawmakers, committee activity provided an opportunity to establish the reputation of being interested in particular issues, as well as giving them the rationale for introducing or supporting specific legislative measures. But Davidson noted that investigative activity involved broader political dimensions as well. Such committees permitted the members to advertise themselves. Sometimes also the creation of investigating committees has reflected jurisdictional competition within Congress, and frequently, if not invariably, investigating committees have been designed to advance partisan fortunes. Committee investigations also have contributed, argued Davidson, to "institutional maintenance" by protecting the interests of the congressional chambers against encroachment from the executive and judicial branches or from lobbying groups. Investigations may also stimulate quiescent groups into political activity, serve as catalysts of public opinion, and even provide a kind of social catharsis for the general public.[4]

We cannot assume that Davidson's generalizations are completely helpful in understanding the congressional behavior of the mid nineteenth century. But they provide hypotheses, explicit and implicit, about the motivations that underlay investigative activity during the Civil War, as well as about the implications and results of such activity. Davidson's congressmen looked back upon an institutional history of almost two centuries and performed their duties during a global confrontation of ideologies; those of Abraham Lincoln's time could recall the deaths of some of the Republic's most illustrious founders and lived to the rhythm of marching feet and the recurrent rumble of artillery beyond the horizon. In such an atmosphere, formal procedures might seem slow, even dangerous, and "earnestness" might all too easily become extremism. These were unusual times, and the committee of investigation was a tested formula for dealing with the unusual; the assault on Charles Sumner, John Brown's attack on the federal arsenal at Harpers Ferry, and James Buchanan's policies all inspired congressional investigators, and their activity was fresh in the memory of each representative and senator who assembled in the Thirty-seventh Congress. These investigations all reflected party maneuvering and conflict, and party competition would not be put to rest during the war for the Union. Despite their common abhorrence of slavery and the unifying pressures of the war, the congressional Republicans were a disparate crew, easily tempted into manifestations of factionalism. Investigative activity might well reflect such divisions, and in the unparalleled mobilization of men and resources soon to take place there would be ample opportunity for conflict as well between the executive and legislative branches. Here too the inquiry might play a role. And although I must caution that Davidson wrote of a different time, the nineteenth-century congressman was also ambitious, also interested in career building, and quite as capable of sensing personal gain as his counterpart of the late twentieth century.

In fact the congressman may engage in various degrees or levels of investigative activity. Individual lawmakers, select committees, subcommittees of standing committees, and their parent bodies all seek information. During the Civil War, standing committees conducted hearings on relevant subjects as a matter of course, and on "Devil's Days," when members might present resolutions on the floor under the House rules, the humblest member of the opposition could submit resolutions of inquiry for the consideration of colleagues.[5] Gaining the approval of a majority of the House was, of course, another matter, but during the war years the representatives were, as the *New York Herald* intimated, highly receptive to suggestions that committees, cabinet officers, and the president should provide answers to questions originating in the legislative branch. Some of the reasons for this will become apparent as we proceed.

Problems of definition and the obscurity of some minor investigative activity impede efforts to provide precise estimates of the number of oversight inquiries during the war congresses and those preceding them. Our tabulations of the number of select House committees in the congresses of the Civil War era do not match exactly with those published recently by Walter Stubbs. Such caveats aside (and disregarding committees concerned with ceremonial activity), the numbers of select or special committees in the Thirty-seventh and Thirty-eighth congresses were 19 and 16, in comparison to the mean of 11.2 found in the five antecedent bodies, the Thirty-second through the Thirty-sixth. The members of the Thirty-fifth Congress particularly favored the use of the select committee, including a goodly proportion of oversight bodies; but taking the congresses of the 1850s as a whole, this particular use of the select committee was less common than during the Civil War, when 15 of 35 select committees were primarily concerned with wrongdoing or improper performance of duties. At the same time, standing committees were supervising similar probes. The Judiciary, Naval Affairs, Military Affairs, District of Columbia, Commerce, and Government Expenditures in the Treasury committees were all involved in the investigative process during the war. Some evidence exists of at least eighteen probes by these groups, quite apart from the Elections Committee's routine consideration of contested or irregular elections. And investigations of wide-ranging scope appear to have been greater in number during the Civil War than in previous congresses.

Apparently also, some committees expanded their perspective during the war. The assorted committees charged with oversight of expenditures in the various departments or bureaus had in peacetime been regarded as little more than symbols of oversight. But the regular legislative session of the Thirty-seventh Congress had not been long under way when Representative William Wall (R., N.Y.) reported a resolution from the Committee on Expenditures on the Public Buildings seeking instruction "to inquire into the probable cost of the Treasury Building extension and Capitol extension, the manner in which the work is being done, and being executed . . . and that said committee investigate and report to this House such facts, in relation to the several matters referred to, as they shall deem proper; and that they have power to send for persons and papers." Not only did this resolution initiate an inquiry of some consequence; it apparently invigorated other committees of this type. A newspaper account of the Thirty-eighth Congress reported such committees busily at work in reviewing the details of departmental expenditures with an interest and diligence unheard of in times of peace.[6]

Although legislators intent on shaping policy or drafting legislation probably always dominated the process of fact-finding during the Civil War, inquiries concerned with fraud, corruption, disloyalty, and the incompetence of public officers generated the most interest, then as now, and had, of course, legislative and political implications that often extended far beyond the ostensible object of investigation. In this chapter we shall examine the scope of this type of inquiry in the war years, note its major manifestations and characteristics, identify some of the lawmakers who were particularly associated with such inquiries, and assess both the general importance of the investigative process and its place in the career-building activity of the individual congressman. Given our state of knowledge, much of the presentation must be purely descriptive and illustrative, providing – as do the other chapters of this volume – a reconnaissance rather than a fully developed exercise in hypothesis testing.

The work of the House Judiciary Committee during the Thirty-seventh Congress provides an instructive introduction to investigative activity during the Civil War. On July 16, 1861, during the special summer session of Congress, the committee members informed Henry May (D., Md.), a representative from Baltimore and a member of the Judiciary Committee, that they had been directed by resolution of the House to investigate the circumstances surrounding his visit to Richmond during the early weeks of the Civil War.

In the early stages of the secession crisis, Marylanders were sharply divided in their loyalties, and to some Republicans Baltimore was little more than a nest of rebels. Had May's journey to the Confederate city cloaked traitorous activity on the part of himself and other Maryland Democrats? Soon May gave testimony before his committee colleagues, as did John F. Potter, the Wisconsin member who at the time was assessing the loyalty of federal government employees. The fact that May had conferred with Lincoln and Winfield Scott, the Union general in chief, before leaving made the situation more interesting. After discussing May's case, the committee members directed their chairman, John Hickman (R., Pa.), to report to the House that they considered May, President Lincoln, and General Scott to be absolved from "the accusation of having held criminal correspondence or intercourse with the rebels."[7]

In their last attempt to exercise oversight powers during the special summer session of 1861, the members of the committee took in hand a House resolution requiring the committee to obtain an explanation from the president ("if not incompatible with the public interest") for the arrest and continuing detention of the police commissioners of Baltimore.[8]

The regular legislative session of the Thirty-seventh Congress had hardly begun in early December when John A. Gurley (R., Ohio) provided the Judiciary Committee with an investigative assignment. A second-term congressman from Ohio, former minister, editor, farmer, and aide-de-camp of General Frémont while in Missouri, Gurley submitted a resolution directing the committee "to inquire if a telegraphic censorship of the press" had "been established in this city" and "if so, by whose authority and by whom it is now controlled; to report if such censorship has not been used to restrain a wholesome political criticism and discussion, while its professed and laudable object has been to withhold from the enemy important information in reference to movements of the army." The committee minutes show that there was some disagreement within the committee as to the intensity with which this inquiry was to be conducted. The radical Republicans – Hickman, John A. Bingham (R., Ohio), and James F. Wilson (R., Ia.) – showed the greatest interest in proceeding vigorously, but not until early January did Hickman, with his colleagues' consent, ask the House to authorize the group to send for persons and papers and to employ a phonographic reporter at the usual rate of compensation.

Once the committee was thus placed in gear, its members conducted an active investigation. Between January 24 and late February 1862 they held many meetings and examined some twenty witnesses, mostly from the Washington press corps, but including also Frederick W. Seward, the assistant secretary of state, and other officials who were closely involved in the censorship process. They recalled several witnesses for further questioning and to give additional statements. Midway in these proceedings, the committee members were forced to divide their forces and agreed that Bingham should take in hand the impeachment of West H. Humphreys, a federal judge from Tennessee. After some differences among themselves, the committee members in late February instructed their colleague Wilson to prepare a report on the "telegraphic censorship of the press" for presentation to the House along with the testimony and the request that the report be printed. In mid March, Wilson's colleagues considered and adopted the report, although Alexander S. Diven (R., N.Y.) gave notice that he would submit a minority report.[9] Of these matters more will be said below.

In early June 1862, the committee involved itself under the leadership of Hickman and Bingham in assessing the loyalty of the two most irritating Peace Democrats in the House, Clement L. Vallandigham (D., Ohio) and Benjamin Wood (D., N.Y.). Hickman's resolution concerning the Ohioan, which requested the House to authorize subpoena privileges and the examination of witnesses on oath or affirmation, was based on a story in the *Baltimore Clipper* alleging that documents incriminating Vallandigham and the two senators from Delaware had been found in a police search of the premises of the newspaper *The South.* Vallandigham denied the truth of the newspaper report so vigorously on the House floor that Hickman withdrew his charge against him.[10] But the resolution that John A. Bingham presented on June 11, 1862, requesting that the committee be allowed to investigate Ben Wood had a very different outcome.

As a result of the inquiry into telegraphic censorship, the committee authorized the payment of some $100 in witness fees, distributed among twenty informants. In assessing the disloyalty of the handsome and articulate young Copperhead from New York, Ben Wood, the committee members took testimony from twenty-seven witnesses, mostly from New York, and expended almost $1,150 in witness fees. The final statements were presented on July 10, 1862, and one day later the Baltimore Democrat Henry May proposed that the resolution of inquiry be reported back to the House "with the opinion of this Committee that there appears [*sic*] to be no sufficient grounds to charge said B. Wood."

The members of the Republican committee majority were unwilling to absolve so irritating a gadfly as Ben Wood, the very prototype of an outspoken urban antiwar Democrat. With the Democrats May and Pendleton of Ohio opposing, they approved a resolution stating that "for want of time for due consideration" a report on the Honorable B. Wood would "be postponed to the next session of Congress." The evidence was to be sealed and placed in the custody of the sergeant-at-arms, and "no inference," committee members cautioned, was "to be drawn from the postponement of the case touching the guilt or innocence of Mr. Wood." Finally on January 22, 1863, they agreed without a recorded vote that "the testimony taken before the Committee on the Judiciary touching the matter of enquiry referred to them relative to Hon. B. Wood be printed." But this apparently was not done; the instructions to the printer still remain in the manuscript volume of testimony, and Wood was denied the pleasure of pointing to a printed document that, in his view, exonerated him from the charge of disloyalty and revealed the excessive zeal of radical Republicans like Hickman and Bingham.[11]

While the Ben Wood case was in train, other investigative assignments came to the committee. On June 26, 1862, Eliakim P. Walton (R., Vt.), newspaper editor and chairman of the House Committee on Printing, rose to a question "affecting the privileges of this House." He obtained the Speaker's permission to have the clerk read an article

from the *New York Tribune* of June 21. The story told of Roscoe Conkling's (R., N.Y.) effort to have his colleagues lay on the table a
resolution offered by Walton from the Committee on Printing that
provided for the payment of $35,000 to the publishers Gales and
Seaton for a stock of the *Annals of Congress.* Conkling failed, and the
Tribune's account of the incident included a sentence affirming, "We
have reason to believe . . . that a careful search for a pliable man was
instituted, and that some persons were approached ostensibly on
behalf of the friends of the resolution with offers of a pecuniary
nature."

Incensed, Walton interpreted the sentence as containing an accusation of bribery, "a breach of the privileges of the House, and by
the act of 1853 . . . a crime punishable with severe penalties." He submitted a resolution to the House calling on the Committee of the
Judiciary to investigate the *Tribune*'s charges. "I have put in the Committee on the Judiciary," explained Walton, "because I want a committee of sharp lawyers." But hot on the trail of Ben Wood, and
involved during these same days in the impeachment of West H.
Humphreys, the "sharp lawyers" of the Judiciary Committee decided
against following a trail that seemed to offer much less interesting
possibilities than the war-related issues that had earlier attracted their
attention. On June 30 they agreed to report Walton's resolution back
to the House with the recommendation that it be referred to a select
committee.[12]

When the Judiciary Committee reassembled in December 1863, the
Ben Wood case still stood unclosed, as we have seen. But at this point
too, its members received instructions to investigate irregularities in
Commissioner Kennedy's administration of the Bureau of the Census.
They took testimony and approved a report on this case in mid Jan-
uary. During February 1863 one of the committee's members, William
Kellogg (R., Ill.), investigated the possibility that the postmaster gen-
eral was "excluding . . . certain matter" from the U.S. mail.[13] The in-
vestigations of the telegraphic censorship of the press and of Ben
Wood's loyalty, however, were the most elaborate conducted by the
Judiciary Committee during the life of the Thirty-seventh Congress.
They deserve closer examination.

James Wilson's report from the Judiciary Committee explained that
a system of press censorship had been instituted in April of 1861,
supervised initially by the Treasury Department, then by the War
Department, and eventually by the State Department. There control
rested at the time of the inquiry. Censorship had begun after leading
members of the Washington press corps met with General McClellan
and, at his suggestion, approved ground rules governing the sub-

mission of news dispatches for telegraphic transmission from Washington to their papers. The most important provision of the short document, which was presumed to serve as a "rule of action" for both censor and press, provided that no matter should be transmitted that might "furnish aid and comfort to the enemy."

Although the officials involved in censoring dispatches were mainly interested in limiting the dissemination of important military intelligence, Wilson and his colleagues alleged that "despatches, almost numberless, of a political, personal, and general character [had] been suppressed by the censor, and correspondents have been deterred from preparing others because they knew they could not send them to their papers by telegraph." In the body of the report Wilson declared the censor completely unqualified for his position but affirmed that he was "not the only person at fault," for the secretary of state had expressed his satisfaction with the way in which the censor was performing his duties. The report ended with a resolution that began by affirming "that the government should not interfere with the free transmission of intelligence by telegraph when the same will not aid the public enemy in his military or naval operations."[14]

Much of the initial investigation by the committee was devoted to establishing the nature of the material that the censor had excised. The first witnesses complained of having to depend on memory alone, since they had not been given a record of expurgated passages. The committee, however, obtained the file of dispatches from the telegraph office, and witnesses introduced a formidable list of such material into the testimony. Wilson used these extracts selectively in preparing his report, seemingly to show both the triviality of the censor's activity and his efforts to protect the Lincoln administration. In retrospect, some of the censor's deletions appear harmless, even ludicrous. One such passage, submitted by Sam Wilkeson, the Washington editor of the *New York Tribune,* puffed Ben Wade by asserting that "the news from Ohio today is, that that great State will insist upon another term of service from the brave senator who has compelled the south to fear and respect the western reserve." But Wilkeson charged as well that he was "not permitted to send anything over the wires which, in the estimation of the censor, the Secretary of State, or the Assistant Secretary of State, shall be damaging to the character of the administration or any individual member of the cabinet, or that would be injurious to the reputation of the officers charged with the prosecution of the war, and particularly those of the regular army."[15] Committee members led other witnesses into making similar allegations.

Contrary to the procedure of some investigating committees of these years, the complete testimony of the witnesses was not printed as an appendix to the censorship report. And if the manuscript testimony hardly bears out the *New York Herald*'s scathing charge that it justified an investigation of the committee, it does provide additional illuminating perspectives. *Herald* writers – notoriously cranky and hypercritical – claimed that the investigation reflected the frustration of the *Tribune*'s Washington chief, Wilkeson, at losing the special privilege accorded to him by Secretary Cameron of sending his dispatches to New York without review by the censor. In his original testimony Wilkeson admitted that he had enjoyed favored status until he transmitted Colonel Charles P. Stone's report on the action at Ball's Bluff before General McClellan had had an opportunity to review it and ask for revisions. And three *Tribune* reporters accounted for a much greater volume of the testimony than did the representatives of any other paper.[16] Committee members, particularly the Republican radicals, probed hard to find evidence that the censorship was designed to protect Secretary Seward and other members of the cabinet. In preparing a report that was critical of the secretary of state, the Republican committee members found common cause with newsmen disgruntled over restrictions they considered excessive. When a definitive history of the radical Republican onslaught on the president and the more moderate members of his administration appears, the contributions of Hickman, Bingham, and Wilson to this investigation will surely be the subject of some attention.

In the committee report, Wilson barely alluded to the investigative incident that threatened to turn the inquiry into utter farce while at the same time pushing it into the borderland between the legislative and executive realms. An excerpt from the president's message of early December 1861 had appeared in the *Herald* before being received by Congress, and the *Tribune*'s Wilkeson spoke in his testimony of the *New York Herald*'s advantage in obtaining "news from the White House . . . from women . . . members of the President's family." In answer to a question from Francis Thomas (BU., Md.) about the *Herald*'s source in obtaining this information, Wilkeson replied, "We understand that it was received from Mrs. Lincoln & . . . was the occasion of a little domestic discord between Mrs. Lincoln and her respected husband before breakfast." The intermediate conduit was supposedly the author and adventurer Henry Wikoff, who was a friend of James Gordon Bennett, the publisher of the *Herald*, and was on cordial terms with Mrs. Lincoln.[17]

Although the identity of the *Herald*'s source was tangential at best, Hickman determined to explore it to the end and subpoenaed Wikoff. The latter admitted that he had passed the information to a *Herald* reporter but refused to divulge his source. On February 10, 1862, Hickman demanded that he answer the committee's question on this subject and gave him two days in which to respond. When Wikoff remained obdurate, Hickman had him brought before the House as a contumacious witness and placed in the custody of the sergeant-at-arms until he should purge himself of contempt. The sergeant-at-arms confined Wikoff in a storeroom used by the Capitol patrol as a depository of odds and ends and the headquarters of its canine members. One of these, a magnificent Newfoundland named Jack, particularly impressed the prisoner. Thus Wikoff passed the night of February 12, the monotony broken by a visit from a curious young lady from the West who was apparently intrigued by this victim of "Capitol punishment."[18]

After eating a "tolerable breakfast" from one of the Capitol restaurants, Wikoff considered his position. His informant had already given him permission to yield to the committee if it seemed advisable, so he claimed, and Wikoff was confirmed in his inclination to follow this course by a visit from his friend General Daniel E. Sickles, who had also been warmly received in times past at the White House – indeed, on the evening before. Sickles pacified the guards by telling them that he was there as Wikoff's lawyer, and in this capacity he advised him to divulge his source. Wikoff now sent word to Hickman that he was prepared to purge himself and soon appeared before the committee. In his account of the proceedings, Wikoff pictured the committee members hanging on his every breath as he prepared to tell the name of his informant, and then collapsing back in their chairs when he named not Mrs. Lincoln but John Watt, the head White House gardener. "The astonishment and disappointment was so deep and manifest," wrote Wikoff playfully, "that it was clear to me as noonday that some one else of more importance had been suspected as the purveyor of the overrated paragraph of the message. Was it, after all, then, a political intrigue?"

The frustrated Hickman did not drop the matter at this point. Sickles was called before the committee and forced to reveal the details of his mission to the White House on the night of Wikoff's incarceration. There he had had Watt reaffirm his permission to reveal his "indiscretion" and incidentally had briefed both Mary Lincoln and the president on developments at the Capitol. The general stubbornly maintained that it was indeed Watt who had inadvertently given Wikoff his information in a friendly conversation. S. P. Hanscom, the correspondent of the *Herald*, who accepted the scoop from Wikoff, affirmed just as stalwartly that the latter had assured him that Mrs. Lincoln was the informant. These events, as well as other dealings with Wikoff, had convinced Hanscom that the Chevalier – as Bennett called him – was not "a gentleman" and indeed would not "hesitate to lie at any time."[19]

By no means all details of this incident are clear. A press report noted that Abraham Lincoln appeared before the committee on the morning of the day when Wikoff purged himself of contempt. If Lincoln did so, the clerk failed to mention the fact in the committee minutes; but perhaps an informal conference did take place at the Capitol and perhaps the premature disclosure of a segment of his message was discussed. Ben Perley Poore was a witness before the committee, and many years later he reminisced of the incident: "Meanwhile, Mr. Lincoln had visited the Capitol and urged the Republicans to spare him disgrace, so Watt's improbable story was received." But the committee was still probing the issue in its questioning of Hanscom some four days later, and on February 20 Hickman opposed the decision of his colleagues to withhold from the House evidence relating to the president's family.

Another and broader issue may have been involved. The committee members had been considering a draft joint resolution offered by Hickman "relating to the powers of the pres[id]ent of U.S." and instructing the chief executive to confiscate the property of rebels, including their slaves. It was a proposal that Lincoln at the time would have considered inappropriate. On February 11, Bingham successfully moved that it should "not be reported to the House." In this motion Bingham received the support of George H. Pendleton (D., Ohio) and May and two moderates, Benjamin F. Thomas (R., Mass.) and Alexander S. Diven (R., N.Y.). Hickman, Kellogg, and Albert G. Porter (R., Ind.) voted nay. Thus the president and the chairman of the Judiciary Committee were at odds on at least two fronts while Wikoff was undergoing his ordeal. Some weeks later Hickman attacked Lincoln bitterly on the House floor, accusing him of shirking his duty and creating discord because he lacked "traits of character necessary to the discharge of grave responsibilities." In later recollections of his relations with Congress, Lincoln mentioned Hickman's hostility to him. If the committee's published report concerning press censorship gave the secretary of state reason for feeling like a victim of the investigative power, the actual proceedings of the committee undoubtedly gave the president grounds for sharing his distaste.[20]

The Ben Wood case reveals other dimensions of investigative activity in the House Judiciary Committee. None who study the history of the Lincoln administration can deny the resilience of William H. Seward, the secretary of state. Taken to task by the Judiciary Committee for his administration of telegraphic censorship during the

spring of 1862, he perhaps welcomed the letter he received later that
year from an obscure informant, A. T. Allen. This gentleman charged
that Representative Ben Wood, proprietor of the *New York News* as
well as a member of Congress, had through his agent William Mackellar employed James B. Kendrick in July 1861 "to proceed to Richmond for the nominal purpose of reporting the proceedings of the
Confederate Congress . . . but in reality to act as a medium for the
communication of important intelligence to the Confederates from
the North." Now the congressmen of the Judiciary Committee could
be sent haring in pursuit of a member of their own chamber, albeit
a detested Peace Democrat.[21]

Seward transmitted the letter from Allen to Bingham of the Judiciary
Committee, who, on June 11, 1862, introduced a resolution, "Whereas
information has been received by the Government that Hon. Benjamin
Wood . . . has been engaged in communicating or attempting to communicate important intelligence to the Confederate rebels, . . . Be it
resolved, That the Committee on the Judiciary inquire into the conduct
of said Benjamin Wood in the premises." The resolution continued
with the standard request for authority to send for persons and papers
and to examine witnesses on oath or affirmation. After some objections to the wording from members of the opposition, the House
approved the resolution and the Judiciary Committee set a vigorous
inquiry in motion.[22]

The evidence collected by the committee in the Wood case includes
various letters that ostensibly relate to Wood's disloyal activities or
to the good character of William N. Mackellar, who was in charge of
the business operations of the *New York News;* the testimony of Kendrick, Mackellar, and other witnesses including Frederick A. Conkling, member of Congress; a sworn statement submitted by Ben
Wood; and a collection of columns from the *News,* apparently intended to show that Wood cherished disloyal sentiments. Wood was
represented in the proceedings by his lawyer, surely appropriately
named, in the eyes of some, Mr. Sly, and after some committee discussion Wood was allowed to cross-examine some of the witnesses.
These were privileges that other congressional investigators of this
House did not allow to witnesses suspected of wrongdoing. The committee did not call Wood to give evidence, and he offered his own
statement voluntarily and under oath.

The basic facts of the Ben Wood case were relatively simple. James
B. Kendrick, on occasion employed as a journalist in the southern
states before the war, wrote to Wood during early July of 1861 and
proposed that he serve as a reporter for the *News* in covering the
proceedings of the Confederate Congress at Richmond. Wood, scent-

ing a scoop, or so he claimed, replied in a letter inquiring about Kendrick's qualifications for such an assignment. In response, Kendrick cited appropriate experience and acquaintance among the leading rebels. Wood referred this letter to Mackellar, citing the usefulness of such coverage and instructing Mackellar to hire Kendrick if he found him impressive. The business manager came to terms with Kendrick and sent letters to two railroads seeking passes for him. The reporter then departed for Louisville, whence he expected to cross through the lines into the Confederacy. During the summer of 1861, however, various executive orders terminated intercourse through the lines, and the arrangement with Kendrick petered out obscurely.

Evidence that Wood had actually sent communications to leading southerners or received letters from such individuals was of course vital to the case against him. Although admitting communication with Kendrick and his instructions to Mackellar, Wood maintained that this was the sum total of his involvement and flatly denied that he had either sent letters south or received missives from that quarter of the compass. Members of the committee devoted much effort to trying to establish the existence of letters that leading southerners had sent to Wood, or that he had addressed to Governor Letcher of Virginia or to Jefferson Davis. Rather dubious testimony was presented to show that the bartender in the building where Kendrick boarded had passed along letters from eminent rebels, but the witness was unimpressive and had not seen the full texts of these communications or the names of the addressees or the senders. The gentleman in Louisville who was to serve as Kendrick's contact above the Union lines claimed that Kendrick bore letters of introduction from John Breckenridge, ostensibly procured or provided by Wood, but these letters could not be produced. A couple of leading New York Democrats were now leaders in the forces of the Confederacy, and efforts were made to tie them to Wood. Committee members searched Wood's editorial writings for expressions of disloyalty, and it was claimed that one of Wood's speeches had been circulated in the South. But as in their pursuit of Wikoff and Mrs. Lincoln, the committeemen overreached themselves. They could not prove that Ben Wood was disloyal.[23]

Although the representative might strongly state his preferences for standing committee assignments to the Speaker, that gentleman had to weigh them against the partisan standing, legislative credentials, and personal qualities of the other members of the majority party in the House. And once the Speaker had made his decisions, the individual member of any standing committee was considerably restricted in his legislative activity by the legislative mandates of the committees on which he served. Service on a select committee might be quite a different matter, however. By long-standing custom, the Speaker usually entrusted the chairmanship of a select committee to the member who had submitted the resolution requesting its formation. If the subject was one of appropriate substance and the need was sufficiently patent to a majority of the House, the congressman might well use the select committee, as had John Covode, to the great benefit of self, party, section, or nation. Select committees of inquiry were active during the first Congress of the Civil War in searching for corruption, inefficiency, or disloyalty in the executive branch agencies and the armed forces.

When the members of the Thirty-seventh Congress met in emergency session during July and early August of 1861, John F. (sometimes called "Bowie Knife") Potter (R., Wis.) and Charles H. Van Wyck (R., N.Y.) discovered problems they believed to be well worth investigating. The select committee on the loyalty of government employees that Potter chaired and the inquiry into fraudulent government contracting that Van Wyck requested and led were to provide both with notice in the press that was well beyond the dreams of most of their colleagues. These committees also provoked mixed reactions among their associates in the House, the officers of the executive branch, and various members of the American public.

On July 8, 1861, Potter moved that a select committee be established "to ascertain and report to [the] House, the number of persons, with the names thereof, now employed in the several departments of the government, who are known to entertain sentiments of hostility to the government of the United States, and those who have refused to take the oath to support the Constitution of the United States." The House empowered the committee to send for persons and papers in its search for rebel sympathizers in the government departments. In addition to Potter, Speaker Grow appointed Haight (D., N.Y.), Samuel C. Fessenden (R., Me.), Egerton (R., Ohio), and Calvert (BU., Md.) to the Select Committee on the Loyalty of Clerks and Other Persons Employed by Government.[24]

Potter and his colleagues set vigorously to work. They met frequently during the course of the summer session and presented a partial report at the end of July. At that time they assured their colleagues that their task was one of great importance and successfully requested permission to continue their sittings during the recess between the end of the summer session and the assembly of the first regular legislative session of this Congress on December 6, 1861. After weeks of meeting "almost daily," the committee took a brief recess at the end of August but soon reassembled to continue its labors until October 8. The committee members had by this time interviewed some 450 witnesses and assembled evidence of disloyalty concerning some 550 government employees.[25]

The procedures that the committee members developed were to cause misgivings both among their congressional colleagues and within the ranks of government workers. Potter requested rosters of all departmental employees from the various members of the cabinet. The secretaries provided these without demur, and the committee members then proceeded to select some "old clerks in various departments, whose loyalty [was] undoubted" and ask them to assess the faithfulness of their colleagues.[26] Once the loyalty of an individual was impugned, however, Potter and his colleagues felt no obligation to confront him or to allow him to refute the charges. Rather they prepared lists of those whom they believed to be compromised without a doubt and those against whom the weight of evidence was less "positive." Potter then sent both lists to the appropriate head of the department for his action. Although they did not state it so bluntly, the committee members apparently desired that those whose names were on the first list should be discharged immediately and that those who appeared on the second should be further investigated at the departmental level.

The overall impact of the committee's labors is difficult to assess. The departmental secretaries did dismiss numerous employees on the basis of the information transmitted to them by the committee. Some who were disloyal in sentiment or who regarded themselves as hopelessly compromised resigned before departmental action was taken. In mid August 1861 the *New York Herald* reported that "upwards of one hundred and seventy clerks" had been dismissed thus far as a result of the activity of the committee. In mid December, Potter reported to the Republican caucus that "only about two hundred had been removed," a number that he considered quite inadequate, charging that there were still between four and five hundred disloyal employees in the various government departments in Washington. Speaking to his colleagues in the House on December 30, he used the larger of the two numbers. Other dismissals followed during early 1862, but the committee report that Congress received in late January did not include the numerical summation that Potter had earlier implied was to be included in it.[27] Whatever the specifics, the committee's activities spread dismay and fright widely in the public employee class in Washington.

The problem the members of the Potter committee addressed was not imaginary. Southerners had come to dominate the Democratic party during the Pierce and Buchanan administrations. Despite the pervasiveness of the patronage system, some government employees of the Democratic regime were retained because of special knowledge or skills or because they had made themselves useful to Republicans while those gentlemen were still the minority. Some of these hold-overs, or members of their families, sympathized with the southern cause, as did others among the permanent residents of the District of Columbia. Through the early months of the war the strains of "Dixie" floated out from many a Washington residence. And during the early months of its existence the Potter committee received commendation in various northern newspapers.[28] By the time Congress reconvened in early December 1861, however, reservations were beginning to develop.

Writing in the *Cleveland Plain Dealer*, "Rolla" argued that the Republicans carried the idea of rotation even to the point of applying it to members of their own party. The Potter committee, this writer alleged, had developed this "cutthroat spirit" allowing "perjured reprobates" to charge "true northern loyal men in office" with "secession sentiments." He noted Lincoln's reaction when one of his prospective appointees was accused of secession sentiment. The president responded that if place hunters believed it possible to get his office, they would "before night prove [him] the vilest secessionist in the country." Congressional Democrats also signaled adverse reaction to the committee in the second session as they groped tentatively for issues that might reflect the legitimacy of a party in opposition. In December, Philip B. Fouke (D., Ill.) tried to submit a resolution to the House that would have required the members of the Potter committee to allow individuals to defend themselves before it. Fouke's attempt failed, but frank complaints soon replaced implied criticism, and Republican voices joined those of the Democrats and border Unionists.

Indeed Potter had long believed that members of his own party were less than fully supportive. Writing to his wife in early September, he reported himself "sustained by the thought that [he was] doing something for [his] poor country, distracted and derided and surrounded by traitors within and without," but of the president and his cabinet he noted that "there is not the most perfect accord between us." Both Mary Lincoln and her husband protested when Potter pronounced John Watt, the White House gardener, disloyal, a charge that the president took so lightly that he was later willing to see the embarrassed horticulturist employed by the Patent Office to obtain agricultural seeds and plants in Europe. "I really think that you are mistaken," wrote Simon Cameron from the War Department in defense of an arsenal employee. Montgomery Blair scrawled on a copy of testimony concerning a postal employee, "This statement is ridiculously false." Even Galusha A. Grow, the Speaker of the House, intervened in behalf of a naval surgeon.[29]

By the time Congress reconvened in early December 1861, Potter was convinced that the executive branch was shamefully ignoring the evidence he and his colleagues had collected. On December 3, 1861, he wrote to the heads of departments requesting that the committee be informed of the removals that they had made since the date of his letter of July 18. Chase in the Treasury and Smith at Interior did not comply, and Potter followed on December 24 with a second letter, reiterating his appeal. On December 30, he introduced resolutions in the House requesting the secretaries to comply with the committee's request. The House approved the resolution concerning Salmon P. Chase without comment, but when Potter moved to the second resolution, the elderly and distinguished Charles A. Wickliffe (UW., Ky.) requested that a copy of Potter's letter of early December be provided. The latter had the clerk read his two communications. An exchange now ensued between Potter and both Wickliffe and Abraham B. Olin (R., N.Y.). Occupying the floor with Wickliffe's consent, the New Yorker expressed his concern about the procedures of the committee. Unless individuals under accusation were made aware of the charges against them and given an opportunity to defend themselves, "the grossest injustice would be committed toward the persons thus implicated." In Wickliffe's view the committee, and the House if it acquiesced in its procedures, was infringing upon the obligations of the cabinet secretaries. Let them manage their clerks and if they did it improperly let them be held accountable. Clerks had a "hard time." "Let us," said Wickliffe, "not divert the great and legitimate powers of this House into an inquisition to find out something against the character of these poor dependent clerks." The old gentleman's colleague Robert Mallory (D., Ky.) then objected to the reception of the resolution concerning the Interior Department, and it was not acted upon.[30]

Potter's response in defense of the committee laid out the lines he was to take in writing the report he would tender to the House on January 28, 1862, although in the heat of the moment he went farther in some respects than he would later. The problem that he and his colleagues were addressing was both real and urgent. At that very time, he said, there were "not less than five hundred clerks still retained who are disloyal to this Government." Given the urgency of the task, the committee members simply could not take the time to follow the kind of procedure their critics were demanding. "Men who are properly charged with disloyalty have no right to come before the committee," he said. "In these times no man should be retained in the employ of the Government against whom there is a reasonable suspicion as to loyalty. [And] no head of Department has the right to require from a committee of investigation . . . evidence against an employe under him strong enough to hang him for treason before he will dismiss him." Nay, said Potter, the proper rule governing retention ought to be: "No man should be permitted by any head of a Department to retain a position in the employ of the Government for a day who was not *known*, beyond all dispute, to be a loyal man. That is the view which the committee has unanimously taken of this question." There was no point in giving men a hearing or in adducing additional evidence; if they were indeed disloyal, they would have no scruples about lying.

In the committee report, presented a month later, Potter still clung to his basic position: Clerks whose loyalty had been impugned should be relieved of their positions immediately. Loyal men who had come under suspicion and lost their jobs because of it had no cause for complaint. "The exigencies of the times demand great sacrifices, even to the extent of fortune and life from all classes; and it is a light exaction to make of men of doubtful loyalty, that they be reduced to the great mass of their fellow-citizens by removal from places of trust and power." He admitted that removals had occurred where "suspicion was slight, or where none was alleged," but "in no instance has any evil consequences followed to the individual other than the loss of the office." Where patriotism was present it soon showed itself, where disloyalty lurked it had been revealed by "desertion to the enemy, or in . . . less disguised manifestations of sympathy with the rebellion."[31]

Although overt dissatisfaction with the work of Potter's committee never revealed itself so clearly again on the floor, discontent remained. When in May 1862 Potter sought to have extra copies of the committee report printed for the use of the House, the motion failed, and although his motion to reconsider that vote was entered, it does not appear to have been brought to a decision. When Potter made his remarks on December 30, he charged that the heads of departments had "not all done their duty," although he hastened to say that he did not believe that this neglect had been "willful" in nature. When Potter announced his intention in caucus in mid December to bring his dissatisfaction with the progress in eliminating subversives into the House, the *Springfield Republican* noted that the move was "not considered friendly to the administration" and added that "many of the clerks reported against" had been "retained by influence of" Republican congressmen.[32]

Late in the winter of 1862, Potter exchanged recriminatory letters in the press with Montgomery Blair, the postmaster general, who took exception to the evidence upon which the committee had adjudged various clerks in Blair's department to have been disloyal. Potter responded that his committee had failed to act in "strict conformity with its functions" only in the degree to which it had allowed rebutting testimony to be presented before it. So to some degree the criticism of committee procedures had borne fruit; the committee had modified its course somewhat. In late May, the *New York Herald* reported that the committee was in session, "giving an opportunity to be heard to those whose disloyalty is impugned by witnesses." By this time some five hundred government employees had been reputedly dismissed. Most of the department heads had acted, so it was said, on the reports from the committee.[33]

As the second session of the Thirty-seventh Congress drew to its close, the *New York Evening Post* noted that there were still southern sympathizers on the federal payroll and cited with approval the firing of an old Democrat who had refused to agree to a plan to have the clerks in his department subscribe a dollar per month from their salaries for the benefit of wounded and sick soldiers in the city. Two days later, the same paper noted that western members were leaving for home well satisfied with the legislative accomplishments of the session and singled out Aldrich of Minnesota and Potter of Wisconsin for special praise. The latter, noted the reporter, had done "good service on the investigating committee . . . and got no thanks for the unpleasant labor, except from the earnest friends of the government."[34]

That the resident Washington community at the outbreak of the war included many who sympathized with the Confederacy, and that some among that number were on the government payroll, we cannot doubt. The possibility that some of these dissidents might engage in espionage was also very real during the early months of the war. Yet the procedures of the Potter committee were a travesty of due process. Potter argued that he and his colleagues tried to guard against witnesses who acted from petty malice, envy, or the desire to profit from the displacement of others. But significant elements in Congress, Republicans as well as members of the Democratic and border state delegations, had strong reservations about the work of the committee, as did members of the Lincoln cabinet. Radical Republican newspapers, however, applauded. The committee report, wrote the *New York Tribune*, would "excite feelings of mingled wonder and indignation."[35]

The frequency with which the number "500" appears in accounts of the committee's work suggests caution in accepting that figure as even an approximate estimate of the dismissals and resignations attributable to the activity of Potter and his colleagues. But surely the number was a considerable one. Unfortunately the committee did not publish a final report, and Harold M. Hyman discovered that it was very difficult to distinguish between departures induced by Potter and his colleagues and those attributable to other causes. He concluded that ninety of the individuals investigated by Potter were no longer on the government payroll in January 1862. Not all of those designated as disloyal paid the penalty that Potter wished. The *New York Evening Post* noted on January 30, 1862, that a large proportion of those referred to in the report would seek to prove that they had been unjustly accused. Several individuals had already been successful in exonerating themselves. If "ordinary means" would not suffice, the *Post* noted, "the female friends of the accused parties are brought to bear upon the sympathies of honorable senators and the heads of departments, and it is an argument which rarely fails."[36]

Some of the more eminent of those identified escaped the fate that the members of the Potter committee had planned for them. One of these was Lieutenant-Colonel William Maynadier of the Ordnance Bureau, who had served in the army since 1827 and had actually refused an invitation to serve in the Confederate army. But Maynadier could be linked to the alleged efforts of Buchanan's secretary of war, John Floyd, to stockpile arms in southern arsenals in preparation for the southern bid for independence. Ostensibly Potter and his colleagues found a basis for their charge of disloyalty against Maynadier in the report of the official investigation of the Floyd case, but that report did not actually implicate the ordnance officer. The *Philadelphia Press* wrote scathingly:

> A garbled statement is made; *incontrovertible* testimony, of the
> Lord knows who, is taken secretly, a grand decision is arrived at
> and announced, and then, fearing that the structure is not strong
> enough, it is finished by the statement that the accused, who
> knows nothing of the case, has not appeared in his defense,
> thereby attempting the despicable subterfuge that conscious guilt
> has kept him silent. Will the House of Representatives endorse
> such proceedings, or will they not rather, in common self-respect,
> immediately purge themselves of such malicious and dishonest at-
> tempts to ruin the fame and reputation of innocent persons? . . .
> Nearly every case before the committee shows that personal ma-
> lignity is at the bottom of it.

If one considers the wording of the initial resolution that authorized the Potter committee, it is clear that its members went beyond their instructions in addition to developing procedures that were almost certain to do injustice to some loyal individuals. Nowhere in their mandate were they instructed to demand an accounting from the executive departments to which they sent the lists of suspected employees.

The members of the House of Representatives implicitly censured the Potter committee by not reconstituting it at the beginning of the Thirty-eighth Congress, in contrast to their treatment of the Joint Committee on the Conduct of the War. Representative Potter's failure to win reelection in 1862 may have dampened the ardor of potential successors, although the Wisconsin representative placed primary blame for loss of his seat on the defection of Roman Catholic and German voters from the Republican party, and others noted the failure to obtain ballots from well-disposed soldiers in the field.[37] Perhaps also the representatives believed that the immediate problem of disloyalty among federal employees in Washington had been eliminated. The various loyalty oaths that Congress developed provided an alternative means of detecting subversion. Certainly the bickering and criticism the committee's procedures produced in the Republican party should have discouraged party managers from endorsing the organization of a new loyalty committee in the Thirty-eighth Congress.

On the same day that Potter moved the formation of a loyalty committee, July 8, 1861, Charles H. Van Wyck proposed the establishment of a committee of five to inquire into the details of government contracting, with power to "send for persons and papers, to administer oaths and examine witnesses, and report at any time."[38] As finally approved, this committee was to have seven members: Van Wyck became chair and was to be aided by Elihu B. Washburne (R., Ill.), William S. Holman (D., Ind.), Reuben E. Fenton (R., N.Y.), Henry L. Dawes (R., Mass.), William G. Steele (D., N.J.), and James S. Jackson (BU., Ky.).[39] Van Wyck, Washburne, Fenton, and Dawes were already chairmen of standing committees. The committee organized itself on July 17 and went to work energetically, seeking a complete listing of contracts from the departments of War and the Navy, and reassembling in late August in New York to begin the task of investigating specific contracting practices and incidents. Though often represented by only one member, or by a subcommittee of the group, the committee pursued its investigations in New York throughout September, and in mid October four members, led by Washburne, reached St. Louis to examine the contracting that had been done in General John C. Frémont's Western Department.

The group held their last hearing in St. Louis on October 31 and after sessions in Chicago and Harrisburg were once again at work in

New York by the end of November, where hearings were held intermittently through December. The new year saw committee members in Boston, and after stopovers in New York and Philadelphia, the group set up shop in Washington for a steady round of testimony through the remainder of January and February. In March the indefatigable investigators were back in New York, as well as in Philadelphia, Cincinnati, Indianapolis, and Chicago. By April the committee was conducting most of its meetings in Washington and would continue to meet regularly until the adjournment of Congress in early July 1862. So dedicated to the urgency of the committee's tasks was Dawes that he did not take the time to go home and visit his wife and family during the Christmas recess of 1861.[40]

The members of the committee submitted their first report on December 17, 1861, and claimed that their expenses of $5,153.38 were already more than offset by a refund of $6,166.48 obtained in reimbursement from a contractor. They presented more than 130 pages of testimony bearing upon instances where they believed that fraud or profiteering had occurred. Here, the members of the House learned of the irregularities attendant upon the purchase and outfitting of the steamer *Cataline* and the excessive profits of those who sold the vessels *Roman* and *Wm. Badger* to the government, as well as the unbusinesslike practices and handsome remuneration of Alexander Cummings and George D. Morgan, the purchasing agents of the War and Naval departments in New York during the early months of the war.

In General Frémont's command the committee members found evidence of conspiracy and profiteering in the purchase of arms, livestock, and military supplies. There, for example, "the most astounding and unblushing frauds had been perpetrated in the purchase of horses and mules . . . and the evidence left no doubt . . . that the quartermaster himself was in collusion with corrupt and unprincipled men." But these practices were not restricted to the West or to materials destined for government forces there. Contracts for the delivery of cattle in Washington and Harrisburg involved "not only evidence of gross mismanagement, a total disregard of the interests of the government, and a total recklessness in the expenditure of the funds of the government, but there is every reason to believe that there was collusion upon the part of the employees of the government to assist in robbing the treasury."[41]

Spurred on by their own enthusiasm, the applause of some colleagues, and elements of the press, the investigators pushed their labors forward after the first report came out. Van Wyck's duties as colonel of the Fifty-sixth Regiment of New York Volunteers led him to surrender the chairmanship to Washburne in 1862, but the latter and Dawes were no less energetic. In their second report, issued at the conclusion of the second session of the Thirty-seventh Congress, the committee members noted that they had examined 350 witnesses; the supporting testimony they submitted covered some 1,600 printed pages.[42]

To their chagrin, the members of the Contracts Committee found that their labors were not to be universally commended, even within the Republican party. Criticism of the purchasing agents of the War and Naval departments was also, indirectly at least, criticism of Secretary Cameron and Secretary Welles. As we shall see, neither of these gentlemen, nor their purchasing agents, lacked sympathizers capable of defending their efforts to mobilize the Union and noting exaggerations or inadequately substantiated charges by the committee. The investigators had been particularly scathing in commenting upon contracting irregularities in General Frémont's department in the West, but many of the general's friends believed that this beleaguered officer had been asked to make bricks without straw or sustenance, and promptly rallied to his defense.

One of the contracts that particularly drew the attention of committee members provided for the purchase on Frémont's behalf of Hall carbines, discarded as obsolete by the army but purchased for a few dollars apiece by one Simon Stevens, who had them altered at little cost and then resold them to the government for more than double his investment. Stevens was initially believed to be a close relative of Thaddeus Stevens's, and although this proved to be untrue, he had indeed read law in the latter's law office and remained on friendly terms with the Radical leader. When Dawes sought to withhold approval of a contract for engraving Treasury notes in early January 1862, Stevens ridiculed the committee, and some days later Dawes defended it with a bitter denunciation of Simon Cameron of Pennsylvania, the secretary of war, and the place of contracts in Pennsylvania politics generally.

On February 7, 1862, Van Wyck called up the report of the Special Committee on Government Contracts and presented three resolutions for the consideration of the House. The first of these requested the secretary of the treasury to refuse to make further payments to "parties interested in the steamboat Cataline." The second requested the same individual to limit the amount paid for five thousand Hall carbines by General John C. Frémont "through Simon Stevens" to $12.50 each. The final resolution maintained that "the practice of employing irresponsible parties having no official connection with the Government in the performance of public duties which may be properly performed by regular officers of the Government, and of purchasing by private contract supplies for the different Departments, where open and fair competition might be properly invited by reasonable advertisements for proposals, is injurious to the public service, and meets the unqualified disapprobation of [the] House."[43]

Committee findings served as the basis of other resolutions critical of the procedures of the executive departments. In late December 1861, Alexander S. Diven (R., N.Y.) introduced a resolution calling for legal action to recapture monies advanced to the contractor who had agreed to construct fortifications for the defense of St. Louis. And William S. Holman, a pugnacious member of the committee, proposed a resolution of censure against Secretary of War Cameron and Secretary of the Navy Welles.

These legislative initiatives provided the occasion for a spasmodic but vitriolic debate on the contributions of the committee during the late winter and early spring of 1862. In the process of these exchanges, Schuyler Colfax (R., Ind.) submitted an amendment to the committee report that implied criticism of the various procedures followed. His resolution suggested that the course of the naval investigating committee of 1850 in providing officers with copies of testimony adverse to them and allowing cross examination constituted practices "worthy of imitation wherever practicable," and "that it [was] contrary to the plainest principles of justice to condemn any citizen upon *ex parte* evidence taken against him by a committee in secret."[44]

When Representative Van Wyck called up the committee resolutions, he delivered a spread-eagle speech, denouncing the peculators who would "coin the grief of the nation into currency, and peril her institutions . . . by conspiring to defraud the people and the Government." He went on to excoriate Alexander Cummings, the War Department's purchasing agent, and to detail instances of contractual graft under the aegis of that department. The sick and diseased soldier who slept at his post was punished with death, he noted, "while the miscreant who holds his festival at this carnival of blood rides in his carriage, drinks champagne . . . dines with Cabinet ministers," and is treated "with deferential respect. Do you say Government cannot banish treason and punish crime?" After moving on to the Naval Department, Van Wyck turned briefly to the California "plunderers" who had clustered about Frémont and to the latter's quartermaster general, Justus McKinstry, "the high priest at this festival of robbery and crime," and ended his oration with a florid invocation of the American flag and the Union cause.[45]

The major congressional critics of the Contracts Committee launched their counter salvoes between the delivery of the Van Wyck speech and the votes on the various resolutions at the end of April.

William M. Davis (R., Pa.) immediately gained the floor to defend his brother, a captain of the Western Quartermaster's Corps whom the committee had accused of buying blankets of inferior quality from his own son. Captain Davis, his brother alleged, had been given no opportunity to clear his name.[46]

Subsequently William D. Kelley (R., Pa.) brought before his colleagues a self-vindicating pamphlet written by Alexander Cummings in defense of his actions as the War Department's representative. And when Diven sought action on the motion that he had introduced weeks earlier, he found himself battered by Colfax, who was certain that "the stern verdict of history" would show Frémont to have been "far more sinned against than sinning." Owen Lovejoy (R., Ill.), an active member of the radical abolitionist faction, meanwhile interjected a protest against the procedures of the "peripatetic inquisitorial committee," lamenting the practice of its members in bringing victims out piecemeal, week by week, rather than following the example of the Spanish Inquisition and having "one general *auto-da-fé*." So furiously did the brickbats fly in defense of Frémont that poor Diven was "rather astonished to know what has become of the resolution which is really the subject-matter before the House." His concern must have increased apace, because Colfax's defense of Frémont drew Francis P. (Frank) Blair, Jr. (R., Mo.), into the debate to reiterate the scandalous state of affairs that the general and his California friends had produced in Missouri. So badly did Blair misstate the case, in Thaddeus Stevens's view, that the old Pennsylvanian shouted in scorn, "Sir, such things in a pettifogger would be detestable, but in a member of this House they are respectable." And broadening his attack, Stevens alleged, "If it were proper I would move to discharge this scandal-hunting committee from any further proceedings, for I believe in my conscience that they have committed more frauds than they have detected. They are spending the country's money and scandalizing the country's best men."[47]

Stevens's indictment, like Kelley's earlier defense of Cummings, was made when the members of the Contracts Committee were absent. On their return, Dawes responded with a slashing defense of the committee that, in turn, inspired more offensive action from its critics. As the debate unfolded during the last days of April 1862, "acrimonious" proved to be much too mild an adjective. There seems to have been a general impression by this time that a motion to terminate the committee would soon be laid before the chamber. On April 29 Elihu Washburne himself took the floor to make a powerful defense of the committee, of which he was now the chairman.[48]

Washburne reviewed the reasons for the formation of the committee and the stern physical labors that its members had performed. When they had taken the time of the House, they had done so in self-defense. And the "unkindest cut of all" had been made by Thaddeus Stevens, the chairman of the Committee of Ways and Means, who "has character enough without ability and ability enough without character to crush almost any committee . . . and yet we survive." He refuted Roscoe Conkling's (R., N.Y.) charge that the committee saved the country only money that would have been recaptured anyway, maintaining that perhaps as much as $12 million had been salvaged as a result of the committee's activities.[49]

Supported by Dawes as well, Washburne noted how small was the actual number of serious mistakes the critics of the committee had been able to discover in their efforts to discredit it. A printer's error was the basis of the charge that the committee had wrongfully accused Alexander Cummings of retaining a large sum of government funds in his own possession. The committee had suggested by inference that Augustus Sacchi, a principal in an irregular contract for the purchase of horses for Frémont's western forces, was the same man as an Italian patriot of that name who was serving without remuneration as a captain on Frémont's staff. Despite this error, none could allege that the contract itself had not been touched with fraud. And finally, the defenders of Frémont alleged that the wording of the Hall carbine resolution suggested that the general was a party to the speculation involved. Washburne demanded to know whether the Republicans proposed to imitate the past example of the Democrats and "cover up and justify fraud." He challenged Conkling to introduce his resolution to disband the committee and warned that the country would look with particular interest upon the vote of Thaddeus Stevens. He denied that the committee members had sought to link Frémont to their investigations and maintained on the contrary that it had been the general's friends who had insisted on bringing him into the debates to such a large degree.[50] Conkling did not offer his resolution.

As the House moved to vote on the committee resolutions on April 30, the first division dealt with Stevens's motion to lay the matter on the table. Only 16 members supported the chairman of Ways and Means. The *Cataline* resolution having been abandoned as no longer of importance, the next item before the House was Stevens's amendment changing the wording of the Hall carbine resolution. That too failed, but only by 6 votes. Fenton, a committee member, likewise failed to win approval for an amendment specifying that the government should be responsible for good-faith advances in contractual relationships. The committee's Hall carbine resolution was then approved by a vote of 103 to 28. Colfax's resolution as to appropriate procedures was accepted, with 41 opposed, mostly Democrats. The resolution deploring the use of "irresponsible parties" in government purchasing won approval without the formality of a roll call. Then came Holman's resolution of censure, now split so that members might consider the cases of Cameron and Welles separately. By a vote of 79 to 45 the House censured Cameron and almost reversed this vote in exonerating Welles.[51]

The story of the Contracts Committee did not end at this point. On February 26, 1862, the House had authorized the committee to investigate the operation of the customs and bonded warehousing system in New York City. Washburne proposed to have this task referred to another committee, but Van Wyck, then stationed in the vicinity of Washington, pleaded that the charge be retained, and volunteered to take evidence for the committee. He began this work on March 11, working with a transcribing clerk and an acting sergeant-at-arms. He did not represent a quorum of the committee, but such procedures had sometimes been followed in the earlier history of the committee. On March 24, Van Wyck received instructions from Chairman Washburne to return and proceed no further with the investigation "until further orders." Subsequently, according to Van Wyck, the remainder of the committee argued that he had taken the evidence already in hand "without authority," and they proceeded to reexamine witnesses where the testimony "affected the official conduct of any such person," in such a way as to allow damaging testimony to be refuted. When the committee majority submitted its report on March 3, 1863, it was bland indeed. No doubt there were abuses in the administration "of a system so vast and varied." Yet, concluded the committee members, "it [was] but just to add . . . that there was no proof before them tending to show that these abuses were more numerous now than they have been heretofore."[52]

Van Wyck submitted a minority report detailing the circumstances under which he had taken evidence and accusing his colleagues of suppressing his findings and blaming Washburne particularly for his treatment. Indeed he accused Washburne of altering the record. Then he submitted extracts from the testimony that he had taken to illustrate his contention that there was substantial evidence of wrongdoing in the public service in New York. In a short conclusion he reflected on the work of the committee in general. "Many frauds have been exposed," he maintained, "the government relieved from many unconscionable contracts, and millions of dollars saved to the Treasury. Yet it is a matter of regret that punishment has not been meted out to the basest class of transgressors. . . . The leniency of the government towards these men is a marvel which the present cannot appreciate and history never explain."

Van Wyck's minority report breathed the fervor with which he and his colleagues had begun their search for malefactors during the summer and fall of 1861. But his colleagues of the committee were no longer receptive. They had besmirched a popular general, revealed the ineptitude of executive departments, brought about the censure of a member of the president's cabinet, and illuminated sordid connections between politics and war contracts. They helped to foster a climate of opinion that contributed to the passage of several ameliorative laws, noted below. But in their energetic righteousness they alienated both elements of the executive branch and powerful radical congressional leaders. Although roll calls limned their victory, they had found themselves fighting for their political lives. They would not allow Van Wyck to lead them into battle again. At their best, the members of the Contracts Committee had shown courage and industry; theirs was a notable contribution. In their indignation, however, they sometimes found it difficult to distinguish between fraud and legal, if unconscionable, profit taking. Years later the U.S. Court of Claims ordered that Simon Stevens be fully reimbursed on his contract for the supply of Hall carbines.[53]

Thus far in this survey we have examined illustrative investigative activity in the House of Representatives initiated during the Thirty-seventh Congress. Inquiry continued on various fronts during the Thirty-eighth Congress, although with somewhat diminished breadth and vigor. The scope of the subject in the Civil War congresses cannot be encompassed in a single article or chapter. In addition to the inquiries already described, representatives, as members of either standing or select committees, inquired into other matters, including the interest of their fellows or government employees in war contracts, charges of disloyalty at the Naval Academy, the abuse of blacks in the District of Columbia, the purchase of steam machinery and ironclads by the Naval Department, corruption in cotton purchasing, illegal trade into the South, the New York Custom House, and wrongdoing in the Treasury Department.[54] We could widen our focus of interest to embrace inquiries into lake defenses, the building of a canal around Niagara Falls, the location of a national armory, the reduction of government expenditures, the compensation of government officers, or the possibility of building a railroad from Washington to New York – inquiries more closely related to the possible development of legislation than to the uncovering of wrongdoing.[55] But we shall conclude our scouting expedition with an examination of ways in which representatives might seek to use committees of inquest to repair their reputations. This subject is best developed by considering the investigations of James M. Ashley (R., Ohio) and Francis Preston Blair, Jr.

"A great fine animal nature – unabashed cheek and a cheery manner," wrote John Hay in description of James M. Ashley, congressman from the Fifth and later the Tenth Congressional District of Ohio, chairman of the Committee on Territories, floor manager of the resolution that became the Thirteenth Amendment when the House passed it in early 1865, and one of the House managers in the impeachment proceedings against Andrew Johnson.[56] During the course of the election for seats in the Thirty-eighth Congress, the *Toledo Blade* published letters written by Ashley in early 1861 that suggested that the Ohioan had "corruptly procured the appointment of F. M. Case as surveyor general of Colorado Territory, for a consideration previously agreed upon." Although the meaning and significance of the letters were hotly debated during the campaign of 1862 in Ohio, Ashley won reelection. On December 4 he introduced in the House a resolution requesting the appointment of a select committee of five to investigate the charges made against him.[57]

Later Ashley told the members of the committee that he had introduced his resolution on the advice of friends and against his own "better judgment," given the fact that his constituents had returned him to the House while thoroughly aware of the charges made against him. He did not believe, he said, "that this committee or the House" had "any right to make inquiries" of him "about this matter, simply to satisfy their judgments as to the correctness of the verdict rendered by [his] constituents."[58] By this time, however, the machinery of investigation was engaged, and the committee report reveals much about the workings of the patronage system of the time as well as the operation of select committees.

On February 2, 1861, Ashley wrote to Francis M. Case, brother of Representative Charles Case of Indiana, then nearing the end of his term as auditor of Paulding County, Ohio. In his letter Ashley brought Case abreast of his efforts to procure for him the position of surveyor general in one of the western territories, preferably Utah. The surveyor general and his assistant there, Ashley believed, could "make a fortune of $50,000 to $100,000 in the four years . . . if he is a good business man." Ashley would want his brother to go with Case as chief clerk, he noted. But he was uncertain as to whether he should represent his nominee as coming from Indiana or Ohio, a question that involved the patronage quotas of the two states and bore on which Indianan, if any, was to fill a seat in Lincoln's cabinet. A letter from Ashley to Case of March 12 reveals that the target territory had become Colorado and that Ashley was actively seeking an endorsement of his protégé from the Ohio legislature. Ashley also instructed Case to provide affirmations of his engineering qualifications and to pledge that members of the Indiana delegation and Ashley jointly would name the subordinates in Case's Colorado office. "Now, Frank," Ashley added, "this is the best office, in my judgment, in the gift of the President, and I would resign to-day if I was sure I could keep it four years. If you get it I want to unite with you as a full partner in land speculations and town sites."[59]

In subsequent letters Ashley urged Case to send supporting letters to him in short order and filled in more details about the position and Ashley's efforts to obtain it. On March 16 Ashley wrote, "The office is $3,000; the second, where I want my brother, $2,000, with half a dozen subordinates, all to be appointed by you." Two days later:

> I have promised all the subordinate places under you to get help, and you must write me at once, authorizing me fully, under your own hand, to make this good. I ask for three of the places myself, and give the rest to other members who are helping me. . . . I want to have an interest with you, if I get the place, in the city and town lot speculation. The Pacific railroad will go through this Territory, and it will be a fortune to us if I can get it. . . . I will probably be chairman of Committee on Territories . . . and then I will know all the proposed expenditures in the Territories, and post you in *advance*.[60]

On March 19 Ashley reiterated his demand that Case give formal assent to the arrangement concerning the subordinate appointments in Colorado and included

> . . . one word as to ourselves . . . brother Eli is to be chief clerk, and my brother William . . . such a position as he can fill. . . . Now, if I get this, I want to be a full copartner with you in the purchase of all the real estate that you may make in that Territory. I have spent a good deal of time and some money to get this place, and if I do get it I trust you will cheerfully go in with me. I have drawn up the enclosed agreement, which I wish you would sign and keep, and copy one just like it.

Faced with the grim prospect of returning to the practice of law, in which he was most "devilish rusty," Case avowed his keen interest in the position and his assent to the details specified by Ashley. "And in the matter of the appointments, you may have them your own way; all of them you can save for yourself, and over and above these the partnership matter in land speculation. . . . God send you success and me the surveyor generalship." And He did, with a little help from friends.[61]

But Ashley would rue his success in securing the surveying plum in Colorado. It is true that his brother became chief clerk and brother William found a place in a surveying crew. And Case did allocate a surveying contract to John Pierce from Ohio, whom Ashley approved. But the fortune in real estate speculation never materialized. When arranging the Colorado surveying appointment, visions of Spanish land grants, available for a song and rich as John Charles Frémont's Mariposa estate, were dancing in Ashley's head, according to Case and Pierce, to whom Ashley had also proposed a partnership in land speculation. But neither Case nor Pierce ventured in real estate in Colorado Territory or believed it necessary to serve as Ashley's eyes in identifying speculative opportunities.[62]

More frustrating to Ashley than the receding glimmer of riches was the fact that his letters to Case appeared in the public press during the course of his bid for reelection in 1862. Somehow they were abstracted from Case's private papers in Colorado and found their way into the hands of the editors of the *Toledo Blade*. Case's role in these developments is less than clear. Although he provided a statement that was used during the campaign by the Ashley forces and his deposition in Ashley's suit against the newspaper was not hostile, Case admitted to feeling that Ashley was too radical in his politics.

Ashley believed that he stood well with Speaker Grow, and the latter provided him with an investigating committee that apparently gave him the benefit of whatever doubt was available. The chairman, Harrison Gray Otis Blake (R., Ohio), was a member of the same state delegation as Ashley. Three others were westerners from Indiana, Kentucky, and Missouri. The lone eastern member was a Democratic banker from New York City. In writing to potential witnesses, Blake requested that they reveal the nature of their evidence before being summoned to appear, and the committee refused to accept as evidence letters that Case had written to third parties. On the other hand, the committee brushed aside Ashley's contention that it had no right to investigate matters on which his constituents had already ruled and forced him to speak to the more troublesome issues raised by his correspondence.

At the very least, Ashley's performance before the committee revealed him to be an avid placeman, greedily eager to convert political influence into personal wealth, and willing to use inside information to further that quest. If he spoke truth in his testimony, his first term in Congress had left him amazingly ignorant of the obligations of the various congressional committees and the operation of the system of land survey administered by the Department of the Interior. Ashley and his part-time clerk, Hezekiah L. Hosmer, emphasized the great pressure for places that the Ohioan faced. They interpreted the rosy picture of imminent riches that Ashley painted as an effort to divert Case's interest from an appointment that Ashley hoped to obtain for another. "Neither Mr. Ashley nor Mr. Case understood [the] agreement or the request which Ashley made in his letters about subordinate appointments, to be so compulsory as that a failure upon the part of Case to comply with them, should operate to deprive Case of the appointment," argued Hosmer. Ashley admitted that his letters were "hastily and inconsiderately written," but denied that he had intended to deceive in his effort to portray Case as coming from Indiana rather than Ohio. He claimed that he had not understood the survey contracting system and that his apparent wish to control it reflected poor word choice and ignorance. He had intended to pay his share for any land that Case or his deputy purchased, and in the end none was acquired.[63]

When queried about his promise to post Case in advance concerning "proposed expenditures in the Territories," Ashley gave a rambling response that touched on his reasons for expecting, as a member of the Committee on the Territories during the Thirty-sixth Congress, to become its new chairman and on his ignorance of the fact, despite this prior service, that the Committee on Public Lands had oversight over the surveys of the public lands. But somehow he failed to address the issue of whether he intended to use inside information to advance his own personal interests.

The key question in the series of eight that members of the committee put to Ashley was the third: whether he had made it a "condition precedent and a consideration for the use of your influence in procuring F. M. Case's appointment, that he 'should contract, in writing, beforehand' to give you an equal interest with himself in all lands purchased by him in the Territory; and, also, that you and your friends should make the subordinate appointments under Case." To which Ashley responded, "I regarded him as a friend, of whom I might, without impropriety, at least without having my motives impugned by him, make the request: 'Now, Frank, I want you to do so and so'; not will you do it if I obtain your appointment, not as a condition precedent, but as an act of reciprocal friendship. I neither intimated, nor intended to intimate, at any time, that, if he declined my requests, I would cease to labor for his appointment."[64] None of the committee members asked Ashley why old friends needed to make written agreements, and it was on the point of conditions precedent that the committee based its finding of innocence. The fact that Ashley had been promoting Case's candidacy prior to sending a written agreement concerning land purchases to him and outlining various requirements as to the disposition of minor offices was taken as proof that there had been no conditions precedent demanded by Ashley, nor "illegal or corrupt" acts upon his part. And so one radical Republican congressman demonstrated how the investigative process could be used to rehabilitate a tarnished reputation.

James M. Ashley sought absolution at the hands of his congressional colleagues and they responded with charity. During the first session of the Thirty-eighth Congress, Francis Preston Blair, Jr., also tried to use the committee process to clear his name, but in his case the quality of mercy was somewhat strained. Indeed, the impetuous Missourian acted as a catalyst of investigative activity on the part of both select and standing committees. Like no other individual in the second of the Civil War congresses, Frank Blair illuminated the importance of the committee system and the investigative process to both the career-building congressman and party managers.

Princeton graduate, trained in the law at Transylvania University, Mexican War veteran of the colorful "Doniphan's Thousand," son of one of the most important political figures in antebellum America, and brother of Lincoln's postmaster general, Frank Blair was energetic, impulsive, and loyal. He threw himself wholeheartedly into the struggle to keep his city of St. Louis and his state of Missouri safely in the Union. Acclaimed for the success of his efforts, he was a serious candidate for the post of Speaker at the beginning of the emergency session of Congress in July 1861. Denied this honor, he chose to be chairman of the House Standing Committee on Military Affairs and performed creditably in that position. Disenchanted by General Frémont's ineffectiveness as commander of the Western Department at St. Louis, Blair played a major role in having the general relieved of command in 1861 and won the enmity of Republican radicals as a result. When he reviewed the general's shortcomings in a major speech in the second session of the Thirty-seventh Congress, no less important a figure than Schuyler Colfax came to Frémont's defense. And Blair was no favorite of Thaddeus Stevens, who considered both him and his brother, the postmaster general, to be much too conservative in their views, despite their free soil antecedents.[65]

At the end of the second session of the Thirty-seventh Congress in July 1862, Frank Blair returned to St. Louis to raise a brigade of troops, becoming colonel of one of the regiments. Assigned with his men to the Army of the West, Blair became a brigadier general of volunteers in August 1862 and a major-general in November of the

same year. He capped some fifteen months of hard service by commanding the Fifteenth Corps in the Chattanooga campaign. In the
meantime the ferocity of the strife among Union politicians in Missouri
had become notorious. The Missouri radicals reviled Blair for his
abandonment of Frémont and supported one of their own against
him when he sought reelection to the House of Representatives from
the St. Louis congressional district. Blair apparently won reelection,
but his enemies accused him of plotting with the Democrats to win
the speakership in a conspiracy in which Emerson Etheridge, the clerk
of the House, supposedly would refuse to accept the credentials of a
sufficient number of Republicans to allow the Democrats and Blair's
friends to organize the House at the beginning of the Thirty-eighth
Congress.[66]

Blair's announced margin of victory over his opponent in 1862,
Massachusetts-born and Harvard-trained lawyer Samuel Knox, was
paper thin and the latter announced that he would contest the election
on the grounds that illegal voters had swelled Blair's total and that
there had been irregularities in the recording of soldier votes. The
radicals were delighted too by the publication of charges that Blair
and a number of his officers had tried to bring a shipment of liquors
through the lines from the North for speculative purposes. Thus when
Blair surrendered his military commission and returned to Congress
at the beginning of January 1864, it was with blood in his eye and a
firm determination to strike back at the members of the party faction
who were threatening his reputation and his seat. He was particularly
incensed at the secretary of the treasury, Salmon P. Chase, who he
charged was a traitor both to the war policies of the administration
and to Abraham Lincoln, whom the secretary was scheming to sup-
plant. More to the point, Blair maintained that he had been falsely
implicated in a contraband-running operation by some of Chase's
western employees while others were in fact guilty of widespread
derelictions of duty.

On February 1, 1864, Blair introduced a resolution calling for a
special committee "with authority to inquire into and report upon the
practical operation and results of the act of Congress regulating com-
mercial intercourse with the states declared to be in insurrection
against the authority of the Government, and whether the regulations
of the Treasury Department . . . as carried out by the Department,
comply with its design." Approval of this would, under normal procedures of the House, have given Blair the chairmanship of the investigating committee, but this the Republican radicals would not
brook. Blair lost his call for the previous question, and Ashley demanded debate, thus sending the resolution over. Still unable to ob-

tain action on his proposal in late February, Blair delivered a sulfurous disquisition on the sins of the radical factions in Missouri and Maryland and upon the inadequacies of Salmon P. Chase's administration of the Treasury Department. He charged that

> ... a more profligate administration of the Treasury Department never existed under any Government; that the whole Mississippi valley is rank and fetid with the fraud and corruptions practiced there by his agents; that "permits" to buy cotton are just as much a marketable commodity as the cotton itself; that these permits to buy cotton are brought to St. Louis and other western cities by politicians and favorites from distant parts of the country, and sold on 'change to the highest bidder, whether he be a secession-ist or not.[67]

In concluding his remarks, Blair discussed the allocation of committee assignments in the House. When he returned to Congress from the "field," he noted, the House representatives on the Joint Committee on the Conduct of the War had not yet been allocated. Benjamin F. Loan (R., Mo.), a radical, resigned his place on the Committee on Military Affairs and was promptly reassigned to the joint committee. Blair perforce returned as an ordinary member to the committee that he had chaired in the preceding Congress. "It would seem, therefore," he remarked, "that the Speaker is not anxious to place me where I could pry into these delicate matters."

Blair contrasted the reception of his charges with that experienced by those who had demanded investigation of the Naval Department. In that case, the secretary had welcomed investigation and the inquiry was placed in the hands of those requesting it. That was the proper mode of procedure. "What I ask in this matter is that the friends of the Secretary of the Treasury will concede what is demanded by parliamentary law, and then I will stand or fall by the result." But to Blair's disgust the radical Republicans denied him the opportunity to use a select investigative committee as a means of taking the offensive against Secretary Chase. Thaddeus Stevens tried to refer the matter to the Joint Committee on the Conduct of the War on the thin ground that this group had been charged with investigating fraudulent contracting in this Congress. The House found that solution unsatisfactory but approved James A. Garfield's (R., Ohio) motion to charge the Commerce Committee with the investigation.[68]

To no one's surprise, the contingent of radicals from Missouri in the House struck back against Blair. I lack space here for a discussion of the whole range of issues on which they differed from Blair and more moderate Missouri Unionists. Although the members of both camps supported the elimination of slavery, their proposed methods were vastly different, and the distinction was further heightened by lingering animosities engendered by Frémont's demotion; by the policies of General John M. Schofield, who succeeded to the Missouri command, and of Governor Hamilton R. Gamble; by the complexities of German ethnic politics; and by rivalries and disagreements among Union politicians relating both to Missouri policies and national presidential politics. When John W. McClurg (R., Mo.) took the floor against Blair on March 9, he introduced a copy of a purchase order signed by Blair and eight of his fellow officers that he alleged was to have been the basis for a profitable speculation in liquors carried illegally into the occupied territory of the South. Blair immediately denounced the document as a forgery, "committed by one of Mr. Chase's agents [of which] publication was procured by another of Mr. Chase's agents, who knew it to be a forgery, in a paper which was in the pay of Mr. Chase. The whole thing can be traced to malice and malevolence." McClurg was undeterred, maintaining that he was giving the "correct and fair interpretation of this whole matter." He denounced Blair and his colleague from Missouri former Governor Austin A. King (D., Mo.) as "former pro-slavery and former anti-slavery leaders . . . united . . . to preserve slavery as long as possible." Such was the opposition that he and other "earnest men, the radicals, who are determined to destroy this accursed institution by the roots, and the rebellion which has grown from it," were facing.[69]

By March 23, McClurg's friends in Missouri had provided him with the original order and invoice, and the application and affidavit for the allegedly speculative purchase of liquors, and he rose to fulfill the "duty devolving on the executioner, whose trembling hand severs the cord that binds to life." To assist him in the process he had had the documents photographed and promised to have copies available within a few days. They were, he maintained, genuine in all respects. Blair promptly rose to move that a select committee be appointed to investigate the charges against him, pronouncing them a "base and miserable falsehood." McClurg, he continued, was an "infamous liar and scoundrel," language that, in the words of the Globe reporter, produced a "[Great Sensation]."[70]

Speaker Colfax selected a committee consisting of William Higby (R., Calif.), Brutus J. Clay (R., Ky.), and John V. L. Pruyn (D., N.Y.). These gentlemen moved rapidly to interview various individuals connected with the case and brought in their report on April 23, 1864. The purchase order had indeed been altered, the committee members said, by, without "any reasonable doubt," Michael Powers, who had volunteered to procure the liquors for Blair and his fellow officers, "probably . . . for the purpose of realizing a profitable speculation under cover of the original." The committee reported "that no violation of law was committed in the premises by General Blair and that the original order was altered and falsified after it had passed from his possession."[71]

Pleading the fact that he was about to leave for the field, Blair asked and received permission to address the House. His remarks were somewhat disjointed and frequently interrupted, but in sum they were a ferocious assault on Salmon P. Chase and his political friends – an attack that was to stimulate still further investigative activity. He noted that he was in the trenches before Vicksburg when the document in question was forged, that he was leading the gallant soldiers of the Fifteenth Corps in the Chattanooga campaign when the forgery was made public and circulated widely in the press to destroy his reputation. He maintained that, although he was complimented in general orders for his conduct during the campaign, he was removed from his command because of the charges that had been made. After a contemptuous summary of McClurg's activity, Blair announced that he did not propose to deal further with the dogs that had been set upon him. He had "whipped them back into their kennel" and would now confront their master, Salmon P. Chase.[72]

The secretary of the treasury, Blair alleged, had been offended by Blair's criticism of the regulation of trade that officers of the Treasury Department administered in Missouri, and his friends had opposed Blair's efforts to have himself put at the head of a select committee to investigate these matters. Chase, Blair charged, had wished to allow the southern states to leave the Union at the outbreak of the war and now supported a "reconstruction" bill that was "intended for the *destruction* of those States." This measure, ultimately known as the Wade-Davis bill, "should have been entitled 'a bill for the permanent dissolution of the Union, to disfranchise the whites and enfranchise the negroes, to prevent any of the states from coming back in time to vote for Mr. Lincoln for President, and to promote the ambition of the Secretary of the Treasury.' "[73]

Blair touched upon the machinations that had denied him a role in the investigation of the Treasury Department, alluded to the "whitewashing" of General Frémont by the Joint Committee on the Conduct of the War, read various personal communications into the record that alleged gross misconduct by officers of the Treasury Department in the West, and described the huge profits garnered by the bankers Jay Cooke and Company in selling government bonds. When the hammer fell, Blair was deriding Chase's denial of interest in being a presidential candidate and maintaining that the candidacy of "that poor creature" Frémont was being promoted so that Chase's friends could threaten the Union convention in Baltimore with an independent candidacy unless Lincoln was discarded and the way thus opened to Chase.

Blair's contributions in Missouri, in the Thirty-seventh Congress, and as an army officer had been outstanding; his frustrations are understandable, but his reactions were extreme and his charges probably overstated. He was, commented the *New York Herald*, "an animal with 'hay on his horns,' whom it would be advisable for men like Secretary Chase to leave alone."[74] The press reported that some of Frank Blair's "admiring friends" presented him with a "sword, with a solid silver scabbard, belt and sash, costing in all $500," following the exonerating committee report and his speech. But when he departed to assume the command of the Seventeenth Corps in Sherman's army, he left his more radical congressional colleagues utterly enraged – all the more so because, as brother of the postmaster general, he could be suspected of having spoken in behalf of the president and the Lincoln presidential candidacy no less than in exoneration of himself. Predictably, McClurg emerged from his "kennel" to try to refute the findings of the Higby committee, arguing that Blair must have been guilty because he took so long to deny the charges and challenging the factual accuracy of Blair's account of the way in which the matter had become public knowledge. Both Higby and his fellow committee member Clay were drawn into further discussion of their report; but more interesting is the way in which Blair continued to activate the investigative process.[75]

Predictions had appeared in the radical press that Samuel Knox, Blair's opponent in the 1862 election, would be successful in the contest that he had brought before the House Committee on Elections for Blair's seat. The committee compiled a substantial body of evidence concerning alleged infractions of electoral procedure on the part of supporters of both contestants. There was wrangling on the floor over the decision of its members to accept evidence from Knox after the expiration of the time allowed for submission and Blair's request for the same privilege. In a dispatch of April 27, 1864, the reporter of the *Springfield Republican* believed the committee deadlocked and Knox's submission of evidence less than completely convincing. But whatever the decision was to be, the president had provided Blair with an honorable alternative by allowing him to return to the army. His opponents in the House were infuriated, and Henry L. Dawes, chairman of the Elections Committee, offered a resolution requesting that the president inform the House whether or not Blair now held a military commission and, if he did, of its nature and effective date.[76]

By April 28, the president's response was in hand. Lincoln blandly informed the members that General Robert C. Schenck (now serving as chairman of the House Committee on Military Affairs) had surrendered his commission during the preceding fall to take a seat in the House "upon the distinct verbal understanding with the Secretary of War and the Executive that he might, at any time during the session, at his own pleasure, withdraw said resignation and return to the field." A similar accommodation had been made with General Blair. Lincoln offered to provide miscellaneous documentation concerning Blair's appointment. The attempt to smoke out Blair had backfired. The nonplussed radical Schenck rose to deny that he would ever have considered returning to the field unless the Senate had reconfirmed his appointment. He successfully moved that the president be requested to provide the documents relating to Blair's appointment mentioned in his response to the Dawes resolution. When these appeared in due course, they were referred to the Committee on Elections. Included among them was a letter from the president to Montgomery Blair concerning his brother in which he referred to "the provocations offered him by insincere time-servers."[77]

On June 10 Dawes was able to obtain votes on companion resolutions, the first proclaiming that Francis P. Blair, Jr., was not entitled to a seat in the House of Representatives and the second to the effect that Samuel Knox was the rightful representative in the House from the First Congressional District of Missouri. Three days later, Dawes brought in the committee report dealing with the resigned commissions of Schenck and Blair. Again the report was in the form of companion resolutions. Since Schenck had resigned prior to the convening of the Thirty-eighth Congress, he was free to serve. Blair, however, had not surrendered his commission until Congress was in session, and had disqualified himself from taking a seat in that body. Stevens commented on the importance of the principle involved, "reversing the established practice of the House heretofore," and hoped that it would be carried over so that there could be consideration of it. This was done, but the House approved the resolutions on June 29.[78]

In the Senate, members submitted resolutions declaring that Blair's resignation of his commission and subsequent service in the House had rendered him ineligible for the rank and emoluments of a major-general of volunteers. These having been referred to the Committee on the Judiciary, its chairman, Senator Trumbull, reported his colleagues' recommendation on June 15. Their resolution ran as follows: "An officer of the United States whose resignation has been duly accepted and taken effect, or who, having been elected a member of either house of Congress, qualifies and enters on the discharge of the duties of a member, is thereby, in either case, out of the office previously held, and cannot be restored to it without a new appointment in the manner provided by the Constitution."[79]

So the committees and assemblies of Congress had spoken. Blair had been too late in surrendering his commission; he had not been entitled to a seat in the House. *But,* said the senators, since he had served, he had no right to return to the army. The Republican radicals who provided the bulk of the votes for these positions had worked out their own formula of double jeopardy for Frank Blair. But the president found no reason to accept the congressional position. Blair marched with Sherman to the sea and did not retire from the army until well after the Thirty-eighth Congress had adjourned for the last time.

Blair's service in the Thirty-eighth House illustrates various aspects of the legislative inquiry process of the time. He would have liked to be assigned to the Joint Committee on the Conduct of the War, and he could have brought to that group field experience that was sadly lacking among its members. But Blair's politics were out of step with those of the committee's established leaders, Senators Wade and Chandler. He sought the organization and chairmanship of a select committee to investigate the Treasury domain of his enemy, Salmon P. Chase, but the Republican radicals again forestalled him. His agitation contributed to such an inquiry, but it would be placed in hands the radicals believed to be safer than those of Frank Blair. When the Missouri radicals accused him of impropriety in the field, he demanded exoneration by special investigative committee and received it, although the Speaker had done him the dubious favor of placing the inquiry under the chairmanship of a man whose penchant for the death penalty as a prosecutor in the Mother Lode country had won him the nickname Bloody Bill.[80]

Despite Blair's vindication, Congress subjected his career to further and less welcome ministrations. The Elections Committee declared for his opponent in the contest for his Missouri seat, and added insult to injury by going against current precedent and declaring that his late arrival due to field service disqualified him from serving; and the Senate Judiciary Committee pronounced him to be without claim to his military commission because he had actually served in the House. The clash of personalities, factional disagreement, president making, and political careers assaulted and defended were all evident in Frank Blair's involvement in the investigative process during the Thirty-eighth Congress. Substantive issues of legislative oversight were surely involved – for example: Was the Treasury effectively administered? Were its western agents corrupt? – but no other series of episodes involving a Civil War congressman so illuminated the political nature of the investigative process.

One other category of investigating committee must be mentioned. In December 1861, the members of the House and Senate approved the formation of an unprecedented joint oversight committee, the Joint Committee on the Conduct of the War. Of all the congressional committees of the Civil War era it has been the most studied. Here I shall merely sketch an outline of its activity for the sake of perspective. Frustrated by military reverses and Lincoln's decision to relieve General Frémont of his command during the fall of 1861, radical Republican senators took the lead when Congress convened in establishing a joint committee to inquire into the conduct of the war. Consisting of three senators and four representatives, this committee served during both war congresses, held 272 meetings, and published eight stout volumes of reports. Although its powers were enlarged during the Thirty-eighth Congress to allow it to investigate contracting in general, the committee, under the belligerent leadership of Ohio's ultra senator, Benjamin F. Wade, devoted its major efforts to the investigation of abortive campaigns or battles and generals who were suspected of providing less than exemplary leadership. The Joint Committee on the Conduct of the War did not allow those called before it to have the benefit of counsel, to examine charges directed against them, to cross-examine accusers, or to take advantage of the Fifth Amendment. In these respects, its members were no more at fault than the investigators on some of the other congressional committees of the time, and at the beginning of the war the law of 1857 did provide congressional witnesses with immunity from criminal prosecution on the basis of their testimony. But Schuyler Colfax's amendment to the report of the Contracts Committee revealed that more enlightened precedents for the treatment of witnesses existed, and so did the practices of some other Civil War committees.

During the Thirty-seventh Congress, the members of the joint committee enjoyed easy access to the president, and they found a similar welcome at the War Department during the whole war. They pressed their advice upon the administration freely, endorsing the cause of favorite generals, including some whose ineptitude in the field was redeemed only by the radicalism of their political views, and arguing vehemently as well for the demotion of those whom they blamed for failure. The members of the committee apparently could claim only one legislative initiative, a bill to allow the president to take control of railroads when military necessity dictated it.

In January 1862 Senator Wade, chairman of the Committee, proposed a new joint rule designed to facilitate the consideration of urgent war measures, which in amended form became Joint Rule 22. This provided that any member of the House or Senate could carry his chamber into executive session by assuring his colleagues that the president wished immediate action on a "matter pertaining to the suppression of the present rebellion"; with the galleries cleared and explanation given, the chamber would vote on whether to consider the proposed measure. If the decision was affirmative, debate was then to proceed under strict secrecy and with each member's time restricted to five minutes. Historians have made little of this measure, but it can be viewed as an effort on the part of Wade to make his investigatory committee into a kind of parliamentary war cabinet that would represent the chief executive on the floor of House and Senate. Who, after all, would be in a better position to represent the president than members of the Joint Committee? But Lincoln blandly ignored the opportunity that Wade so kindly provided, and Joint Rule 22 stood uninvoked for the duration of the war.

To many historians the activity of the Joint Committee has seemed to typify the impetuous, unforgiving immoderation of the Republican radicals in Congress. Those who have centered their attention on the committee specifically, however, have not been united in condemnation of Wade and his colleagues and their contributions to the Union war effort. Their first serious chronicler found them to be "partisans, but . . . men of energy; . . . often rash and impetuous, but their hearts were in the struggle. If their service as a council be discounted . . . there was still their great service in giving publicity . . . to faulty military and questionable political transactions." In his book-length study *Lincoln and the Radicals*, T. Harry Williams tipped the balance against the committee members; he portrayed them as the cutting edge of the Jacobin forces who dueled with Lincoln in their efforts to control the military policies of the administration and "conquered" him in every controversy. A generation later, Hans L. Trefousse argued that the committee's activity "made it easier for Lincoln to bring about necessary changes. . . . Despite its errors, it performed a significant service . . . one of persuasion rather than action." Still more recently, another dedicated scholar concluded, "Aside from reaffirming the right of Congress . . . to supervise expenditures by the Executive branch . . . and aside, perhaps, from establishing the outer limits to which a congressional investigation might go in trampling individual civil rights – the Joint Committee . . . accomplished nothing either of immediate good or of lasting significance."[81]

We cannot doubt that the committee served *pour encourager les autres* to some degree, but Lincoln left no testimonials to the effect that it did, as Trefousse suggests, make his task easier. He seems to have suffered its ministrations, as he suffered so much else, making the best of it with wry resignation. Perhaps – almost certainly – he would in secret have echoed Gideon Welles's diary entry "I distrust Congressional committees. They exaggerate." But during the spring of 1864 he accepted the evidence that Senator Wade and Daniel W. Gooch (R., Mass.) of the joint committee assembled concerning the massacre of black Union soldiers at Fort Pillow as definitive. His retaliatory formula, however, fell far short of what congressional fire-eaters might have preferred and in the end was never applied.[82] The episode is symbolic of Lincoln's relations with the committee; its activities undoubtedly influenced him but seldom with the end result that congressional radicals would have found most satisfactory.

Congress renewed the joint committee's mandate at the beginning of the Thirty-eighth Congress and even expanded it by adding oversight of military contracting procedures to its duties. The action was in part a political gambit; a committee so fully occupied with other matters could hardly be expected to stir up messy details of contracting in congressional backyards. But the decision of the chambers also illustrated the fact that the committee had, for the most part, avoided the pointed criticism in the majority party that some of the House investigating committees had inspired, in large measure because the investigative thrust of this group was essentially outward with fewer of the linkages back into Congress than, say, the Contracts Committee had. Its ostensible targets of opportunity were military men, often of Democratic lineage, or, failing that, suspected incompetents. William Parker Cutler's (R., Ohio) diary of 1862–63 reveals the respect that he and other members of the House showed for men like Covode, Gooch, and George W. Julian (R., Ind.) who were serving on the joint committee. Cutler deemed conversations with them, and their statements in caucus, well worth noting.[83] Such men enjoyed the enhanced status that those possessed of inside information usually hold and were, we can believe, role models for other aspiring investigators.

During the discussion of the work of the Contracts Committee, Alexander S. Diven questioned the usefulness of investigative committees, and Roscoe Conkling denounced them in scathing terms. The inquiry, however, was an integral part of congressional activity during the Civil War. Here we have examined the activities of only some of the wartime inquiries, though admittedly the more influential ones. In sum, they were important not only for their contribution to the administration of the war effort but also because of their factional and partisan implications and the ways in which their activity might affect the individual congressional career. If commentary in the press and letters in the Potter and Dawes papers are indicative, the inquiries also had considerable impact on public opinion. The committees in addition could well provide a chapter in any full-scale treatment of the civil rights of congressional witnesses.

Historians will probably always differ on the importance of the Joint Committee on the Conduct of the War. For better or for worse, its members influenced the selection of major army personnel during much of the war as a result of the pressure they placed on the executive branch and the impact of their work and reports on public opinion. Once their methods of operation and style became generally known, they must have done much to invigorate the Union generals. Whether or not the Contracts Committee saved the country as many millions of dollars as its members claimed, it was a major force in purifying the system of government contracting during the war and in rendering it more efficient. As a result of the activities of that committee, men lost their positions and suffered damaged reputations – even Simon Cameron, a member of the president's cabinet. Who can doubt that Potter and his companions raised the level of loyalty among government employees in Washington during the early years of the war? And if these particular committees worked in the areas of greatest visibility and concern, others fulfilled important tasks and had significant impact. The probes of various standing committees similarly affected both the course of government and the fortunes of individuals.

Critics could rightly scoff that the investigators did not maneuver significant legislation through the houses, but they did have some impact upon the institutional structures of the federal government. Joint Rule 22 was now to stand amid the other formal procedures of the Congress, though disregarded by an uncooperative president. The sequences of contract investigation initiated by Van Wyck and the House ultimately revealed that Senator Simmons of Rhode Island had charged a commission for helping a constituent to obtain a contract. Henceforth, such activity would be forbidden in a law that was amended during the third session of the Thirty-seventh Congress to cover "any agent of the Government of the United States." The House recorded by internal resolution its collective opinion of the ways in which government purchasing and contracting were to be conducted and for good measure censured the secretary of war for his shortcomings in this regard. The members of both the second and third sessions of the Thirty-seventh Congress approved substantial measures designed to eliminate fraud in contracting. The statute of March

2, 1863, prescribed penalties for civilians as well as for government officials involved in offenses. And a joint resolution of July 1862 called for public listing of information concerning government contracts that fell outside normal advertising and bidding procedures. Under a law of 1857, witnesses could not be held criminally responsible for acts to which they testified before congressional committees. As members of the Contracts Committee came to suspect that volunteer witnesses were insuring themselves against prosecution, their colleagues sharply modified that guarantee of immunity.[84]

The era when individuals appearing before congressional investigating committees would seek refuge in the First or Fifth Amendment had not yet arrived, but critics accused the committees of refusing to allow the witnesses to be accompanied by counsel, to cross-examine, and to be informed of accusations against them. All three of the major select committees appear to have been delinquent in allowing such prerogatives, although the members of the Contracts Committee defended their procedures vigorously. Potter's committee seems to have been the worst in these respects; for all practical purposes, the redoubtable gentleman from Wisconsin treated hearsay as fact. If Schuyler Colfax's resolution be taken as a measure of the best of past practice, the treatment of witnesses by the investigators of the Thirty-seventh Congress illustrated retrogression in the treatment of men called to testify concerning their own behavior. In accepting the Colfax resolution and in the coolness they ultimately displayed toward the Potter committee, the representatives condemned some of the alleged abuses of the early war years. Crisis, of course, fosters radical solutions, and so it was here. Although the Judiciary Committee allowed Ben Wood the use of counsel, and apparently some right of cross examination, the behavior of its members during the investigation of press censorship was hardly exemplary.

The committees of inquiry invariably included representatives from the opposition, Democrats and Unionists, evidently in proportions similar to those of the standing committees. Sometimes these individuals were very able men and participated actively in the work of investigation. Of the Democrats, William S. Holman was particularly effective. But we would be naive to assume that representatives did not see the opportunity for partisan advantage in committee activities. The reports of the Joint Committee on the Conduct of the War were mined by many a Republican politician for proof of Confederate depravity or the worthlessness of Democratic generals. Evidence from the Van Wyck and Potter committees could be used to illustrate the vigor and probity that characterized a Republican Congress and administration. The Republicans of the Judiciary Committee burned with eagerness to show the treasonable lengths to which a New York Democrat like Ben Wood would go. To their chagrin, the prize eluded them; they could prepare no report indicting the Democrats as personified by Wood and extolling the Republicans as reflected in the energetic patriotism of Hickman, Bingham, and Wilson.

Early in the Thirty-eighth Congress, the Democrats tried to turn the investigative process to their advantage. Fernando Wood, a leading Peace Democrat, proposed the creation of a special committee to investigate assorted charges against military officers, the Navy Department, various branches of the Treasury, and the "general demoralization and incapacity" thought to "pervade the executive branch of the Government."[85] Appalled at the prospect of a Democrat heading such a committee, the Republicans added the surveillance of contracting to the duties of the Joint Committee on the Conduct of the War and ultimately launched investigations as well of the Navy Department, the New York Custom House, and other Treasury operations.

If Republicans sometimes found investigative activity useful in their continuing conflict with the Democrats, some of them were also prepared to turn it against their moderate associates in the executive branch. The radical leaders of the Joint Committee on the Conduct of the War provided the outstanding example of such behavior, but the Judiciary Committee's investigation of press censorship was clearly hostile to both the secretary of state and the president. And indeed elements of the administration viewed most of the oversight investigations as inimical to some degree. Lincoln reputedly accused Dawes of the Contracts Committee of having "done more to break down the administration than any other man in the country."[86] That comment may have gained in both scope and asperity in its circuitous passage into the public press, but the wave of congressional investigative activity must have appeared to Lincoln and some of his cabinet officers to be part of a concerted effort by Congress to expand both its policymaking and its oversight powers at the expense of the executive. And indeed, in the court of inquiry, the court-martial, and the executive commission of inquiry and adjudication, the administrative branch of the federal government possessed the tools necessary to do much of what the investigative committees were doing.

Party factionalism also colored committee activity. The investigations of the Treasury Department during the Thirty-eighth Congress illustrated reaction in part to Democratic charges but also responded to the charges of Francis P. Blair, Jr., against Salmon P. Chase, the secretary of the treasury. Blair still regarded himself as a supporter of the administration, whereas Chase was preferred by many radical

Republicans as a replacement for the moderate Lincoln. The Missouri radicals circulated the charge of profiteering against Blair, and he sought and obtained a committee of investigation to vindicate himself. But since Blair linked Chase to the radical opposition he faced in his home state, the radical cause at both state and national level was at issue in these proceedings. On other occasions inquiries provoked responses that invoked dimensions of factional conflict, even though the investigation was ostensibly focused elsewhere, as in the furious defense of the radical General Frémont inspired by the president's decision to remove him from his post and by the activity of the Contracts Committee.

At the beginning of this chapter we briefly reviewed Roger H. Davidson's assessment of investigative committee roles in the modern era. The conditions of imminent crisis and the relatively short tenure expected by the congressman of the Civil War era make the two periods less than fully comparable. But the partisan aspect that Davidson mentions was clearly present during the Civil War. His concept of "institutional maintenance" also represents a useful focal point for the war years - although "institutional aggression" might have found more favor with the president. Certainly, too, Davidson's emphasis on the usefulness of committee service in the advancement of individual fortunes can easily be transferred to the period of the Civil War.

In these chapters we are examining the interplay of individual politicians, institutional structures, and political events. For the individual congressman of the Civil War period, the opportunity to lead an eye-catching committee, or to share prominently in the work of one, might have very important consequences. One's fellow representatives could be impressed, party leaders gratified, and constituents reassured that they had sent a good man to Congress. As John Covode had discovered, if the subject of inquiry was sufficiently arresting, committee leadership might turn a state or regional leader into a national figure. On the other hand, the investigating committee might provide the beleaguered politician an opportunity to rehabilitate a damaged reputation. James M. Ashley and Frank Blair gambled that committees of inquiry would clear their names, and if the result was less satisfactory than each might have preferred, both had grounds for arguing that they had been vindicated.

If indeed the select committees might provide substantial political opportunities and rewards, these off-the-floor prizes were not equally available to all, even in the majority party. Fourteen of the nineteen chairmen of nonceremonial select committees during the various sessions of the Thirty-seventh Congress were congressional veterans.

On the other hand, the fact that five freshmen could win chairman-ships of select committees illustrates the fact that an aggressive or well-connected representative might well obtain an opportunity to demonstrate his abilities on special assignment. Yet in general the special committee, whether geared primarily to oversight or to leg-islative preparation, was dominated by veterans, sometimes chairmen of standing committees. All four of the Republican members of the Contracts Committee headed standing committees, including two of the most important, Commerce and Elections. Daniel W. Gooch and George W. Julian, the two most important representatives on the Joint Committee on the Conduct of the War, were both veteran congressmen.

It is difficult to assess the relative significance of the various aspects of a politician's career. But certainly special committee assignments during the Civil War became part of the career record of men destined to be significant political powers. The Republicans of the Contracts Committee included a future secretary of state, a governor of New York, and a long-serving senator, as well as Van Wyck, whose political career was destined to have its ups and downs but brought him back to Washington after the war as both representative and senator. Both Roscoe Conkling and James A. Garfield chaired select committees of the House during the Civil War. On the other hand, John F. Potter pursued subversives with ruthless vigor during the early sessions of the Thirty-seventh Congress, but the benefits in enhanced reputation were insufficient to counter the demographic changes in his constit-uency: He was defeated in 1862. Hickman and Bingham, the most energetic probers of the Judiciary Committee in the Thirty-seventh House, failed to return to the next Congress. An important committee assignment was, therefore, no unrestricted passport to further polit-ical success. Select committee service could enhance reputations, and careers already impressive could justify the creation of committees of inquiry. Representatives might see their careers threatened, saved, or reinforced by the work of such bodies. Investigative activity was, then as now, an important element in the machinery of Congress, in the federal government, and in the calculations of the individual career-building politician.

But why should rational politicians in a period of unalloyed party patronage politics have behaved as some of the investigators did during the Thirty-seventh Congress? Quite obviously they irritated or alienated other important individuals or elements in their parties. Did the national crisis temporarily unsettle the minds of calculating politicians? Was personal rectitude or policy position valued more strongly than party harmony? Were the benefits of sensational disclosure thought to be greater than the payoffs in personal advancement and patronage that might be gained by pleasing colleagues or members of the administration? Were the boundaries of party tolerance more flexible then than we currently assume, or the process of party realignment less far advanced than the victory of 1860 might suggest? Did the more reckless investigative committee members perhaps carry minority party tactics into their roles as members of the majority? There are suggestions certainly that an increasing number of Republicans came to recognize that inquiry could be counterproductive. By the third session of the Thirty-seventh Congress, the Contracts Committee was a purring tabby. Investigation continued during the Thirty-eighth Congress, and the Blair case provoked no little acrimony, but other major activity seemingly failed to produce as much collegial confrontation as the contracts, loyalty, and press censorship inquiries had inspired. Investigative activity was recognized to be a two-edged sword.

4 "God alone can guide us": authority structures in the House of Representatives

There have been several periods in America's history when the Union was sorely tried, the federal system put to extreme test. The First Congress met in such a time, as did the Seventy-third Congress, in 1933. The men of 1789 essayed a unique task; they had to vitalize structures visualized to that point in thought and discourse alone. Still, despite their magnitude, the dangers that the founding legislators confronted were also vague and unfocused. In 1933, on the other hand, the threat was clear; a devastating depression threatened to obliterate the economic security and pride of millions of Americans. Even so, most will agree that the Civil War provided the greatest challenge to the American Republic. The pledges of Union had been violated; one-time citizens were in arms against it; its very existence hung in the balance.[1] How did the Congress of these years react to the crisis? Did its members willingly follow President Lincoln's lead? Did they find in their own system of internal governance the direction and will to contribute positively to the Union effort?

The Seventy-third Congress and those of the Civil War years, the Thirty-seventh and the Thirty-eighth, provide opportunities to study the American government under extreme stress. The Democratic majorities in Franklin Delano Roosevelt's first administration were so cowed by events, it has been said, that they accorded their president the famed one hundred days of grace when executive recommendations were treated with special deference. Apparently Lincoln experienced no such period of willing acquiescence. Why not? Granted, the institutional circumstances are not exactly comparable. On April 15, 1861, the day after Major Robert Anderson was allowed to evacuate Fort Sumter, Lincoln issued a proclamation calling seventy-five thousand militiamen to the colors and, in a final paragraph, summoning both houses of the Congress to assemble in session on July 4. Almost three months of acute war crisis had passed before the members of the Thirty-seventh Congress assembled in their humid chambers on the nation's birthday. Little more than a month later, most of them were on their way back to their constituencies, not to reconvene until December 2, 1861. Thus the country was deep in conflict with the rebels before the congressmen had logged one hundred days of legislative activity, and they had long intervening periods in which to observe and evaluate the national administration's course and to build up a strong head of steam. But these facts provide only a skeletal context for the differences of opinion that prevailed between Congress and the executive branch on issues relating to the war.[2]

In some respects Congress behaved during the Civil War as one might expect. The emergency, we may speculate, would quicken the pace of legislative activity or encourage efforts on the part of congressmen to make institutional adaptation. Such developments apparently occurred in the House of Representatives.

The evidence upon which we can base a judgment about the pace of legislative activity and lawmaking during the Civil War is not easily assessed, because formal measures of house or floor activity do not reflect the full workload of the congressmen. Many, for example, were directly involved in the process of recruiting soldiers in their states. Related matters, such as the procurement of arms and supplies and draft quotas, demanded their attention. An increased flow of requests for assistance or intervention from constituents must also have increased the number of morning and Saturday visits by congressmen to the various federal departments.[3]

During the war years, the number of legislative measures (bills and joint resolutions) the members introduced was slightly lower than in the two preceding congresses. However, the number of joint resolutions introduced during the wartime congresses was almost double the average of the previous decade. War-related resolutions accounted for much of the change. And there was a striking increase in the volume of internal House resolutions; representatives averaged 951 resolutions in the two wartime congresses, whereas the average for the 1850s was but 423. And much of this increase involved interaction with one or other of the executive departments.

The number of measures introduced in the House failed to portray legislative activity accurately in another way as well. The introduction of bills or joint resolutions often represents position taking that reflects little real intent or hope on the part of lawmakers that specific legislation will be the outcome. But during the Civil War there was a sharp increase in the number of public measures approved. The two congresses passed on the average 420 public measures; their predecessors of the preceding five congresses had perfected only 146.[4]

There were various illustrations of institutional reaction to the war crisis. During the emergency summer session of the Thirty-seventh Congress in 1861, the members accepted the Holman resolution limiting the attention of the lawmakers to financial, military, and naval measures – those matters judged essential to successful prosecution of the war. Later the members of the House, and the senators ultimately, reinterpreted the definition of a quorum to allow effective operations on the floor. As we have seen, a most unusual joint committee was approved to monitor the conduct of the war by the administration during the second session of the Thirty-seventh Congress. Lawmakers agreed to a joint resolution, emanating from that committee, providing that the houses might go into immediate secret session on report that the chief executive desired prompt consideration of confidential matters. Congressmen bound themselves to take a more rigorous oath of loyalty to the Union than hitherto. The chambers united to forbid members to accept commissions for "procuring contracts, office or place" after Senator Simmons's activities in this respect were revealed and Senator Hale's acceptance of a fee for representing a constituent in his differences with the War Department brought a ban on that kind of arrangement.

The House members placed new restrictions on the admission of members to seats and on state participation in the electoral college, and initially accepted military service as a valid excuse for absence without pay. The representatives and senators both expelled colleagues believed to be disloyal and attempted to expel others. The representatives expanded the duties of some minor committees and ultimately increased the number of standing committees. The Thirty-eighth House made the momentous decision to split off the consideration of appropriations from the Ways and Means Committee and added three other standing committees to the roster. Greater use was made in these congresses of select committees, and their investigative activities were expanded. Although there was probably never a serious chance of passing it, Congress carefully discussed George H. Pendleton's (D., Ohio) bill providing that the departmental secretaries should be given the right of the floor to answer questions about their departments. And finally, the members probably tolerated more rigorous application of the previous-question motion and other restrictions on debate than otherwise would have been acceptable to them.[5]

So there is evidence of the kinds of institutional reactions to stress that we might have expected. But why was there no hundred days of grace for Lincoln or, more precisely phrased, no sustained closing of party ranks in support of executive policies? There can be no definitive answer to the question. Optimally it should be answered in a framework involving the other crisis congresses, perhaps including as well those that fashioned the great sectional compromises of the antebellum era. Here our view must be more restricted. But we can perhaps develop a fuller understanding of the issues involved if we examine the structure of leadership and authority in the House of Representatives during these traumatic years and add our findings to what we already know about the nature of congressmen, the career-enhancing politicians who fought the legislative war for the Union. Some readers may wish to argue that the congressional situations during the spring of 1933 and the war sessions of 1861–62 are not comparable. That contention is supported by the fact that the emergency measures of 1933 were under discussion in Congress while Roosevelt was still allocating the major patronage that came with the change in administration – a situation quite different from Lincoln's. Whatever the merits of this position, it does not significantly diminish the importance of examining the internal workings of the chambers and their bearing upon executive-legislative relations. These are important issues irrespective of whether or not it is feasible to analyze our great political crises comparatively.

Disdaining at a time of such extremity to prearrange the matter in party caucus, the Republicans in July of 1861 elected Galusha A. Grow (R., Pa.) to be Speaker of the Thirty-seventh House of Representatives. Entering state politics as law partner and political protégé of David Wilmot, famed author of the Wilmot Proviso, Grow was a compromise candidate in his congressional district in 1850, winning election to the Thirty-second Congress. He was just twenty-eight years of age. During the mid 1850s he joined the growing band of Republicans in the lower house and responded to the bullying of Representative Laurence M. Keitt (D., S.C.) by knocking him down. After another brush with sensitive southerners, he armed himself with a revolver and accepted John F. Potter (R., Wis.), fortified with both handgun and Bowie knife, as a bodyguard before testing the uncertain climate of the House at the opening of the next morning hour. Chairman of the Committee on Territories in the Thirty-sixth Congress and firmly antislavery in sentiment, he was more moderate in his posture than some of his early Republican associates and had the passage of a homestead bill as his great policy interest. Although the charismatic Francis P. Blair, Jr. (R., Mo.), also campaigned for the position of Speaker on the basis of his important role in holding Missouri in the Union, the *New York Herald* noted Grow's "superior claim . . . by thorough knowledge of parliamentary debate and tactics." The reporter continued, "In all responsible positions he has held in Congress, Mr.

Grow has never committed a blunder, not even when he knocked down Keitt." But when Blair responded to serenaders with a ringing speech, the *Herald* thought his words were "like the notes of a trumpet sounding the charge" and proclaimed him "just the man for Speaker."[6]

Many viewed the selection of Grow as a happy augury. When the First Congress had assembled, its members had selected Muhlenberg of Pennsylvania as their presiding officer. Now, in a time of even greater peril, Pennsylvania had provided another stalwart son to guide the House in deliberation. Grow's speech of acceptance was emotional – "somewhat overwrought" in the view of the *Springfield Republican* – but it suited the temper of the time, as did his first official act. He ordered the bust of ex-Speaker James L. Orr of South Carolina, now a confirmed Confederate, banished from its niche in the Speaker's room and replaced by the marble likeness of John Quincy Adams, the "Old Man Eloquent" of the antislavery cause. When Grow brought the proceedings of the House to a close in March 1863, he had not had a decision reversed from the floor, and the motion of thanks was approved unanimously, a collegial gesture that was by no means routine in House practice.[7]

Although his Thursday evening receptions were impressive and his talent for the symbolic gesture was well developed, Grow was apparently no more than adequate – if that – in his capacity as Speaker. Although floor business proceeded relatively smoothly, he gained a reputation for being a scold.[8] He did not claim for himself any exceptional contribution to wartime legislation other than his continuing support for the homestead bill. The Robert Todd Lincoln papers suggest less interaction between Grow and Lincoln than between the president and Grow's successor, Schuyler Colfax (R., Ind.).

Major newspapers seem to have carried little adverse comment of Grow initially. Ultimately the most telling criticisms of the Pennsylvanian concerned his committee assignments. Examination of his roster of chairmen suggests that New England fared least well of the various regions (see Table 2), obtaining roughly 11 percent of the positions though providing more than 24 percent of the Republican strength in the House. The Middle Western proportion of chairs was only slightly in favor of that region, whereas border and Middle Atlantic states in particular exceeded their share by substantial margins. The chairmanships of the Middle Atlantic states amounted to 43.2 percent of the whole, translating into sixteen slots, of which Pennsylvania obtained six and New York ten. Soon midwesterners at least were bitterly critical of Grow and the Pennsylvania delegation. The *Chicago Tribune* mirrored their complaints in a long column of late

Table 2. *Number of committee chairmen by region*

	Northeast	Middle Atlantic	Border states	Middle and far west
Thirty-seventh Congress				
Large committee	1	10	3	8
Small committee	3	6	1	5
Total chairs	4 (11%)	16 (43%)	4 (11%)	13 (35%)
Percentage share of party strength	24	37	6	33
Thirty-eighth Congress				
Large committee	3	7	3	9
Small committee	6	4	1	4
Total chairs	9 (24%)	11 (30%)	4 (11%)	13 (35%)
Percentage share of party strength	24	26	16	34

February 1863 in which the paper blamed Grow, his Pennsylvania colleagues, and the committee structure for the failure of the western ship canal project, so dear to the hearts of Chicagoans.

Carrying the analysis beyond chairmen, the *Chicago Tribune* editor noted that there was no true westerner on Ways and Means. Representative Valentine B. Horton (R., Ohio) came from the southeastern part of his state and did not represent the feelings of the northwest. Pennsylvanians had also drawn high-ranking positions below the chairman on important committees, thus laying claims for preferred treatment should they be reelected. The *Tribune* tried to show as well that such favoritism had been extended into the organization of select committees. Grow had, believed the Chicago editor, demonstrated "unfairness and partiality."[9]

Meanwhile the Pennsylvania legislature imaginatively "improved" the boundaries of Grow's congressional district in the decennial redistricting, and the Speaker failed reelection. Although his defeat was a "loss to the Union cause in the next Congress," regret at the *Tribune* office was "materially tempered and modified by . . . disapprobation of his course towards the West during his Speakership."[10] In his troubled department, Simon Cameron, Lincoln's beleaguered secretary of war, had also found Grow insufficiently supportive. Since Cameron resiliently reemerged as a major force in Republican party politics in Pennsylvania, Grow's sojourn in the wilderness was a long one. Declaring for the seat of a deceased representative while the preeminent Pennsylvania boss of the time was tarpon fishing, Grow returned to the House in 1894 and served until 1903, providing one of the final illustrations of the way in which Civil War contributions could be transformed into political rewards.[11]

Grow's successor as Speaker was Schuyler Colfax (R., Ind.), a four-term congressional veteran who had tested the waters of the Speaker's race in 1861 and gracefully withdrawn after evaluating the strength of his opponents.[12] Colfax was a highly energetic chairman of the Post Office Committee during the Thirty-seventh Congress and was always friendly and cooperative with colleagues. In November and early December of 1863 he called in his political IOUs and easily outdistanced Elihu B. Washburne (R., Ill.) despite the pleas of the latter's friends that their candidate deserved the Speaker's chair because his continuous service in the House was longer than that of any of his colleagues and because his parliamentary skills were unmatched in the chamber. As a former newspaperman, Colfax had maintained good relations with the press corps on Capitol Hill, and its members tendered him a congratulatory dinner soon after he accepted the Speaker's gavel. The reporters gave him much more attention than they had paid to Grow, extolling the brilliance of the Friday night receptions – brilliant enough to make even Mrs. Lincoln envious, or so that lady was reported to have said – where widower Colfax's mother and sister presided. Although Colfax barred spirituous liquors from the House side of the Capitol, the reporters lauded his skills in the House chamber; at the conclusion of the second session of the Thirty-eighth Congress the residents of the House press gallery "united, without distinction of party, in a letter to Speaker Colfax . . . expressive of their gratification with the courtesy, dignity, and ability which he exhibited in the discharge of the important duties of the Chair, while at the same time they appreciated not less the virtues which adorn[ed] his private life." Colfax was guest of honor at various testimonial gatherings, including one at which his Indiana friends gave him a service of silver, and Congress named a street for him, breaking the practice to that time of using only letters or numbers for the purpose.[13]

Henry J. Raymond, editor of the *New York Times*, cautioned Colfax, "Don't give us committees for the Presidency. Do justice to all shades of opinion, put your heel on the Copperheads remorselessly." Colfax apparently did take his responsibility for naming the House committees very seriously. He consulted cabinet members as to their preferences on the committees with which they had to deal, and spent two days locked in a private cubbyhole in the Capitol, considering the most appropriate placement of colleagues on the various standing committees. Region, locality, and prior service in the House had of course to be recognized, as well as individual experience and capacity.

"I made some of them [the Committees] over 20 times before they suited me," he wrote. Some Democrats he assigned to "respectable Committees but where they could not embarrass the War or the Administration." In this statement he seems to admit having ignored the practice usual in the late 1850s of allowing the opposition to fill minority committee slots according to their own caucus priorities. At the time, the *Herald* detected a "disposition" on the part of "war democrats . . . to arrange amicably with the republicans the places on the various committees," and there was apparently therefore some prior consultation between Colfax and the opposition. Others agreed that Colfax's task of allocating committee assignments was not an easy one. The *Chicago Tribune* noted "great pressure for positions on the Committee of Ways and Means." Another paper wrote of the committees in general, "Much difficulty attended their formation, as there was more than the ordinary amount of talent and ability."

The general reaction to Colfax's labors was favorable; regional balance was apparent and westerners were "jubilant." The evidence of dissatisfaction that surfaced during Grow's term as Speaker was not duplicated in the Thirty-eighth House, although Ben Perley Poore ("Perley"), correspondent of the *Boston Journal* and clerk of the Senate Committee on Foreign Relations, reported some irritation with the prominence of New Englanders in "directing legislation." Colfax did not apparently make up the committees with any view to influence the Republican presidential choice of 1864.[14] He would win the post of Speaker twice more before becoming Ulysses S. Grant's running mate in 1868.

There was, however, an anomalous side to Schuyler Colfax. He had supported the conservative Edward Bates initially for the presidency in 1860, but he convinced radical colleagues that he shared their views. Secretary of the Navy Gideon Welles noted in his diary that Lincoln considered him to be "a little intriguer, – plausible, aspiring beyond his capacity, and not trustworthy." The diary of Lincoln's secretary John Hay also mirrored White House uncertainty as to where Colfax's loyalties lay within the party. For the most part Colfax appears to have walked among the contentious groups and factions in Congress and the Republican party with inspired delicacy. Secretary Chase, Lincoln's major rival for the presidential nomination in 1864, had touted Colfax for Speaker, but the latter assured Lincoln that he was not a passenger on the Chase bandwagon. He delighted the radical Republicans of both houses by descending from the Speaker's chair to move the expulsion of a Copperhead representative, Alexander Long (D., Ohio), but he kept his lines open to the moderate elements in the House by fair dealing on the floor and to the executive office by staying after the presidential receptions for family chats with the Lincolns. When Colfax was reported in January of 1864 to have declared himself in support of Lincoln's presidential candidacy, however, he denied the story, saying that such a choice appeared to be a "popular way to go," or in the words of his formal statement, sentiment "seemed to be manifesting strongly in favor of President Lincoln's renomination."[15]

Colfax's influence on the development or passage of specific legislation is unclear. Reporters noted his official and social activity but did not report specific instances when his rulings or his diplomacy changed the course of major policy development. If he tried to improve the lines of communication with the departmental secretaries and the president, he seems not to have used these contacts to reinforce the legislative processes. Nor did he overtly seek to restrain radical firebrands like Henry Winter Davis (R., Md.) who declared war on Secretary Seward or who wished to launch investigative fishing expeditions in departmental offices. His resources of knowledge and diplomacy seem to have enhanced his reputation without allowing him to contribute in a major way to healing the breaches in party alignment. As a career builder, Colfax must be evaluated as much more successful than Grow. Perhaps also he was a greater force in the House during his later terms as Speaker than during the sessions of the Thirty-eighth Congress. Judgment on that score must rest, pending intensive scrutiny of his whole career as Speaker, but in the meantime we can note that political scientists have categorized both Colfax and Grow as "figurehead" Speakers.[16]

The Speaker aside, where indeed did the individual representative look for guidance in legislative matters? Most important in formal terms were the committees and the floor leader. Both Galusha Grow in the Thirty-seventh Congress and Schuyler Colfax filled thirty-seven standing committees, assigning nine members to twenty-two major groups and up to five to an additional fifteen minor committees. These committees were, however, anything but bastions of stability and accumulated expertise. The qualifications of the chairmen highlight the situation. The mean congressional service of the chairs of the nine-man committees in Grow's term was 3.2 years and of the smaller groups only 1.7. Of the thirty-seven committee chairmen named for the Thirty-seventh Congress, twenty-one had not served on their committee during the preceding Congress. Nor was the situation much different in the Thirty-eighth Congress.[17]

If discontinuity was the general rule for chairmen, that was also true for rank-and-file committee members. Just under 15 percent of the members of both large and small committees were returned at the beginning of the Thirty-eighth Congress. Since only 11 percent of the members of House standing committees in the Thirty-fourth Congress had fulfilled the same assignments in the preceding House, we cannot argue that this turnover was unique. But "leadership untempered by experience" is the phrase that best captures the essence of the committee authority structure during the Civil War and the decade that preceded it.

Several newspapers noted an unusual meeting of standing committee chairmen at Speaker Grow's residence on Tuesday, December 10, 1861, "relative to the progress of the business of the House." Discussion centered on the timing and duration of the Christmas recess, the length of the session in general, and the degree of freedom that was to be allowed in debate. Perhaps the gathering mirrored disaffection among the chairmen of the standing committees. There was an "increasing tendency to refer pet measures to special instead of regular committees," and this assembly may have been an attempt on Grow's part to soothe ruffled feelings. The most detailed report of the special meeting made no mention of irritation among the chairmen of standing committees, nor did the discontent inspired by the use of select committees curb their use.[18] Select committees, both legislative and investigative in nature, were an important part of legislative activity during the Civil War, providing their chairmen and more aggressive members with opportunities to influence both administrative and legislative outcomes and to increase their own political visibility to a degree that would have been impossible within the standing committee structure alone. Nevertheless, the caucus of standing committee chairmen, if used regularly, might well have served as a device for ensuring solidarity in the legislative party, but Speaker Grow apparently did not assemble it again.

In selecting the chairman of the Committee of Ways and Means and de facto floor leader, Galusha Grow followed convention and offered the post first to Frank Blair, his major rival for the speakership, and then to Colfax, who also had significant support for that spot. Both men preferring other assignments, Grow turned to his colleague the veteran legislator Thaddeus Stevens (R., Pa.). Students of American government have considered the Pennsylvanian one of the greatest of the chairmen of Ways and Means, an "autocratic floor leader of the most pronounced type," fully equal to the challenge of heading the most important House committee in the years of its greatest challenge.[19]

Press opinion of Thaddeus Stevens was mixed. Never a great admirer of Stevens, the *Springfield Republican*'s editor printed an early judgment from Washington. "To make so imprudent, so severe and

satirical a man, as Mr. Stevens, chairman of the most important committee of the House, was certainly very indiscreet. He is very able,
but not popular. Why cannot our public men, in and out of Congress,
learn how to be good natured and affable? . . . Schuyler Colfax, for
example, . . . is radical in his views and votes, but he is always gentlemanly and courteous. His enemies like him." "Perley" of the *Boston
Journal* termed Stevens a "sarcastic and bitter Pennsylvanian, who at
times rivals John Randolph, and who ill brooks any opposition to his
wishes." Other writers failed to see the resemblance between Stevens
and the eccentrically vituperative Virginian, but his prepared
speeches were usually marked by "withering sarcasms, quaint denun-
ciations, and humorous jibes," noted one. Although not invariably
hostile to Stevens, the *New York Herald* admitted "that the ability to
use bad language was born in Mr. Stevens like original sin." Sometimes he could be amusingly self-deprecatory, as when protesting, "I
cannot write," in extenuation of refusing to act as a teller and in wry
admission of the notorious illegibility of his handwriting, but his usual
style was marked by corrosive sarcasm and headlong attack. He may
have kept some colleagues in line by fear alone.[20]

Stevens was adept at recognizing the minimal amount of debate
that would satisfy his colleagues. For a period during the long session
of the Thirty-seventh Congress, he set Saturday aside as a day when
representatives could unburden themselves by making speeches on
issues of particular interest to them. He imposed restraints on those
who sought to use the floor for mere "position-taking" or blatantly
party purposes by generous use of the previous question and motions
providing for termination of debate in the Committee of the Whole
for the State of the Union at the end of a stated period – in one
instance only "one-half minute."[21] There were always during the Civil
War a majority of Republicans, border state Unionists, and War Democrats who believed that Congress had to provide the taxes, borrowing, and circulating media essential to a vigorous war effort. In this
respect Stevens was fortunate; the majorities were there if appropriately summoned.

But even among the most patriotic of men there could be differences
as to the equitable distribution of taxes and on the most appropriate
ways of achieving ends desired by all. During the long session of the
Thirty-seventh House, Stevens clashed bitterly with Representative
Dawes (R., Mass.) and other members of the Select Committee for
the Investigation of Government Contracts when they assailed various contractors from the Keystone State, including Simon Stevens,
a former clerk in the Pennsylvanian's law office. More important is
the fact that Stevens was less than complete master of the Ways and

Means Committee, which was made up of men of "diverse views upon subjects of taxation." Indeed it was said that he and the next-ranking Republican member, Justin Morrill (R., Vt.), disagreed "in almost everything."[22] In contrast, although there were differences within the Senate Finance Committee, its chairman, William Pitt Fessenden, apparently suppressed his reservations when in the minority. Stevens carried minority proposals to the House floor and put them to the vote of his colleagues, sometimes meeting defeat there also. In the long session of the Thirty-seventh Congress Stevens lost 31 percent of his motions on which the roll was called.

Fessenden participated freely in debates on measures that fell outside the general purview of the Finance Committee, but he did not take a proprietorial interest in them. Stevens mixed much more actively in the efforts to develop radical southern policies than did the senator, promulgating his doctrine of captured territories and steering his own bill on the recruitment of black regiments to passage during the third session of the Thirty-seventh Congress. During that session also he introduced a resolution proclaiming that members of the legislative or executive branch who proposed to make peace or advised the acceptance of peace proposals that failed to ensure the integrity of Union territory as it had existed at the beginning of the war "were guilty of a high crime." Stevens was, in other words, a major spokesman of radical doctrine in the House.[23]

Stevens was also an unabashed critic of the president and the moderate members of his cabinet. In party caucus in December 1861, he delivered a stinging denunciation of Lincoln and the western politicians who had "misrepresented" him to the other Republicans at the convention of 1860. In caucus again in January 1863, Stevens threatened to bring before the House a vote of lack of confidence in the cabinet. When the president and his moderate secretary of state journeyed to the ceremonies at Gettysburg, leaving the secretaries of war and treasury in the capital city, Stevens quipped mordantly, "Let the dead bury the dead," and in 1864 he referred to Isaac N. Arnold (R., Ill.) as the only Lincoln Republican in the House of Representatives. In their floor leader the Republicans had a man who demanded loyalty from his colleagues in the chamber but was himself a model of insubordination.[24]

The formal bridge between the party and the chamber floor was the party caucus, and the story of that institution during the Civil War gives us a good deal of insight into party matters and leadership during those years. The history of the legislative caucus dates to the colonial period; it emerged in the U.S. Congress as early as 1790.

Political leaders of the early national period used it both as a means of marshaling support for legislative measures and policy and as a device for consolidating the strength of presidential candidates.[25] By the time of the Civil War, the political party caucus was used to perform a number of different but related functions. These can be designated as (1) organizational, when party members met to agree upon party slates for the major appointive positions in the chambers – Speaker through doorkeeper in the House; (2) legislative, when party members agreed upon the content of legislative measures or planned legislative strategy or tactics; (3) electoral, when the party caucus tried to develop political strategies designed to enhance the fortunes of candidates in forthcoming elections or to foster the candidacies of presidential nominees; and (4) advisory, or monitory, when the caucus took positions relative to the policies, procedures, or personnel of the executive branch and sought to influence executive activity. In all such areas of political activity, the individual member of the Thirty-seventh or Thirty-eighth Congress might presumably expect guidance from the discussion and decisions of the party caucus.

When the Republicans met in the special session of July 1861, the press assumed that they would convene initially in caucus to agree on party nominations for Speaker and clerk. This the party did not do, and Galusha A. Grow (R., Pa.) and Frank Blair (R., Mo.) faced each other in floor balloting. Apparently the decision to proceed in this way reflected the belief that manifestations of partisan activity should be eliminated during a national emergency of such magnitude. On the morning following Grow's selection, however, the Republicans did meet to find a basis of agreement on the candidates for sergeant-at-arms, doorkeeper, and postmaster.[26] During the remainder of this short session, caucusing in the Republican party was apparently of little significance. The major newspapers noted no activity of this kind, although the Democrats were reported to have reached general agreement in a caucus of July 9 that they would support the government firmly and not delay congressional proceedings with long speeches.

The regular session of the Thirty-seventh Congress met in early December of 1861. Radical Republican congressmen were incensed by Lincoln's action of that fall in countermanding a proclamation issued by General Frémont in Missouri freeing the slaves of rebels there and by his excision from the secretary of war's report to Congress of a passage endorsing the use of the army to free slaves. These events stimulated caucusing among the radicals of the party in behalf of vigorous legislation to prosecute the war, to punish southerners, and to move the cause of emancipation forward. The *Boston Evening*

Journal's "Perley" reported an "important conference," apparently of radical Republicans, relating to appropriate policy regarding the slaves of rebels in the early days of December, and another meeting of radicals took place on December 5. The *New York Times* noted that party leaders had been resisting the call of a general party caucus, fearing that "differences between the conservative and radical wings on the slavery question would be widened," but one took place on Saturday, December 7, to "harmonize the conflicting views . . . on the disposition of the runaway slaves" who were streaming into Union encampments.[27]

But attendance proved light at that meeting. Only eleven were present, according to some accounts, and the group adjourned after delegating a committee of five to call another meeting on the following Monday evening. About forty members of House and Senate met at that time under the gavel of Senator Samuel C. Pomeroy (R., Kan.) and listened to Thaddeus Stevens denounce the administration and the party members of the Northwest for having assured them that Lincoln was a "true and sound Republican." The drift of discussion in various ten-minute statements was in general radical, although Alexander S. Diven (R., N.Y.) opposed using the caucus as a forum for criticizing the administration and offered resolutions endorsing strict adherence to the Philadelphia and Chicago platforms as guides to party policy. More popular was the resolution of John A. Bingham (R., Ohio) urging that the party enact a sweeping confiscation bill aimed at "all the property of rebels and of their aides and abettors – lands, slaves, and everything." The meeting agreed to postpone a vote on this recommendation in hopes that a larger assembly could be arranged. "The conservatives who were present," reported the *Herald*, "left the caucus in evident disgust, and the radicals retired . . . dejected at the cold reception of their scheme for the construction of a great abolition party."[28] Two nights later, the caucus reassembled with Senator Clark (R., N.H.) in the chair and some sixty Republicans present – an attendance deemed large by the *New York Tribune*. After two hours of discussion, those present unanimously adopted the Bingham resolution.

The fragmentary newspaper reports suggest that the discussions in the two adjourned sessions of the Republican caucus were wide-ranging. Representative Potter gave a progress report on his investigation of subversives among the employees in the federal departments. Senator Trumbull (R., Ill.) spoke in behalf of liquidating and reorganizing the Supreme Court, and others considered the appropriate role of parties in a time of civil strife and the degree of support owed by Congress to the administration and particularly to Lincoln.

But these caucuses were essentially legislative in intent and dominated by the radicals of the party. The *Herald* termed the Wednesday night meeting a "radical caucus" but predicted that there would be no further activity of this sort for some time.[29]

In early February, the Republican senators caucused in a morning session and selected William P. Fessenden (R., Me.) and four colleagues to serve as a committee "to determine the order of business and hours of adjournment, and to secure the attendance" of majority members for the duration of the session. There is no evidence that the representatives used a caucus to establish a steering committee of the same sort.[30]

Though endorsed in the December caucuses, the measure for confiscation of southern property was still mired in the legislative process in late April 1862, and colleagues successfully besought John F. Potter (R., Wis.) to call a meeting "as chairman of the Republican caucus." With Colfax in the chair, representatives listened to eighteen colleagues give five-minute speeches. The roster included party wheelhorses such as Stevens, Frank Blair, and William Kelley (R., Pa.), but less prominent figures like William Parker Cutler (R., Ohio) also addressed the group. Opinion in favor of confiscation or emancipation in some shape was "unanimous," and "those few who doubted" expressed willingness to abide by the "general opinion." "Unexpectedly harmonious," the group resolved in favor of referring all the relevant measures before the House to a select committee of seven as Abraham B. Olin (R., N.Y.) had that day proposed, it having become obvious that the confiscation issue was too complex to be resolved in committee of the whole. Those present agreed that a majority of this group should be "friends of a decided confiscating and liberating policy." This action was not of itself sufficient to bring the confiscation bill rapidly to fruition. Almost two months later, on June 17, a "caucus of republican senators . . . determined to bring the emancipation and confiscation bills upon the carpet shortly."[31]

The last major caucusing among Republicans during this session occurred during the closing ten days. Called for the evening of July 7, a party caucus attracted only between forty and fifty representatives and senators; the small number was attributed to inadequate notice and an evening storm. Several days later, the adjourned meeting of this assembly drew between fifty and sixty Republicans, who listened to colleagues representing a wide range of viewpoints on southern issues. The members present were much interested in electoral matters, and Bingham moved that a committee of five senators and five representatives be selected to prepare a political address that would be laid before a further adjourned meeting of the caucus on Saturday evening, July 12, 1862.[32]

The names of the committee members, selected apparently by Socrates N. Sherman (R., N.Y.), were, noted the *New York Tribune*, "sufficient guaranty for the thorough Republicanism of the address which they will prepare." The committee was ultra in tone. The five senators were strong radicals, and the House members included the radicals Bingham, Stevens, and Potter. Aaron A. Sargent (R., Calif.) was the most moderate of the representatives; his votes on slavery issues placed him at about midpoint on the conservative-radical continuum. The committee members appointed Bingham to be committee draftsman. He prepared an elaborate statement defending the party record during the past session and calling for the use of black Americans as soldiers. When the caucus assembled, however, Colfax moved to have it consider his short resolution calling (in paraphrase) upon all loyal men to stand by the Union, to unite heart and hand against its armed enemies, to sustain the president and the administration, to punish traitors and treason, and to crush the rebellion so that no flag of disunion should ever be raised again. To this end the cooperation of all men who loved their country was invited. Taken aback at this celebration of mother, home, and country, Stevens requested that the Bingham document be at least considered, and this was done. But the Colfax proposal carried the day with few dissenting votes. Colfax was regarded as radical but sensible on southern issues, and his action reflected a division within the party on electoral strategy – one faction trying to commit the party as a whole to an advanced radical position and one seeking to create a broad base of party support that would include pro-Union men of varying attitudes on southern issues.[33]

The correspondent of the *Chicago Tribune* applauded Colfax's action, asserting that the caucus was an appropriate vehicle for selecting doorkeepers and the like but that using it to create a party creed was going too far. Colfax was a "wag, and his drollery was never put to better use than last night," wrote the reporter. If Republican caucuses provoked the scorn of the *Tribune* correspondent, Democratic caucuses had impressed him little more. Recurrently during the spring, he noted, the Democrats had tried to hold conservative caucuses. All had "ended in a snarl, leaving matters worse than they were before."[34]

When the Republicans assembled for the third legislative session of the Thirty-seventh Congress in early December of 1862, they were in a mood to demand from the administration changes in policy. Lincoln's preliminary Emancipation Proclamation in September had seemed to answer radical demands to some degree, but the fall state elections had gone badly. Now there seemed a strong possibility that the Democrats would be organizing the lower house in the Thirty-eighth Congress a year hence. Military operations were discouraging. Both radicals and moderates based their differing explanations of the sad outlook upon the failure of the administration to follow more effective policies. This situation provided the background for interesting caucus activity in both Senate and House of Representatives.

While Burnside's Army of the Potomac painfully extricated itself from the disaster at Fredericksburg, unrest in the Senate reached the point of explosion. Colleagues asked the chairman of the Republican Senate Caucus, Henry B. Anthony (R., R.I.), to call a meeting subsequent to an early adjournment of the chamber on Tuesday, December 16. In his diary Senator Orville H. Browning (R., Ill.) recorded the proceedings at this and subsequent meetings on the seventeenth, twenty-second, and twenty-third of the month. Radical senators had identified Secretary of State Seward as the root cause of ineffectiveness in the cabinet, and Fessenden, a centrist over the long haul, volunteered that a member of the cabinet (Salmon P. Chase) "had informed him that there was a back stair & malign influence which controlled the President, and overruled all the decisions of the cabinet," an influence that he understood to be Mr. Seward. Although more moderate members of the caucus tried to temporize, the best they could do was suggest that a fact-finding deputation be sent to the president and win an adjournment before a vote was taken on the motion of want of confidence that James W. Grimes (R., Ia.) proposed. On the next day the senators backed away from the suggestion that the president be asked to resign and instead approved Ira Harris's (R., N.Y.) resolution "declaring . . . that a reconstruction of the cabinet would give renewed confidence in the administration" and Sumner's recommendation that a committee of seven "call on the President and represent to him the necessity of a change in men and measures." Of those present, only Seward's good friend Preston King (R., N.Y.) failed to vote for both resolutions.[35]

Lincoln's skillful defense of Seward – forcing Chase to testify to the harmony and good order in the cabinet before the senatorial committee and balancing the resignations of Chase and Seward so that he needed to accept neither – is one of the best-known and most dramatic incidents of the Lincoln presidency. Senator Fessenden prepared a detailed description of the confrontation, perhaps because, as he wrote, "the story of the last few days will make a new point in history, for it has witnessed a new proceeding – one probably unknown to the government of the country." The exchange between the senatorial caucus and the chief executive was the most extreme Civil War illustration of caucus efforts to exercise a monitory role.[36]

Although the members of the senatorial caucus were almost unanimous in supporting the course of action adopted and although the temperate Jacob Collamer (R., Vt.) headed the delegation, moderates were obviously less content with the proceedings than were the radicals. Secretary Chase's stock fell among the centrist senators at least – Collamer noted flatly in reporting to the caucus that the secretary of the treasury had "lied."[37] Among the radical senators, however, the knowledge that the president had outwitted them must have rankled and strengthened their desire to effect changes in both policy and personnel in the executive offices. But apparently the reaction among Republican moderates in the Senate caucus was sufficiently strong to deter the members from making common cause with the House Republicans, who were soon themselves involved in a round of angry caucus activity.

In mid January 1863, Grant was bogged down before Vicksburg and military affairs were still discouraging. Horace Greeley and Wendell Phillips descended upon Washington and conferred earnestly with various representatives and senators. And on the evening of Saturday, January 17, 1863, some fifty House Republicans caucused and, after transacting some business, adjourned until Tuesday evening, January 20. The *Herald* reported that "Republicans of known conservative proclivities were left out," and representatives who did not attend were said to be ignorant of the proceedings. But the *New York Tribune* reporter believed "it safe to say" that the business involved "the shaping of the course of Congressional proceedings for the residue of the session." This writer also noted the "public impression" that the meeting had been called "to effect a change in the Cabinet."[38]

The fragmentary diary of William Parker Cutler provides more details. He did not record anything about the January 17 meeting, but he was present on Tuesday evening. He noted that committees had been appointed at the previous meeting to consider (1) the policy to be followed in admitting members elected to Congress from the seceded states, (2) the question of enacting a uniform election law (relating to the soldier vote), and (3) "measures proper for a more vigorous prosecution of the war." The reports of these committees made up the agenda of the Tuesday night caucus.[39]

Sentiment, Cutler reported, was against "premature admission" of members from states under military government and in favor of a uniform election law. Members expressed concern about the newspapers that were being read by the soldiers of the Army of the Potomac, the *Herald* and the *World* almost exclusively, it was believed. The request of the third committee for the removal of the last meeting's "injunction of secrecy" so that committee members could communicate with the president and department heads sparked a general discussion of the disorganization believed rampant in both cabinet and army. A New York member protested, however, when it was alleged that rioting was imminent in New York City.

At a third meeting, on January 27, Valentine B. Horton (R., Ohio), chairman of the committee charged with canvassing ways of infusing vigor into the administration, reported that his committee saw no way of accomplishing its objective and asked on his colleagues' behalf that its members be discharged. The members again discussed the issue of newspapers for the soldiers at length and the degree of culpability assignable to the Quartermaster's Department. The focus of discussion then shifted as Stevens took the floor to argue that "all the trouble" was with the cabinet and "gave notice that he would at next meeting of the caucus move a Resolution of want of confidence in the Cab." James M. Ashley (R., Ohio) then asked the group to agree on a new cabinet and propose it to the president. As a beginning, he suggested the former congressman and Speaker of the House, currently a general in the army, Nathaniel Banks; Galusha A. Grow; and Salmon P. Chase. Theodore M. Pomeroy (R., N.Y.) protested that this action would take them "outside of constitutional limits," and Stevens replied that he was willing to allow the president to "name a new cabinet." Horton attributed much of the current difficulty to the president, who played men off against each other. "The cabinet men are brought to a deadlock by the President – the President is tripped up by his Generals." And "God alone" could "guide us through these terrible storms of doubt uncertainty treachery imbecility & infidelity." Stevens responded that "he had given [God] up lately."

On February 7, the caucus reassembled and took up the newspaper issue once again. The committee that had been authorized to confer with the secretary of war reported two articles of war, allowing the suppression of papers giving aid or comfort to the enemy, punishment of the proprietor, and sale of the press. General "Joe" Hooker, reported William D. Kelley (R., Pa.), was eager to cooperate in keeping treasonous papers out of the hands of the troops in his Army of the Potomac. Hereafter reference to Republican caucusing fades from Cutler's diary entries and also from the newspapers.

Security in these meetings of early 1863 was tight. Only Cutler's decision to start keeping more elaborate diary entries in December of

1862 has preserved a reasonably full record of events in this series of caucuses. Some conservative Republican members did not receive invitations, at least initially, and those attending enjoined secrecy upon each other and refused to enlighten absent colleagues about the content of the discussions. Such strategy on the part of the moving spirits in these meetings suggests that they were much more interested in formulating and advancing radical policies than in using the caucus as a harmonizing agency. Horace Greeley visited Washington at this time, but his role in precipitating the proceedings is unclear. That radical Republicans provided the leadership and driving force in the caucusing is apparent. But not all radicals were involved, and the failure of the senatorial maneuvers of December must have had a dampening effect upon the movement.[40] Like the meetings of senators in December 1862, these gatherings involved the caucus advisory function, but electoral and legislative functions were also in play. As in much of the general and House caucusing, the attendance was unimpressive. The first meeting in the series was "slimly attended," and fewer than seventy members were on hand at the largest meeting. This was characteristic of House and general party caucusing during the Civil War.

A somewhat different type of party conclave also occurred in January 1863. More than a hundred Republicans, mostly from the House and Senate, congregated at an evening rally and banquet in Washington on January 26, and John Covode (R., Pa.), the presiding officer, received the gift of a gold-hilted sword. General Simon Cameron was the subject of a friendly toast, giving him an opportunity to respond in a healing exchange designed to assuage the pain that loss of office and censure in the House must have caused him. A nonmember, William B. Mann, addressed the group, as did Secretary of the Interior Usher, Senators Lyman Trumbull and John Sherman (R., Ohio), and Representative Daniel W. Gooch (R., Mass.). One newspaper used the word "caucus" in describing this gathering, another the term "reunion," but given the circumstances and the attendance of nonmembers of Congress, the meeting is more properly considered a party rally.[41]

At the beginning of the Thirty-eighth Congress, Republican representatives approached organizational caucusing differently than in July 1861. The situation was quite dissimilar. There was widespread fear that the clerk of the preceding body, Colonel Emerson Etheridge, would so narrowly interpret the terms of an act of that Congress concerning the content of the representatives' credentials that various Republican delegations might initially be denied their seats. The Democrats and border state men could then organize the House and, incidentally, retain Etheridge as clerk. Lincoln himself had taken steps to prevent such an occurrence, sending warning notes to leading members of threatened delegations as to the proper elements in the governors' certificates of election. But the possibility that Etheridge was conspiring with the Democrats and the necessity of planning strategy to counter it must have reinforced the normal desire to have the party candidates for Speaker and clerk agreed on in advance in a chamber in which the formal Republican majority was smaller and less firm than in the last Congress. Caucus and organization proceeded, however, without untoward incident. State electoral successes in the spring of 1863 and Lincoln's patient policy of supporting border state Unionists, whose representatives now elected to go into the Republican caucus, had reversed the gloomy forecasts of late 1862, replacing possible Democratic ascendancy with an administration margin of some twenty-five votes. On December 5, the party caucus selected Schuyler Colfax as its candidate for Speaker and, with the House organized, reassembled to choose candidates for clerk, sergeant-at-arms, doorkeeper, and postmaster on the evening of December 7, 1863.[42]

House caucusing thereafter focused on a variety of matters. The chairman, apparently the cautious Yankee Justin Morrill, refused to call the caucus when a significant number presented him with a signed request to meet in order to consider the elimination from the cabinet of the moderate postmaster, Montgomery Blair. Past experience, and the failure of senatorial colleagues with similar intent a year earlier, made Morrill and many colleagues reluctant to exercise the advisory function of the caucus in this way.[43] But in February of 1864 caucus activity increased. On February 3, a House caucus assembled to focus interest and strategy on several legislative measures: (1) the bill repealing the 1862 resolution amendatory to the confiscation bill that Lincoln had requested in return for signing that legislation; (2) proposed changes in the Enrollment Act of 1863 that had instituted compulsory military service for the first time in the history of the United States army, particularly the proposal to terminate the right of draftees to commute their service into a monetary payment; and (3) the bill prepared by Henry Winter Davis enunciating the radical Republican plans for bringing the rebel states back into the Union, ultimately known as the Wade-Davis bill. In addition, members had to be selected to fill the vacancies on the National Republican Committee in preparation for the presidential campaign of 1864. Estimates of the turnout at this caucus vary widely from a "small attendance" to ninety – the latter surely an overgenerous guess or a misprint. The group decided to involve the "unconditional Union" senators in the selection of committeemen and adjourned, pending a call for a general Republican congressional caucus, which reporters forecast would be the "first definite trial of the relative strength of the Lincoln and Chase wings of the party."[44]

The adjourned caucus was reconvened on February 8, and Senator Daniel Clark (R., N.H.) took the chair. Representative Ashley sketched the background of the need for filling Republican National Committee vacancies, and Representative Nathaniel B. Smithers (R., Del.) submitted a resolution outlining a method by which the new members might be chosen. But then a wide-ranging discussion followed concerning the appropriate strategies for the presidential campaign. Support from every loyal quarter was essential, thought various leaders who favored changing the national committee's name to "National Union Committee." Senator James R. Doolittle (R., Wis.) reported that the name "republican had been laid by in all the states." He noted that it was essential to attract votes from War Democrats. Representative Robert C. Schenck (R., Ohio) went so far as to suggest that the name be "The Free Union Party" and that there be a new national committee, a new organization, and a new platform. He so moved, and Representative Ashley worried that his colleague and others of like mind were exceeding their mandate. The sole obligation of the caucus, he reminded the group, was to provide names for filling the vacancies on the national committee. Schenck's motion was defeated: yeas, twenty-three; nays, thirty-one. Finally the caucus agreed that openings in the committee should be filled by the appropriate state delegations and that seven men should be selected to administer the distribution of campaign documents.[45]

For the remainder of the first session of the Thirty-eighth Congress, House caucusing mainly involved legislative matters. A resolution to allow the Treasury to sell surplus gold, recommendations of the Committee on Ways and Means, soldiers' pay and bounties, the reconstruction issue and the Davis bill on that subject, the tax bill, the request for congressional seats on the part of Arkansans elected to Congress under the provisional military government of that state, the question of repealing the commutation clause of the enrollment acts, and the loan bill, authorizing additional borrowing by the federal government – all were subjects of caucus discussion and, on occasion, agreement as to appropriate legislative tactics. At the meeting of the caucus on March 15 those present decided to hold a weekly assembly "so as to insure more concerted action," but the press recorded fewer meetings than observance of the rule would have required. The reporters also noticed "slim attendance" and adjournments to attract larger turnouts. Indeed in the week following the decision to put the caucus meetings on a regular schedule, the *Herald* noted, "It is almost impossible now to induce a full attendance in any Congressional caucus. The members are tired of that old, slow motioned machinery, and pay little attention to it." In mid April, however, the *New York Tribune* reported "full attendance at the Union or Republican caucus ... the object being to arrange and expedite the business of the House." If the participants in such meetings sometimes achieved agreement on legislative strategy, they did not apparently place strong emphasis upon party discipline in implementing decisions. "There is want of unity of action among the Union men," reported the correspondent of the *Chicago Tribune*, and when fifty-plus members discussed the legislation pending on the draft, they took "no definite action" and were "left free to so act on the bill reported from the Committee on Military Affairs" as they "may think proper." And in such disunity the chairman of Ways and Means led the way, declaring that he would "not be bound by the caucus."[46]

Having examined major aspects of the authority structures in the House of Representatives, let us consider the informal groupings in the Republican party that have attracted the most attention from historians – the division into radicals and nonradicals, designated variously as moderates and conservatives. Little stressed through several generations of Civil War historiography, this distinction was given new life by such progressive historians as Howard K. Beale, James G. Randall, and T. Harry Williams in their accounts of the Civil War and reconstruction.[47] Harsh and vindictive in their attitudes toward southerners, the radicals, or Jacobins – or ultras, as they were also called – enunciated policies of immediate emancipation, confiscation of rebel property, and harsh terms of reconstruction for the rebel states. They harassed generals whom they believed to be slow or who had West Point, southern, or Democratic antecedents. They found Lincoln's military and civil policies inadequate and planned a postwar Union where men from northern finance and industry would provide the leadership. They tried to dispense with Lincoln after his first term and replace him with a candidate who would more fully share their attitudes and policy preferences. Opinions among the progressive historians differ somewhat as to Lincoln's success in coping with the radicals, but T. Harry Williams portrayed them as victorious over Lincoln in every encounter. "The wily Lincoln," wrote Williams, "surrendered to the conquering Jacobins in every controversy before they could publicly inflict upon him a damaging reverse. Like the fair Lucretia threatened with ravishment, he averted his fate by instant compliance."[48]

After 1950, historians began to change their evaluation of the radicals. The ultras, noted some, were not so different from Lincoln and the nonradicals as had once been argued. Others, often biographers, began to give the radicals higher grades than formerly because they were – so it could be argued – the members of the Republican party who were most in tune with the moral imperatives of the day. If radical measures were sometimes draconian, the motives of the framers were pure and their objectives correct. They were, thought Hans L. Trefousse, Lincoln's "vanguard for racial justice."[49]

Other scholars placed the radicals in somewhat different perspective. David Donald wrote, "The Radical Republicans were only one of the many factions that pulled for control of the Lincoln administrations. Because they were noisy and conspicuous, their historical importance has been overrated." Reviewing the literature recently in one of the most authoritative overviews of the Civil War of our generation, James M. McPherson wrote in 1982: "Although the radicals never constituted a majority of Republicans, they were the most aggressive faction in the party. A vigorous determined minority with a clear vision of what it wants and how to get it always has an advantage, especially in time of crisis."[50]

It is still unclear how factionalism worked to structure the legislative process and party management during the Civil War. The sources suggest that division in the Republican party affected a wider range of lawmaking activity and influenced relations between the executive and legislative branches more extensively than those seeking to downplay the distinction between radical and moderate have admitted. The implications of the differences between the radicals and their moderate colleagues in the Thirty-seventh House of Representatives have been studied closely in only a few major areas of public policy.[51] In fact, our general understanding of these matters has not yet overtaken the methodological advances in legislative analysis made during the years between 1955 and 1975. It was then that scholars introduced the technique of roll call scaling, along with a number of other simple quantitative methods that gave historians of the U.S. Congress an analytical capacity hitherto unavailable. Both the techniques and the initial findings of those who have used them call us to reformulate our thinking about policymaking during the Civil War in ways that have only just begun.[52]

In 1963 Glenn M. Linden defended a dissertation called "Congressmen, 'Radicalism,' and Economic Issues, 1861–1873" in which he tried to identify radicals, nonradicals, and unaligned Republicans in both the Senate and the House of Representatives from 1861 to 1873 and to test the proposition that the radicals stood united in support of a particular economic program, as Howard K. Beale had suggested. Linden searched the literature for identification of Republican radicals and legislative measures that represented a test of their views, and broadened the scope of his inquiry to include votes on amendments to the selected measures, "plus others considered appropriate," totaling seventy-six votes in the House of Representatives. Having identified radical positions in each of the roll calls, Linden calculated the percentage of votes on which congressmen agreed with the radical responses. He showed that historians had failed to identify some radicals and argued on the basis of his analysis that party voting dominated the votes on the test measures. Voting on economic measures was quite different, however. In this category representatives showed a strong tendency to vote with those members from the same geographical section, irrespective of party. To Linden must go the credit for launching the first systematic analysis of Civil War voting patterns. But his group boundaries were arbitrary and, potentially at least, his method might associate individuals together whose voting records were quite dissimilar – indeed completely so at the center of his scales.[53]

Meanwhile William O. Aydelotte and other faculty and graduate students at the State University of Iowa had begun to apply the Guttman scale, group-cohesion and likeness scores, and cluster-bloc analysis in their studies of legislative voting.[54] Among these techniques, the Guttman scale possessed definite advantages over the identification of positions and the percentage scoring that Linden and others had used, and allowed us to move far toward definitive solution of the identification problem in the study of the Republican radicals in Congress. The progressive historians had failed to identify the positions of many lawmakers and sometimes disagreed in their identification of radicals. Systematic use of scales across considerable numbers of roll calls tended to reveal the reasons underlying omissions and anomalies. In part the earlier problems of identification were linked to uncertainty about how radicalism could be defined. Scaling allowed scholars to posit an operational definition of radicals that set semantic quibbles aside: During the Civil War, radicals in Congress were individuals whose votes generally placed them in Guttman scales on southern issues at or close to the pole of the scales farthest removed from that occupied by Democrats from the loyal slave states.

Once identification of the radicals had been made more precise, the way became clear for types of analysis hitherto impossible in anything but impressionistic fashion. The easiest hypothesis to test was the one that posited a specific economic dimension to Republican radicalism. In its most comprehensive formulation, that hypothesis failed to stand. My research on the Senate during the Civil War showed that it was possible to develop a comprehensive picture of radical-moderate disagreements on both major and minor issues and to highlight those incidents and measures that particularly exacerbated the differences. Scaling identification of radicals and moderates in the Senate, for example, allows us to argue that radicals and moderates did indeed differ in their behavior in the Senate caucus crisis of December 1862. But much remains to be done. In particular, committee composition in terms of radical or nonradical dominance, with the resulting implications, has not thus far been systematically examined for either chamber. Only when we reach the point where all the lawmakers of the Civil War congresses are identified by scale score on all important issues and committee activity is assessed in these terms shall we have reached the point where a truly systematic evaluation of the political and legislative factionalism of the Civil War is possible.

But there are other implications of the new methodology particularly relevant to this inquiry. The Donald or McPherson metaphor of embattled groups conjures up a mental picture of several clusters of encircled wagons from which fire is directed not only at the enemy line but back and forth between the clumps of wagons and, particularly from one position, at the command post directed by a tall gentleman in frock coat and stovepipe hat. The scales reorient our thinking. We now see our legislative warriors in extended line, with component parts threatening to break apart and move farther away from, or closer to, each other or the command post. Or, in more prosaic terms, instead of more or less cohesive groups in conflict with one another, we see our actors arranged in lines or attitudinal continua in which opinion on policy ranged from advocacy of extreme solutions to positions much more congruent with the status quo. As a moderate committed to his own policy initiatives, Lincoln, in the twin capacities of legislative and party leader, had to try to extend the range of his supporters both ways along the congressional continuum.

What does this revised conception of the congressional situation tell us about the members of the House of Representatives and patterns of authority? Voting scales show us that there was a kind of ordered diversity of opinion, and they reveal attitudinal tendencies sufficiently strong to be reflected in voting activity. But how many who showed particular tendencies of this kind actually participated in factional activity designed to unseat Lincoln or otherwise influence party policy? Michael Les Benedict has made a useful distinction between legislative and political radicalism, explaining that political realities or personal assessments could make radicals or moderates seek alliance with groups or constituencies with which they were not necessarily in full accord. Thus both Kansas senators voted a radical position, but James H. Lane kept on good terms with Lincoln while Senator Samuel C. Pomeroy, his colleague and rival for patronage, called for the replacement of the president by Secretary of the Treasury Salmon P. Chase. In the House of Representatives, radical congressmen like Owen Lovejoy (R., Ill.) and William D. Kelley supported the chief executive while other radicals excoriated him. We know that among individuals found at both ends of the spectrum of Republican opinion there were efforts to mobilize those of like mind. Some of the more radical Republicans tried to use the party caucus to bind the party in support of their policy preferences. Apparently they failed. In other caucusing activity, the Union Democrats attempted to detach more conservative Republicans into a conservative coalition designed to block the passage of extreme legislation, and some even dreamed of creating a conservative party.[55] They unquestionably labored in vain.

In the House, just as in the Senate, there were men who were consistently radical on most issues relevant to southern problems and others whose positions relative to their colleagues' changed over time, in the direction of either greater harshness or a more moderate stance. In the House of Representatives during the Thirty-seventh Congress, there were at any given time probably a majority of Republicans who were more extreme in their policy views than was the president. Table 3 is a scale based on twenty-four roll calls relating to aspects of the slavery question during the second session of that Congress. The center, or scale-type, column identifies eighteen combinations of voting responses in which the underlying policy positions become increasingly extreme or radical as we read downward. The names at the left identify illustrative Republican congressmen whose voting placed them in the various scale types, and the adjacent numerals in parentheses show the number of Republicans in that category. The voting of the eleven members of type 16A differed from those in 16B only to the degree that each member of the A group recorded one nonscaling response whereas those in B voted a perfect pattern of opposition to Charles Delano (R., Mass.) and his colleagues in type 00. Grouping scale types into larger categories can provide food for argument, but this scale does show clearly that about one-third of the ninety-five Republicans demonstrated a distinct tendency to break from the radical position and that more than one-fifth were opposed to the polar radicals on one-half or more of the votes. The fact that these moderates on occasion voted with the Democratic and border state members obviously restricted the radicals' freedom of movement in legislative activity. In both the Thirty-seventh and the Thirty-eighth House the opposition was sufficiently numerous so that defection of moderate Republicans could place the radicals in the minority.[56] There was diversity within the party, and no faction achieved a clear ascendancy. The radicals were strong enough in both houses of Congress to force the chambers to perfect legislation that went well beyond the desires of moderate or conservative colleagues and the president. But as Chapter 2 shows and William Parker Cutler's account of caucusing illustrates, they were never sufficiently dominant to win approval of legislation that the more extreme committee chairmen thought most desirable. Although Congress refused to follow the executive lead in major areas of legislation, no leader or group could sufficiently control the levers of either party or of Congress to assert clear dominance.

In part Republican intransigence must have reflected the congressmen's understanding of constituency opinion. In 1984 David Donald reaffirmed his earlier hypothesis "that a congressman's radicalism varied with the degree of security he felt about his chances of being reelected," and this he linked to the member's margin of victory, using data from the second session of the Thirty-ninth Congress. But Michael Les Benedict could not find a similar relationship when he examined the electoral margins of all those who, according to scale analysis, voted consistently radical or moderate positions during the years 1863–69. It follows logically from Donald's hypothesis that Republicans from marginal constituencies would be disproportionately moderate in their floor voting. But when we use the slavery and confiscation voting scales from the second session of the Thirty-seventh Congress to identify radicals and moderates, the correlation between radicalism and constituency electoral margin was only .146. By this measure, victory margins accounted for only about 2 percent of the variation in the voting on the floor of the House of Representatives. The explanation of radical voting behavior cannot be as simple as Donald has suggested.[57]

Although the Republicans of the House of Representatives had majorities sufficient in both Civil War congresses to pass the legislation deemed essential to the war effort, there was significant disunity in the party on the issues related to broader questions of southern policy, race, and civil rights. In confronting such problems, Republican congressmen disagreed among themselves and with the suggestions of their titular leader, Abraham Lincoln. The radicals of the House and Senate referred to themselves as earnest men; they tended to justify

Table 3. *Thirty-seventh Congress, second session: Republican House Slavery Issue Scale with illustrative members*

Roll call I.D. and response

Distribution	259	286	287	160	161	288	171	221	249	69	243	149	150	271	82	191	170	72	248	220	241	166	239	240
	N	N	N	Y	N	N	Y	Y	Y	Y	Y	N	Y	Y	Y	Y	Y	N	Y	N	Y	Y	Y	N
Delano (5)	X	X	X	X	X	X	X	X	X	X	X	X	X	X	0	0	X	X	X	X	X	X	X	X
Diven (1)				X	X	X	X	X	X	—	X	—	X	X	X	X	0	X	X	X	0	X	X	X
Phelps, T. G. (1)				X	0	0	0	—	—	—	—	0	X	X	0	—	X	X	X	0	X	X	X	X
Dunn (2)							X	X	X	X	X	X	0	X	X	X	X	X	X	X	X	X	X	X
Stratton (3)									X	X	X	X	X	X	0	0	X	X	X	X	X	X	X	X
Nixon (1)										X	X	X	X	X	0	0	X	0	X	X	X	0	X	X
McKnight (3)										X	—	X	X	—	0	X	X	0	X	X	X	0	X	X
Porter (1)						X						X	—	0	X	—	X	X	X	—	X	X	X	X
Worcester (2)												X	X	X	X	X	0	—	X	X	X	0	X	X
Blair, F. P. (1)					X							X	X	X	X	X	0	—	X	X	X	0	X	X
Olin (4)								X					X	X	X	X	X	—	X	X	X	—	X	X
Verree (1)											X					X	X	X	X	X	X	—	X	X
Gooch (10)																				X	X	—	X	X
Pomeroy (10)																					X	0	X	X
Arnold (15)																						X	X	X
Stevens (8)																							X	X
Julian (11)																								X
Hickman (17)																					X			

Source: Inter-University Consortium for Political and Social Research, United States Congressional Roll Call Voting Records, 1789–1987 (Thirty-seventh Congress).

SLAVERY SCALE: ITEM DESCRIPTIONS

259 To recommit H.R. 472 to a special committee with instructions to report on the amendment offered as substitute for the bill.

286 To amend H.R. 472, a bill to free from servitude the slaves of rebels... which substitute amendment strikes out all after the enacting clause of the said bill and inserts that all persons held in service by any person connected with the rebel government shall now be free.

287 To pass the substitution to H.R. 472 [as above].

160 To table a resolution providing that a select committee of nine be appointed to inquire and report to the House whether a plan can be proposed for the gradual emancipation of all the African slaves, and for the extinction of slavery in the states of Delaware... by the people or local authorities. ...

161 To pass [at a later date] the above.

288 To pass H.R. 472 as amended.

171 To amend a motion limiting the time of debate on S. 108 to allow one hour, instead of one minute, for debate.

221 To table the substitute for H.R. 374 [a bill freeing all slaves in all territory of the United States].

249 To table H.R. 472.

69 To table a resolution providing that the secretary of war revoke the first section of General Order Number 3, dated Nov. 20, 1861... which section prevents fugitive slaves from coming within the lines of the Union Army.

243 To pass H.R. 472.

149 To amend a motion to postpone consideration of H.J. Res. 48 [to cooperate with and financially aid any state which may adopt the gradual abolishment of slavery]. ...

Roll call I.D. and response

Scale type	259	286	287	160	161	288	171	221	249	69	243	149	150	271	82	191	170	72	248	220	241	166	239	240
	Y	Y	Y	N	Y	Y	N	N	N	N	N	Y	N	N	N	N	N	N	Y	N	Y	N	N	Y
00																								
01	0	0	X						X		X		X											
02	X	0	0	X					X	X	X													
03	X	X	X	X	0	X																		
04	X	X	X	X	X	X	X																	
05	X	X	X	X	X	X	X	0																
06	X	X	X	X	X	X	X	X	X		X		X											
07	X	X	X	X	0	X	—	X	X	X	X					X			X					
08	X	X	0	X	0	X	0	0	X	X	X						X							
09	X	0	0	X	X	0	—	X	X	X	X	X	X						X				X	
10	0	X	X	X	X	X	0	X	X	—	X	X	0	0									X	
11	X	X	X	X	X	X	X	X	X	0	X	X	X	—	0	0	X	0	X				X	
12	X	X	X	0	0	X	X	X	X	X	X	X	X	X	X	0	0	X	X	0				
13	X	0	0	0	X	0	0	0	X	X	X	0	X	X	0	0	0	0	X	0	X			
14	X	X	X	X	X	X	0	X	X	0	X	X	X	0	X	0	X	X	X	X	X	X		
15	X	X	X	X	X	X	X	X	X	X	X	X	X	X	X	X	X	X	X	X	X	X	X	
16A	X	X	X	X	X	X	X	X	X	X	X	X	X	X	X	X	X	X	X	X	X	—	X	X
16B	X	X	X	X	X	X	X	X	X	X	X	X	X	0	0	X	X	0	X	X	X	X	X	

150 To postpone consideration of H.J.Res. 48, until Monday next. [A resolution to cooperate with and financially aid any state which may adopt the gradual abolishment of slavery.]

271 To pass a resolution providing that the judiciary committee be instructed to report a bill repealing the fugitive slave law approved September 18, 1850.

82 To adjourn . . . during debate on a resolution to prohibit officers in the military service of the U.S. from using any portion of their forces for the purpose of returning fugitives from service or labor; and to provide for the dismissal of such officers as may violate the said article.

191 To postpone . . . H.R. 126, a bill to manumit and liberate from servitude, the slaves of all persons who shall engage in or aid and abet armed rebellion against the U.S.

170 To limit the time of debate on S. 108, a bill for the release of certain persons held to service . . . in the District of Columbia. . . .

72 To table a resolution providing that the President be respectfully requested to direct General Halleck to recall his order prohibiting Negroes from coming within the lines. . . .

248 Call of the house, made during debate on H.R. 472.

220 To adjourn, motion made during debate on H.R. 374.

241 To amend H.R. 472 by providing for the penalty of death or imprisonment and the freeing of slaves owned by any person convicted of treason against the U.S.

166 To amend H.R. 312 by providing that any person who shall claim to own the service or labor for life of any person . . . shall pay . . . the sum of two dollars.

239 To amend H.R. 472. [Amendment of Francis P. Blair, Jr., including freedman resettlement].

240 To amend H.R. 472 by providing that any commanding military officer whose district embraces any states in rebellion shall invite all persons within his lines to be enrolled in U.S. service, and that any slaves liberated by this shall entitle the owner to compensation.

their positions in moral terms. And one who is driven by moral imperatives is uneasy in compromise. Ironically, the rightness or wrong-
ness of placing conditions on the reentry of the Confederate states
was never really at issue. In these years all – or almost all – Republicans
agreed on ultimate ends. In each case the troublesome questions were
about the proper means of achieving objectives deemed appropriate.
The great challenge facing the Republicans was to apply the arts of
politics to produce solutions upon which the party members could
unite in amity.

Had there been no Civil War and no legislation relating to that
conflict specifically, the legislative record of the Thirty-seventh Congress, taken individually or in company with that of its successor,
would have represented a great achievement. Homesteads on the
public domain, land grant colleges, a transcontinental railroad system,
a significantly revised tariff structure, a system of national banks, and
a department of agriculture – what a calendar of interests served and
futures shaped! And in addition the hard-working representatives
and senators of these congresses considered, shaped, and approved
the many laws and resolutions necessary to fight and win a war in
the field. Perhaps the measures forecast in the national Republican
platform of 1860 – the free soil agenda – moved forward more easily
because war issues distracted the attention of the hard-pressed lawmakers. But the legislative record of these congresses in sum was
remarkable. Even so, the members of the Republican party in the
House of Representatives fell short of unity in those policy areas that
provided the greatest challenges. Scaling illustrates the diversity of
positions found among congressmen and indicates the grounds for
coordinated factional activity. When we examine the authority structure of the House we find Speakers of modest attainments and regional dissatisfaction with committee assignments. Continuity in
committee leadership and personnel was lacking. Investigative self-
seeking was rampant. The chairman of Ways and Means was at odds
with colleagues both in and out of committee. A promising effort to
use the committee chairmen to coordinate legislative activity was
discontinued.

Party was the great lubricant of the legislative process, but it failed
to provide the kind of authoritative caucus guidance that would have
welded the legislative party together. The caucus attempted to exercise all of the potential caucus functions, but with few positive
results. Its most constructive contribution lay in its endorsement of
the Unionist strategy for the 1864 election. If it served as a safety
valve, allowing malcontents, often the most distinguished among the
members, to air their grievances, those very statements often worked

to reinforce distrust of the executive branch. The Republicans did use the caucus to establish some legislative priorities, but the more radical elements tried to use it as a means of dragooning moderate colleagues. That effort failed, and the record of the caucus is replete with adjournments, instances of poor attendance, and expression of dissatisfaction with caucus initiatives or with the caucus as an institution. On one occasion a future Speaker sabotaged the carefully prepared address that a previous meeting had authorized. On another the floor leader dismissed the usefulness of the caucus by refusing flatly to be bound by its decision.

A cooperative, forceful, and united leadership structure in the houses of Congress could perhaps have given Lincoln his hundred days of grace. But neither the congressional authority structure nor the party caucus could mobilize the Republican congressmen either to follow Lincoln in united cohort or to achieve a dominant congressional consensus. Given the self-seeking nature of the congressmen, their constituency orientations, their belief in congressional prerogatives, and the fact that they were molded as politicians in an era that pointedly rejected the politics of compromise, the possibility of accepting presidential initiatives unquestioningly probably never occurred to them.

5   *Conclusion*

When the Civil War broke out, the federal representatives and senators had been making their annual pilgrimages from their states to
the nation's capital for seventy years. They had traveled in fair
weather and foul, on horseback and by stagecoach, coastal vessel,
canal boat, and river steamer, and finally on the cars of the wonder
of its age, the railroad. Usually in December of each year they settled
into the boarding messes, hotels, and private homes of the capital
city and set themselves to the tasks of national governance. Sometimes
their labors brought them little but tedium, enlivened perhaps by the
occasional clash of personalities, but on occasion the lawmakers faced
grim crises when their decisions defined the realities and meaning of
the American Republic. Through time, these men shaped the ways
in which the Congress of the United States did business and were
themselves shaped to some degree by the experience. But through
those seventy years none of the people's representatives faced a more
fateful task or future than those who filled the legislative chambers
of the Capitol during the Civil War. Yet their concerns, their perspectives, their individual objectives, and their collective labors are
still too little known to us. This little collection of essays is an attempt
to reconnoiter some of the possibilities for understanding the congressmen, their relations with one another, and their interaction with
Lincoln, through an understanding of Congress as an institution.

In this volume I have, in effect, posed four major questions: What
was the political preparation of the federal politician of the middle
period? What did the men who served in the congresses of the Civil
War expect of President Abraham Lincoln? What was the nature of
the activity of congressmen off the floor during the Civil War? And
who among the congressmen was in charge in these years and to
what effect? The answers given here are manifestly incomplete, yet
sufficient I believe to confirm my suggestion that the view from Capitol Hill may be highly rewarding to the student of the Civil War.

Few congressmen of the American middle period, we have found,

142

were destined to return to the Capitol for many subsequent terms of service. Congressional labor was by no means, however, a diversion or anomaly in the careers of such men. Trained to some degree at the local level, and particularly at the state level, in the art of government, they found myriad ways of impressing their constituents and other state politicians who chose them as Speakers of the assembly or presiding officers of the senate in the state legislatures. Election to the Congress of the United States was a natural progression for those who best demonstrated general abilities, skill in riding the tides of partisan politics, and a knack of capitalizing on family or other personal attributes and connections, and who were amply endowed with luck that put them in the right place at the right time and the wit to recognize that fact. If such men were exceptionally endowed, they might emerge in Washington as part of the relatively small core group of national public figures who survived for a considerable time in Congress, the presidential cabinet, and the diplomatic corps. But the median service of the representatives of the 1850s and 1860s was only two years. Few of them, we suspect, viewed the years as wasted, but they can hardly have believed that their election was the beginning of long-term legislative service in Washington.

All through the middle period, about half of the congressmen would subsequently serve in other public positions. Sometimes these later assignments were elective at other levels or in other branches of government, but frequently they were patronage places, the rewards of a political system that as in no other era of our history, made non-elective appointments a matter of partisan influence and prerogative. Congressional service opened the door to other political opportunities.

The historians of the Civil War era have rightly made it clear that this was a period of strong ideologies. It was also a time when the politics of power and place was preeminent. And many who played the game, whether ideologue or placeman or a mixture of the two, as was probably most common, were but lightly broken to it by the responsibilities of public officeholding. We have seen that there were southern and northern differences in the institutional systems of politics, as reflected in the careers of politicians from North and South. Although these differences were of some significance, it is not clear that they were becoming substantially greater at mid century. From the scattered evidence – suggestive rather than definitive – in Chapter 1, the more striking and growing divergences between the congressional delegations from North and South apparently lay in the realm of values and political strategies. This transformation, in turn, was most directly attributable to the general and political socialization of a new generation of political leaders. That socialization produced more men who were less able or willing to develop formulas of political accommodation or compromise. In their hands, the increasingly unstable federal political system disintegrated into civil war, and such leaders, or others like them, played a major role in shaping the policies of both the Union and the Confederate government. The members of the Republican party were, in northern phraseology, earnest men, but few if any of them were not also politicians, playing the game by the rules of the time. These men carried a heritage of minority party intransigence into the wartime congresses and were all the more encouraged to hold hard to extreme positions by the evidence of threat and crisis that they saw all around them.

Although the roles of President Abraham Lincoln were many, he was most important in the eyes of the representatives and senators, I argue, as the general director of the system by which federal patronage was dispensed, and as an intervenor who could influence subordinate government officers in their behalf. Lincoln's contributions to establishing and effecting the legislative agenda and formulating Union ideology were much less appreciated by many members of his party, but his efforts in these respects powerfully influenced the development of war policies and the political fortunes of the Republican and Union parties. The challenge of establishing a wartime legislative agenda and melding it with the free soil program to which the party had committed itself in its national platform imposed strains on the ties between president and the members of Congress that peacetime presidents did not have to experience. In effect, this task presented both legislators and chief executive with the opportunity to improvise, and representatives and senators could put in play extreme proposals that would never have found favor as national platform planks.

Now too, in the face of the crisis and unparalleled mobilization of men and resources, the location of the appropriate boundaries between executive and legislative powers and functions naturally became an issue of compelling interest. As he squared to his tasks, Lincoln defined the relations between the executive and legislative branches in terms consonant with Whig theory, but the actual record shows a much more active and manipulative president than any good "Whig in the White House" should have been. Lincoln seldom got exactly what he wanted from his party supporters on Capitol Hill; on the other hand, he was not "conquered" at every turn, as has been suggested. Moderate forces in Congress and Lincoln's own actions meant that in the end much crucial war legislation was compromise legislation – as legislation usually is. Nor did Lincoln seek to revamp the party that had brought him to power and, in effect, try to read extremist politicians out of the party. He accepted support from wherever it was offered, helped radicals in their reelection bids, and admitted that if he must choose between moderates and radicals in Missouri it was the latter who stood closest to the true needs of the time.

Most political historians willingly admit that, even as today, debating and voting in the chambers of Congress or in the committee of the whole represented only part of the congressman's Washington duties during the nineteenth century. Indeed, for many representatives, perhaps on-the-floor activity was one of the less important aspects of their role. Few historians, however, have closely examined or described off-the-floor activity during that century – the representation of constituency interests before the departments, the related interaction with increasingly important lobbying interests, and the work in standing or select committees. Such emphasis in part has reflected historians' prevailing interest in the development of policy, as contrasted with concern about institutional functioning. But committee decision making has always played an important role in formulating and refining floor agendas, and it is curious that historians have not devoted more attention to the standing committees at least. Chapter 3 investigates the involvement of members of the House in the oversight activity of the Judiciary Committee and various special committees during the Civil War.

Although the work of investigating committees did not have all of the implications found in such activity today, their labor during the Civil War was an important part of the congressional process. The investigations had partisan and factional implications of great significance and provided representatives with the means for both evaluating and influencing executive policies. Here too the boundary lines between the branches were at issue, and an investigator like John Hickman, steeped in the minority tradition of legislative guerrilla activity, could push into areas where feelings of sensibility and party solidarity were gravely compromised.

Just as the successful procurement of patronage might ensure the further development of a representative's political career, so could investigation be turned to career-building ends. In Chapter 1 we noted the importance for the individual congressman of obtaining positions of leadership, which, if successfully filled, paved the way for further preferment, and the usefulness of special issues or political challenges that might likewise produce advertisement of superior talent. Investigative activity fulfilled a similar function; a dramatic investigation, rich in revelation or achievement, could transform a little-known politician into a national figure. Such inquiries might also make a representative highly unpopular with party leaders, as Chapter 3 illustrates. Choice committee assignments tended to be the prerogatives of relatively senior members of the House, a reminder of the fact that in politics, as elsewhere, "them as has, gets." Finally, the congressmen could use the committee of investigation as a means of clearing themselves of damaging accusations of impropriety. Given the highly charged nature of Civil War politics, the political stakes in that kind of investigation might extend far beyond the boundaries of career preservation, as the Frank Blair investigation revealed.

Who was in control of the House of Representatives during the Civil War? At one level of analysis the answer is, of course, obvious – the members of the Republican party had a considerable majority during the sessions of the Thirty-seventh Congress and a slimmer, but adequate, numerical advantage during the sittings of the Thirty-eighth. But who provided the leadership, refined the agenda, formulated the legislative strategy, mobilized the voting majorities, and coordinated the activities of the House with those of the Senate and the executive branch? Of course, there was a formal structure of leadership and working committees, whose functions had been developed through the years, and an elaborate set of House rules to provide guidance. Chapter 4 is primarily concerned with some of the ways in which the serving members breathed life into the institutional arrangements.

How effective were the two Speakers in providing leadership? I suggest that they were competent men, Colfax more so than Grow, but not individuals who used their office to galvanize their colleagues to purposive action. An eminent social scientist categorized them as figurehead speakers. Thaddeus Stevens, as chairman of the Committee on Ways and Means and party floor leader, has fared better at the hands of scholars – one of the great chairmen of Ways and Means, say most. Yet this judgment has rested on rather little intensive analysis of his performance. His policy preferences placed him among the most radical members of the House, and some argue that centrists are more effective in mobilizing majorities. That he was strong of will and that he had an agenda, none can dispute. But he was also vituperative and uncompromising; voting divisions fell against him to a surprising degree; he meddled in areas of legislation outside his committee domain; and within that arena he faced opposition from other party members. On occasion Stevens was at war with his president and scornful of opinion in the party caucus. He was obviously less of a unifying force in the legislative party than the ideal floor leader would be. When we examined the committee leadership and members in general, we noted lack of experience and rapid turnover in even the most important of committees. And in Chapter 3 we discovered the abysmal ignorance with which James M. Ashley assumed the chairmanship of the Committee on the Territories at the beginning of the Thirty-seventh Congress.

Elements of the Republican House membership, particularly those of radical persuasion, tried to use the party caucus to bring direction and discipline into legislative proceedings. Reconstructing that story is not easy, but apparently these efforts were more successful in providing occasions for therapeutic expressions of irritation than in mobilizing support for radical measures or in devising means of energizing the administration. In a series of secret caucuses in early 1863, the chairman of a subcommittee dedicated to the latter purpose asked in complete hopelessness for the discharge of his committee. The chairman of Ways and Means used the caucus as a forum in which to vent his own choler but refused to accept its advice on legislative matters. When the first session of the Thirty-eighth Congress adjourned *sine die* on July 4, 1864, Attorney General Bates exclaimed, "God be thanked!" and added, "But, both house[s] being destitute of a *leader*, every thing is in confusion, and every little clique and faction aspires to rule." He could with justice have said the same of the Thirty-seventh House. Even so, he admitted that the Thirty-eighth Congress "passed some necessary and proper laws" and that the members of its predecessor "with unhesitating liberality . . . granted all our demands for men, money, means and appliances."[1] Seventy years of development had produced a legislative mechanism with a formal structure of position and role that enabled even an assemblage of heterogeneous, short-serving, crisis-ridden, and contentious men to achieve major objectives.

Still, it is fair to say that there was a leadership crisis in the national government during the Civil War; against such a background the efforts to use scaling to establish relative ideological and policy preferences in the congressional chambers are important. Members presumably acted in conformity with the dictates of their own internal monitors to a greater degree than they would have done if a strong leadership pattern had existed. On those basic southern issues related to slavery in its broadest connotations, about a third of the Republicans of the Thirty-seventh Congress were moderate in their approach. If the party was to have an effective majority, these men had to be retained in roll call voting whenever possible. They were a brake that restrained their more radical colleagues. But as a result neither group could expect that the policies adopted would completely satisfy it. Leadership, insofar as it was manifest, was diffused in the House of Representatives during the Civil War.

As I noted, the chapters in this volume represent a reconnaissance and certainly do not fully describe the world of the Civil War congressman. But it is instructive to remember that while great armies marched to victory or disaster and major and fateful policy issues gripped the attention of federal lawmakers, administrators, and many of the general public, those same legislators fulfilled their institutional roles to their own best advantage and thought of patronage, personal power, and career advancement. If Owen Lovejoy was the most effective Republican abolitionist on the floor of the House until his death in the Thirty-eighth Congress, we must remember that he was as avid for patronage as any of his colleagues and did not scruple to see to it that a Democratic brother-in-law was retained in place. James M. Ashley, floor manager for the Thirteenth Amendment and hailed as the "Great Impeacher" for his efforts to bring down a president, dreamed of western land speculations on the basis of inside knowledge and avowed that he would give up his seat could he be assured of holding the position of surveyor general in a western territory for as many as four years. This was how the system worked, and we must appreciate these personal imperatives and institutional contexts if we are to understand the congressman's Civil War.

Appendix: Representatives and senators who died in office, 1844–1865

ADAMS, JOHN Q. (Sen., rep., Mass.) 2–23–48

ANDREWS, CHARLES (Rep., Me.) 4–30–52

ASHLEY, CHESTER (Sen., Ark.) 4–29–48

ATHERTON, CHARLES G. (Sen., rep., N.H.) 11–15–53

BAILEY, GOLDSMITH F. (Rep., Mass.) 1862

BAKER, EDWARD D. (Rep., sen., Oreg.) 10–21–61

BARROW, ALEXANDER (Sen., La.) 12–29–46

BAYLEY, THOMAS H. (Rep., Va.) 6–23–56

BELL, JAMES (Sen., N.H.) 5–26–57

BINGHAM, KINSLEY S. (Rep., sen., Mich.) 10–5–61

BLACK, JAMES A. (Rep., S.C.) 4–3–48

BOSSIER, P. E. J. B. (Rep., La.) 4–24–44

BOWDEN, LEMUEL J. (Sen., Va.) 1–2–64

BRADLEY, EDWARD (Rep., Mich.) 8–5–47

BRENTON, SAMUEL (Rep., sen., Ind.) 3–29–57

BRINKERHOFF, HENRY R. (Rep., Ohio) 4–3–44

BRODERICK, DAVID C. (Sen., Calif.) 9–16–59

BROOKS, PRESTON S. (Rep., S.C.) 1–27–57

BUELL, A. H. (Rep., N.Y.) 1–29–53

BURROUGHS, SILAS M. (Rep., N.Y.) 6–3–60

BUTLER, ANDREW P. (Sen., S.C.) 5–25–57

BUTLER, CHESTER P. (Rep., Pa.) 10–5–50

CALHOUN, JOHN C. (Rep., sen., S.C.) 3–31–50

CAMPBELL, BROOKINS (Rep., Tenn.) 12–25–53

CLAY, HENRY (Rep., sen., Ky.) 6–29–52

CLAYTON, JOHN M. (Sen., Del.) 11–9–56

COOPER, THOMAS B. (Rep., Pa.) 4–4–62

DICKINSON, RUDOLPHUS (Rep., Ohio) 3–20–49

DOUGLAS, STEPHEN A. (Rep., sen., Ill.) 6–3–61

DROMGOOLE, GEORGE S. (Rep., Va.) 4–27–47

ELMORE, FRANKLIN H. (Rep., sen., S.C.) 4–11–50

EVANS, JOSIAH J. (Sen., S.C.) 5–6–58

EWING, PRESLEY U. (Rep., Ky.) 9–27–54

FAIRFIELD, JOHN (Rep., sen., Me.) 12–24–47

FOWLER, ORIN (Rep., Mass.) 9–3–52

FRICK, HENRY (Rep., Pa.) 3–1–44

FULTON, WILLIAM S. (Sen., Ark.) 8–15–44

GOODE, WILLIAM O. (Rep., Va.) 7–3–59

HANCHETT, LUTHER (Rep., Wis.) 11–24–62

HARMONSON, JOHN H. (Rep., La.) 10–24–50

149

HARRIS, THOMAS L. (Rep., Ill.)
11–24–58

HENDERSON, J. PINCKNEY (Sen.,
Tex.) 6–4–58

HERRICK, RICHARD P. (Rep., N.Y.)
2–4–46

HICKS, THOMAS H. (Sen., Md.)
2–14–65

HOLLEY, JOHN M. (Rep., N.Y.)
3–8–48

HORNBECK, JOHN W. (Rep., Pa.)
3–4–47

HUNTINGTON, JABEZ W. (Rep.,
sen., Conn.) 11–1–47

KAUFMAN, DAVID S. (Rep., Tex.)
1–31–51

KELLOGG, ORLANDO (Rep., N.Y.)
8–24–65

KING, DANIEL P. (Rep., Mass.)
7–25–50

KING, WILLIAM R. (Rep., sen.,
Ala.) 4–18–53

LEWIS, DIXON H. (Rep., sen., Ala.)
10–25–48

LOCKHART, JAMES (Rep., Ind.)
9–7–57

LOVEJOY, OWEN (Rep., Ill.) 3–25–64

MCCONNELL, FELIX G. (Rep., Ala.)
9–10–46

MEACHAM, JAMES (Rep., Vt.)
8–23–56

MILLER, JOHN G. (Rep., Mo.)
5–11–56

MONTGOMERY, JOHN G. (Rep., Pa.)
4–24–57

MOORE, HEMAN A. (Rep., Ohio)
4–3–44

MUHLENBERG, HENRY A. (Rep.,
Pa.) 1–9–54

NES, HENRY (Rep., Pa.) 9–10–50

NEWMAN, ALEXANDER (Rep., Va.)
3–2–49

NOELL, JOHN W. (Rep., Md.)
3–14–63

NORRIS, MOSES (Rep., N.H.)
1–11–55

PEARCE, JAMES A. (Rep., sen., Md.)
12–20–62

PENNYBACKER, ISAAC S. (Rep.,
sen., Va.) 1–12–47

PEYTON, JOSEPH H. (Rep., Tenn.)
11–11–45

PORTER, ALEXANDER (Sen., La.)
1–13–44

QUITMAN, JOHN A. (Rep., Miss.)
7–17–58

RANTOUL, ROBERT (Rep., sen.,
Mass.) 8–7–52

READ, ALMON H. (Rep., Pa.) 6–3–44

RUSK, THOMAS J. (Sen., Tex.)
7–29–57

SCHWARTZ, JOHN (Rep., Pa.)
6–20–60

SCRANTON, GEORGE W. (Rep., Pa.)
3–24–61

SIMS, ALEXANDER (Rep., S.C.)
11–22–48

SNODGRASS, JOHN F. (Rep., Va.)
6–5–54

SPEIGHT, JESSE (Rep., S.C.) 5–1–47

SPINK, CYRUS (Rep., Ohio) 5–31–59

TAYLOR, WILLIAM (Rep., Va.)
1–17–46

THOMPSON, BENJAMIN (Rep.,
Mass.) 9–24–52

THOMSON, JOHN R. (Sen., N.J.)
9–12–62

UPHAM, WILLIAM (Sen., Vt.)
1–14–53

WOOD, AMOS E. (Rep., Ohio)
11–19–50

Notes

Key to abbreviations

Basler, CW	Basler, Roy P., ed., *The Collected Works of Abraham Lincoln*. 9 vols. and supplement. New Brunswick, N.J., 1953–55
BU	Border state Unionist
CG	U.S. Congress, 28–39 Congress, *Congressional Globe*. Washington: Congressional Globe Office, 1844–67.
D.	Democrat
HRJCMB	House of Representatives, Judiciary Committee Minute Book
R.	Republican
RTLC	Robert Todd Lincoln Collection of Abraham Lincoln Papers
UU.	Unconditional Unionist
UW.	Union Whig

Introduction

1 Allan G. Bogue, *The Earnest Men: Republicans of the Civil War Senate* (Ithaca, 1981), 40–41.
2 Stephen Vincent Benét, *John Brown's Body* (New York, 1928), 81.
3 *The Federalist: A Commentary on the Constitution of the United States* (New York: Modern Library, 1937), 337.

Chapter 1. The paths of power

1 Roy F. Nichols, *The Disruption of the American Democracy* (New York, 1948); James G. Randall, "The Blundering Generation," *Mississippi Valley Historical Review* 27 (June 1940), 3–28.
2 The literature is a large one. In the absence of an updated bibliography of the politics of the nineteenth century, reference is best made to the contributions listed in the notes of such recent works as Alan M. Kraut (ed.), *Crusaders and Compromisers: Essays on the Relationship of the Antislavery Struggle to the Antebellum Party System* (Westport, Conn., 1983); Richard L. McCormick (ed.), *Political Parties and the Modern State* (New

Brunswick, N.J., 1984); Stephen E. Maizlish and John J. Kushma (eds.), *Essays on American Antebellum Politics, 1840–1860* (Arlington, Tex., 1982); and Joel H. Silbey, *The Partisan Imperative: The Dynamics of American Politics Before the Civil War* (New York, 1985).

3   85 Cong., 2 Sess., House Document no. 442, *Biographical Directory of the American Congress, 1774–1961* (Washington, 1961). Issued in various earlier editions, this great compendium contains sketches of almost all federal representatives and senators up to the date of publication. Carroll R. McKibbin converted these materials to machine-readable form; they are available in the Archives of the Inter-University Consortium for Political and Social Research, Ann Arbor, Michigan. The original compilers did not include some important categories of information, and there are also some errors in the sketches. Researchers should verify these biographical data whenever possible. My own impression, however, after detailed examination of the data relating to the Civil War senators, is that errors in the sketches are not so numerous as to invalidate trend line analysis. Early-nineteenth-century information in the sketches is probably somewhat less reliable than that bearing upon twentieth-century figures.

4   These eighty-three careers represent about 5 percent of the congressional careers in the years 1844–65. We would not expect the incidence of death among serving congressmen to be such as to make the careers of decedents unrepresentative of careers in general, except that the opportunity for subsequent private or public office was foreclosed. Some years ago I participated in the preparation of a quantitative collective biography of all the members of the House of Representatives between 1789 and 1960, organized by decadal cohort. (See Allan G. Bogue, Jerome M. Clubb, Carroll R. McKibbin, and Santa A. Traugott, "Members of the House of Representatives and the Processes of Modernization, 1789–1960," *Journal of American History* 63 [September 1976], 275–302.) Most of the comparable career and biographical characteristics of those who died in the House or Senate during the middle period are very similar to those found in the broader collective biography. Lawyers were present in almost equal percentages in both, and differences in the means of the two groups were usually markedly less than ten percentage points. The main deviance between the various measures in the two groups lies in the proportions who served in state offices. Of those who died in office, 87 percent had so served, whereas the percentage for all representatives was just above 60. Much of that difference is explained by the presence in the decedent group of a substantial number of southern senators who did not serve in the House of Representatives but had held state office.

5   33 Cong., 1 Sess., *CG*, 19–26. See William S. Ashe, p. 26; Edward Everett, p. 20.

6   37 Cong., 2 Sess., *CG*, 37–39, 45–49. See Zachariah Chandler, p. 37; Daniel Clark, p. 38; Fernando C. Beaman, p. 46; Bradley F. Granger, p. 47.

7   33 Cong., 1 Sess., *CG*, 146–48. See Christian M. Straub, p. 148.

8   31 Cong., 1 Sess., *CG*, 1810–11. See Thaddeus Stevens, p. 1810.

9   The basic data used in this career summary are those found in the *Biographical Directory of the American Congress*. The broader trends referred to are derived from Bogue et al., "Members of the House of Representatives," and from an unpublished comparison of the biographical characteristics of the regional delegations in Congress conducted by Bogue, Clubb, and Traugott. I draw upon this unpublished study with the kind permission of Clubb and Traugott. The fact that the findings in these analyses conform in general to those derived from the data of the decedent group strengthens my confidence in the illustrative usefulness of the latter sample.

10 Seymour M. Lipset, *The First New Nation: The United States in Historical and Comparative Perspective* (New York, 1963); Bertram Wyatt-Brown, *Southern Honor: Ethics and Behavior in the Old South* (New York, 1982); Carl Degler, "The Two Cultures and the Civil War," in Stanley Coben and Lorman Ratner (eds.), *The Development of an American Culture* (Englewood Cliffs, 1970), 92–119; Rollin G. Osterweis, *Romanticism and Nationalism in the Old South* (New Haven, 1949). Anne Norton, *Alternative Americas: A Reading of Antebellum Political Culture* (Chicago, 1986), is an intriguing recent contribution to the literature. I have made no extreme claims for the representative nature of this particular sample of federal legislators, although I note that the characteristics of its members were similar to those of their era in other collective biographies, in particular the Bogue et al. analysis of all representatives who served between 1789 and 1960. That sample revealed some of the same contrasts between northern and southern lawmakers that we find here. For those who are interested in statistical tests, the chi-square value derived from analysis of thirteen variables relating to the background and training of the southern and northern members of our group of eighty-three was 21.9 with 12 degrees of freedom, providing a significance level of .05.

11 David R. Mayhew, *Congress: The Electoral Connection* (New Haven, 1974); Samuel Kernell, "Toward Understanding 19th Century Congressional Careers: Ambition, Competition and Rotation," *American Journal of Political Science* 21 (November 1977), 669–93.

12 Anson Burlingame, 36 Cong., 1 Sess., *CG*, 753–54; Solomon Foot, 32 Cong., 2 Sess., *CG*, 310, and 34 Cong., 2 Sess., *CG*, 27; Emery D. Potter, 28 Cong., 1 Sess., *CG*, 619.

13 Thomas H. Benton, 28 Cong., 1 Sess., *CG*, 225–26; Isaac N. Arnold, 37 Cong., 1 Sess., *CG*, 37; Orville H. Browning, 37 Cong., 2 Sess., *CG*, 53.

14 The valedictory materials for Senator Porter appear in 28 Cong., 1 Sess., *CG*, 225–26, 228. Salmon P. Chase, 31 Cong., 2 Sess., *CG*, 29.

15 Richard K. Meade, 30 Cong., 1 Sess., *CG*, 42; John S. Millson, 34 Cong., 1 Sess., *CG*, 1501; James M. Mason, 34 Cong., 1 Sess., *CG*, 1500. For the relationship between constituency and long service see Table 1.

16 James M. Ashley, 37 Cong., 2 Sess., *CG*, 48. These spatial mobility data need not surprise us. They fall well within the limits apparent in the large body of mobility literature based upon manuscript census analysis

that stretches in line from James C. Malin, "The Turnover of Farm Population in Kansas," *Kansas Historical Quarterly* 4 (November 1935), 339–72, to Hal S. Barron, *Those Who Stayed Behind: Rural Society in Nineteenth-Century New England* (Cambridge: Cambridge University Press, 1985), and John M. Faragher, *Sugar Creek: Life on the Illinois Prairie* (New Haven, Conn.: Yale University Press, 1986). I have myself made some contribution to this research; see *From Prairie to Corn Belt: Farming on the Illinois and Iowa Prairies in the Nineteenth Century* (Chicago: University of Chicago Press, 1963), 8–28.

17 Ambrose H. Sevier and Edward Cross, 28 Cong., 2 Sess., *CG*, 73–75.

18 Joseph R. Chandler, 31 Cong., 2 Sess., *CG*, 7; Garrett Davis, 39 Cong., 2 Sess., *CG*, 1119.

19 Two books in particular provide a conceptual background and source references for thinking about this question: James Willard Hurst, *The Growth of American Law: The Law Makers* (Boston, 1950), and Heinz Eulau and John D. Sprague, *Lawyers in Politics: A Study in Professional Convergence* (Indianapolis, 1964), noting particularly ch. 1, pp. 11–30. More recently Kermit Hall has touched on this subject in *The Politics of Justice: Lower Federal Judicial Selection and the Second Party System, 1829–61* (Lincoln, 1979).

20 Preston S. Brooks, 32 Cong., 1 Sess., *CG*, 1641.

21 George Scranton, 37 Cong., 1 Sess., *CG*, 18–21; John Schwartz, 36 Cong., 1 Sess., *CG*, 3214–15, 3222–24; Pierre E. J. B. Bossier, 28 Cong., 1 Sess., *CG*, 585–86; Sampson W. Harris, 30 Cong., 2 Sess., *CG*, 18.

22 Calvin Colton, *The Life and Times of Henry Clay*, 2 vols. (New York, 1846), I, 113.

23 John Reynolds, *My Own Times: Embracing Also the History of My Life* (Chicago, 1879), 159, 189; and see particularly p. 283: "The convention system was not established until 1834. Anyone who wanted to run for office could do so. All who ran for Congress did so without having held a convention." Richard P. McCormick, *The Second American Party System: Party Formation in the Jacksonian Era* (Chapel Hill, 1966), is still the best place to begin investigation of the growth of political parties during the 1820s and 1830s. Although I disagree with some of his interpretation, Sean Wilentz provides a recent listing of major contributions to the Jacksonian literature in "On Class and Politics in Jacksonian America," in Stanley I. Kutler and Stanley N. Katz (eds.), *The Promise of American History: Progress and Prospects*, *Reviews in American History* 10 (December 1982), 45–63.

24 Joseph R. Chandler, 33 Cong., 1 Sess., *CG*, 24.

25 John W. Crisfield, 37 Cong., 3 Sess., *CG*, 298.

26 Philip Johnson and John W. Killinger, 37 Cong., 2 Sess., *CG*, 1687.

27 Samuel R. Curtis, 36 Cong., 1 Sess., *CG*, 900; Charles Sumner, 36 Cong., 1 Sess., *CG*, 3214.

28 Isaac S. Pennybacker, 29 Cong., 1 Sess., *CG*, 219.

29 James W. Bradbury, 30 Cong., 1 Sess., *CG*, 73; Alfred Ely, 36 Cong., 1 Sess., *CG*, 2806.

30 Zeno Scudder, 32 Cong., 2 Sess., *CG*, 28–29; "Luther Hanchett," 37 Cong., 3 Sess., *CG*, 103–5; "Thomas H. Bayly," 34 Cong., 1 Sess., *CG*, 1500–3.

31 "John R. Thomson," 37 Cong., 3 Sess., *CG*, 11–12.

32 As measured by the maximum difference between the regional means of the biographical characteristics of all representatives and senators serving between 1789 and 1861.

33 Thomas S. Bocock, 35 Cong., 1 Sess., *CG*, 2014. On the subject of southern values see the references in note 10 and also William R. Taylor, *Cavalier and Yankee: The Old South and American National Character* (New York, 1961); Edwin L. Ayers, *Vengeance and Justice: Crime and Punishment in the Nineteenth Century American South* (New York, 1984). For a biography of Quitman see Robert E. May, *John A. Quitman: Old South Crusader* (Baton Rouge, 1985).

34 Lawrence M. Keitt, 35 Cong., 1 Sess., *CG*, 337; Philip Philips, 33 Cong., 1 Sess., *CG*, 26; Sydenham Moore, 35 Cong., 2 Sess., *CG*, 230; "Memorial Resolutions," 35 Cong., 2 Sess., *CG*, 224; Thomas Y. Walsh, 32 Cong., 2 Sess., *CG*, 1643.

35 David Donald, *Charles Sumner and the Coming of the Civil War* (New York, 1960), 278–311.

36 John B. Haskin, 36 Cong., 1 Sess., *CG*, 752.

37 Lafayette S. Foster, Solomon Foot, Benjamin F. Wade, and Robert Toombs, 36 Cong., 1 Sess., *CG*, 749. Jack K. Williams, *Dueling in the Old South: Vignettes of Social History* (College Station, Tex., 1980), and Kenneth S. Greenberg, *Masters and Statesmen: The Political Culture of American Slavery* (Baltimore, 1985), 23–41, describe the place of the duel in southern life. The concern with it in this chapter is of course as an indicator of sectional value differences.

38 Milton S. Latham, 33 Cong., 1 Sess., *CG*, 24; Guy M. Bryan, 35 Cong., 1 Sess., *CG*, 2721; Clement C. Clay, 35 Cong., 1 Sess., *CG*, 30; Andrew P. Butler, 30 Cong., 1 Sess., *CG*, 582; Horace F. Clark, 35 Cong., 2 Sess., *CG*, 411; Robert C. Winthrop, 31 Cong., 1 Sess., *CG*, 622.

39 Roger A. Pryor, 36 Cong., 1 Sess., *CG*, 844.

40 Augustus R. Wright, 35 Cong., 2 Sess., *CG*, 228.

41 Bernard C. Steiner, *Life of Henry Winter Davis* (Baltimore, 1916), 25, 51; Josiah B. Grinnell, *Men and Events of Forty Years: Autobiographical Reminiscences of an Active Career from 1850 to 1890* (Boston, 1891), 29–36.

42 This typology is borrowed from the work of Douglas Yates, who used it in an analysis of presidential leadership. I offer it here in a suggestive sense in the belief that a similar, if not identical, schema might well be applied to the congressmen of the mid nineteenth century. See Yates, "The Roots of American Leadership: Political Style and Policy Consequences," in Walter D. Burnham and Martha W. Weinberg (eds.), *American Politics and Public Policy* (Cambridge, Mass., 1978), 140–68.

43 I must thank Peter Knupfer for discussing his research on the nature of political compromise in the middle period with me.

Chapter 2. Lincoln and the "disorderly schoolboys"

1 The first scholarly monument is John G. Nicolay and John Hay, *Abraham Lincoln: A History*, 10 vols. (New York, 1890). Illustrative modern scholarship includes James G. Randall, *Lincoln the President*, 4 vols. (Richard N. Current completed vol. 4) (New York, 1945–55); Richard N. Current, *The Lincoln Nobody Knows* (New York, 1955); David Donald, *Lincoln Reconsidered: Essays on the Civil War Era* (New York, 1956); Stephen Oates, *With Malice Toward None: The Life of Abraham Lincoln* (New York, 1977); and Cullom Davis, Charles B. Strozier, Rebecca M. Veach, and Geoffrey C. Ward (eds.), *The Public and the Private Lincoln: Contemporary Perspectives* (Carbondale, 1979). John L. Thomas (ed.), *Abraham Lincoln and the American Political Tradition* (Amherst, 1986), appeared after my work was well advanced.

2 O. J. Hollister, *Life of Schuyler Colfax* (New York, 1886), 209–10.

3 James G. Randall, *Lincoln: The Liberal Statesman* (New York, 1957); Norman A. Graebner (ed.), *The Enduring Lincoln* (Urbana, 1959), 67–94; Jacques Barzun, *Lincoln's Philosophic Vision*, Twenty-first Annual Robert Fortenbaugh Memorial Lecture (Gettysburg, 1982); Jeffrey Tulis, "On Presidential Character," in Joseph M. Bessette and Jeffrey Tulis, *The Presidency in the Constitutional Order* (Baton Rouge [ca. 1981]), 283–313.

4 Clinton Rossiter, *The American Presidency* (New York, 1956), 15–43.

5 Abraham Lincoln, "Draft of Address for Sanitary Fair at Baltimore," ca. April 18, 1864: Basler, *CW*, VII, 303.

6 Harry J. Carman and Reinhard H. Luthin, *Lincoln and the Patronage* (New York, 1943), is an encyclopedic analysis of appointments during the Lincoln administration. My concerns are somewhat different, however, and the detail and generalizations here are based primarily on my own reading of the Lincoln correspondence in Basler, *CW*, and in RTLC.

7 Abraham Lincoln to Caleb B. Smith, July 6, 1861: Basler, *CW*, IV, 442; Lincoln, "Memorandum of Interview with William P. Fessenden," July 4, 1864: ibid., VII, 423. See also William O. Stoddard, Jr. (ed.), *Lincoln's Third Secretary: The Memoirs of William O. Stoddard* (New York, 1955), 70–71, 107.

8 Isaac N. Arnold to Abraham Lincoln, March 12, 1861: RTLC; William D. Kelley and Edward J. Morris, lists, April 1861: ibid.

9 George H. Yeaman to Abraham Lincoln, January 13, 1862: RTLC.

10 "Memorandum: Appointment of Edgar Harriott," February 17, 1863: Basler, *CW*, VI, 107–8.

11 Abraham Lincoln to John P. Usher, August 27, 1864: Basler, *CW*, VII, 521–72. Lincoln to William H. Seward, August 11, 1861: V, 366–67; July 8, 1861: IV, 442; August 10, 1861: IV, 481; December 4, 1861: V, 56. Lincoln to Edwin M. Stanton, December 6, 1862: V, 543; October 11, 24, 1862: V, 458, 475; January 16, 1864: VII, 133. Lincoln to Frederick F. Lowe, February 29, 1864: VII, 214–15. Lincoln to Edwin M. Stanton, April 14, 1865: VIII, 413. Lincoln to Caleb Smith, November 18, 1862: V, 500n.

"Memorandum...Stephen Baker," April 15, May 3, 1862: V, 188–89.
"Memorandum...William H. Acker," July 11, 1861: IV, 446.

12 James R. Doolittle to Abraham Lincoln, ca. March 8, 1862: Basler, CW, V, 149.

13 Abraham Lincoln to William H. Seward, January 17, 1862: Basler, CW, V, 102; Lincoln to Seward, December 4, 1861: V, 56; Lincoln to Seward, September 4, 1861: IV, 509; Lincoln to Seward, December 9, 1861: V, 62; Lincoln, "Memorandum...John C. Henshaw," April 5, 1861: IV, 321.

14 Abraham Lincoln to William Sprague, May 10, 1861: Basler, CW, IV, 365.

15 On Howard, see Abraham Lincoln to Salmon P. Chase, March 2, 1863: Basler, CW, VI, 122–23; Lincoln to Chase, August 14, 1862: V, 375 and notes; James Dixon to Abraham Lincoln, August 11, 1862: RTLC; Lincoln to James Dixon, August 15, 21, 1862: Basler CW, V, 376, 385–86.

16 Abraham Lincoln to Lafayette S. Foster and James Dixon, December 21, 1863: Basler, CW, VII, 82–83. Another perspective on the Connecticut appointments is found in Howard K. Beale (ed.), The Diary of Gideon Welles: Secretary of the Navy Under Lincoln and Johnson (New York, 1960), I, 78, 81–82, 235, 239.

17 Abraham Lincoln to Samuel C. Pomeroy, May 12, 1864: Basler, CW, VII, 338.

18 Abraham Lincoln, "Response to a Serenade," November 10, 1864: Basler, CW, VIII, 101; Lincoln to Morton Wilkinson, June 20, 1864: VII, 403; Lincoln to John C. Ten Eyck, September 19, 1864: VIII, 12.

19 Abraham Lincoln to Simon Cameron, June 17, 1861: Basler, CW, IV, 409–10; Lincoln to Edwin Stanton, March 12, 1861: VII, 241; Lincoln to William Pickering, October 7, 1861: IV, 550; Lincoln to Stanton, January 12, 1863: VI, 55.

20 See Donald W. Riddle, Congressman Abraham Lincoln (Urbana, 1957), 180–97. Abraham Lincoln to Richard Yates and William Butler, April 10, 1862: Basler, CW, V, 186; Lincoln to Andrew Johnson, July 27, 1864: VII, 466; Lincoln to William H. Seward, March 7, 1862: V, 147. The expression "true men" is in John Hickman to John A. Bingham, April 1, 1861: RTLC.

21 Abraham Lincoln to William H. Seward, February 16, 1864: Basler, CW, VII, 188; Lincoln to William Jayne, February 26, 1864: ibid., 206–7.

22 Samuel Shellaberger to Abraham Lincoln, February 27, 1863: RTLC; Harrison G. O. Blake to Abraham Lincoln, March 4, 1863: ibid.

23 David Wilmot to Abraham Lincoln, undated: Basler, CW, VI, 52n; Lincoln, "Memorandum" (concerning Thomas M. Wilmot), December 10, 1862: V, 549.

24 William Kellogg to Abraham Lincoln, April 8, 1863: RTLC; Lincoln, "Endorsement," April 11, 1863: Basler, CW, VI, 167.

25 Abraham Lincoln to John Z. Goodrich, March 13, 1865: Basler, CW, VIII, 351–52 and note.

26 Charles Sumner to Montgomery Blair, May 25, 1863: RTLC; Abraham Lincoln to Salmon P. Chase, July 18, 1861: Basler, CW, IV, 452; Salmon P. Chase to Lincoln, July 19, 1861: ibid.; Lincoln to Chase, November 8, 1862: V, 490–91.

27   Tyler Dennett (ed.), *Lincoln and the Civil War in the Diaries and Letters of John Hay* (New York, 1939), 181.

28   Abraham Lincoln to George G. Meade, October 8, 1863: Basler, *CW*, VI, 506; Dennett, *Diaries and Letters of John Hay*, 68.

29   Abraham Lincoln to Edwin M. Stanton, March 18, 1864: Basler, *CW*, VII, 254–56; Lincoln to Ulysses S. Grant, March 9, 1865: VIII, 347–48; Lincoln, "Endorsement Concerning Garrett Davis," February 13, 1865: ibid., 293–94.

30   Abraham Lincoln to Major-General Pope, November 10, 1862: Basler, *CW*, V, 493 and note; Lincoln to H. H. Sibley, December 6, 1862: ibid., 542–43; Lincoln to Joseph Holt, December 1, 1862: ibid., 537–38.

31   Abraham Lincoln to Samuel R. Curtis, January 5, 1863: Basler, *CW*, VI, 36–37.

32   Charles Wickliffe to Abraham Lincoln, July 5, 1862: RTLC; Lincoln, "Endorsement: Request of C. T. Benton": Basler, *CW*, VII, 171–72; Godlove S. Orth to Lincoln, October 16, 1863: RTLC.

33   Abraham Lincoln to Oliver P. Morton, October 13, 1864: Basler, *CW*, VIII, 46; Lincoln to Edwin M. Stanton, January 22, February 2, 1865: ibid., 232, 257n.

34   Abraham Lincoln to Edwin M. Stanton, February 22, 1865: Basler, *CW*, VIII, 311–13; Lincoln to Gideon Welles, August 28, 1864: VII, 522–23; Lincoln to Welles, January 26, 1866: VIII, 240; "Order Annulling Sentence of Benjamin G. and Franklin W. Smith," March 18, 1865: ibid., 364; *Diary of Gideon Welles*, II, 124–25.

35   Abraham Lincoln to William P. Fessenden, December 15, 1863: Basler, *CW*, VII, 67; Lincoln to Thaddeus Stevens, August 10, 1864: ibid., 491; Lincoln to Thomas D. Eliot, February 28, 1865: VIII, 323–24; "Stay of Execution for Nathaniel Gordon," February 4, 1862: V, 128–29.

36   Isaac Arnold to Abraham Lincoln, July 2, 18, 1864: RTLC; Lincoln to J. L. Scripps, July 4, 20, 1864: Basler, *CW*, VII, 423–24, 453; William Kelley to Abraham Lincoln, June 19, August 3, 1864: RTLC; Lincoln to Cornelius A. Walborn, June 18, 1864, and note: Basler, *CW*, VII, 400; "Memorandum of Interview with Cornelius A. Walborn," June 20, 1864: ibid., 402; Lincoln to Morton McMichael, August 5, 1864, and note: VII, 480–81; Lincoln to Ward Hunt, August 16, 1864: VII, 498; Lincoln to Henry W. Davis, March 18, 1863: VI, 140–41.

37   Philip B. Fouke to Abraham Lincoln, March 24, 1863: RTLC; Lincoln to Samuel L. Casey, February 8, 1864: Basler, *CW*, VIII, 595 and note; "Draft of Order Concerning Samuel L. Casey," February 29, 1864: VII, 213–14.

38   Abraham Lincoln to Edwin M. Stanton, June 5, 1862: Basler, *CW*, V, 261; Lincoln to Salmon P. Chase, June 25, 1863: VI, 294; Lincoln to William Kellogg, June 29, 1863: ibid., 307 and note.

39   James E. Kerrigan to Abraham Lincoln, February 17, 1862: RTLC; Lincoln to John A. McClernand, September 10, 1862: Basler, *CW*, V, 413 and note; "Authorization for William J. Allen," September 16, 1862: ibid., 427.

40 David Donald, "Abraham Lincoln: Whig in the White House," in Graeb-
    ner, *The Enduring Lincoln*, 47, 52, 55, 65; Mark E. Neely, Jr., *The Abraham
    Lincoln Encyclopedia* (New York, 1982), 245. The subject is, of course, more
    complex than these quotes may suggest. While in opposition, Whigs said
    a good deal about the proper role of the president. Harrison's much
    derided inaugural address apparently reflected the views of both Henry
    Clay and Daniel Webster on these matters, although Clay went so far
    ultimately as to advocate modification or even abolition of the presidential
    veto. See Harrison's inaugural address in James D. Richardson (ed.), *A
    Compilation of the Messages and Papers of the Presidents, 1789–1897* (Wash-
    ington, 1897), IV, 5–21, and Calvin Colton (ed.), *The Works of Henry Clay:
    Comprising His Life, Correspondence, and Speeches* (New York, 1904), VIII
    and IX. Of the two great Whig senators, it was Webster, rather than
    Clay, who was allowed to edit Harrison's oration, giving that worthy
    the opportunity to boast of the number of proconsuls whom he had slain
    in the process. Freeman Cleaves, *Old Tippecanoe: William Henry Harrison
    and His Times* (New York, 1939), 333–40, deals briefly with the speech
    and its political context. The best general account of Whig thought cur-
    rently available is Daniel W. Howe, *The Political Culture of the American
    Whigs* (Chicago, 1979). See also Thomas Brown, *Politics and Statesmanship:
    Essays on the American Whig Party* (New York, 1985).

    But the Whigs had little opportunity to develop working guidelines in
    such matters while the party was in control of the administration. During
    his quest for the presidency, Zachary Taylor made ritual obeisance to
    the Whig conception of a diminished executive role, but when Old Rough
    and Ready lost his last battle, his term of presidential service had been
    short and he was resolutely struggling to force federal lawmakers to
    accept his views on the sectional crisis of 1850. "Any 'weak executive'
    notions he had long since discarded," wrote his most insightful biog-
    rapher (Holman Hamilton, *Zachary Taylor: Soldier in the White House* [In-
    dianapolis, 1951], 384). So the predictive utility of past events in
    forecasting Lincoln's executive behavior appears to be a good deal more
    fragile than the confident assertions of controlling Whiggery quoted in
    the text might suggest.

    This chapter was prepared and delivered as one of the Becker Lectures
    in the spring of 1986 before Stephen B. Oates's essay "Abraham Lincoln:
    Republican in the White House" became available to me (see Thomas,
    Abraham Lincoln and the American Political Tradition, 51–97). I find much
    to agree with in this important reevaluation and use some of the same
    evidence, but my perspective and emphasis obviously differ from
    Oates's, and I believe that he, like Donald, has somewhat misunderstood
    Lincoln's use of the veto power. Nor has he (nor was it perhaps necessary
    for his purposes) noted the significance of the party platform and Lin-
    coln's views on it or his importance as an implicit as well as an explicit
    agenda setter for Congress. Nor do I believe that Donald's position that
    old party positions still retained force or charm subsequent to party

realignment is as unreasonable as Oates suggests. The formula is suspect in this case, but for other Civil War politicians and on other matters it seems at times to have held.

41 Abraham Lincoln to Lyman Trumbull, December 10, 1860: Basler, *CW*, IV, 149–50; Lincoln to William Kellogg, December 11, 1860: ibid., 150. See also Lincoln to Elihu B. Washburne, December 13, 1860: ibid., 151.

42 Abraham Lincoln, "Speech at Pittsburgh": Basler, *CW*, IV, 211–12; "First Inaugural Address – First Edition and Revisions": ibid., 250; "Final Text": ibid., 263.

43 Abraham Lincoln, "Manuscript Prepared for the Pittsburgh Speech": Basler, *CW*, IV, 214.

44 37 Cong., 3 Sess., *CG*, 785.

45 There is a concise treatment of these matters in Allan G. Bogue, *The Earnest Men: Republicans of the Civil War Senate* (Ithaca, 1981), 263–66. See also Randall, "The Rule of Law Under Lincoln," *Lincoln: The Liberal Statesmen*, 118–34, 229–36.

46 William S. Holman (D., Ind.) introduced this resolution. For the text see 37 Cong., 1 Sess., *House Journal*, 46.

47 Dennett, *Diaries and Letters of John Hay*, 144–45.

48 John Hay to John G. Nicolay, August 7, 1863, in Dennett, *Diaries and Letters of John Hay*, 76. Seward's role and activities were subjects of continuing interest to his colleague Gideon Welles, who dwelt on them in many diary entries and was moved – so he said – by Charles Francis Adams's "Memorial Address on the Life, Character, and Services of William H. Seward" to write a small book in response. See Gideon Welles, *Lincoln and Seward: Remarks Upon the Memorial Address of Chas. Francis Adams on the Late Wm H. Seward* (New York, 1874), and Beale, *Diary of Gideon Welles*, 3 vols., passim. For Welles's comment on Lincoln and the departments see II, 264.

49 Abraham Lincoln to Horace Greeley, March 24, 1862: Basler, *CW*, V, 169; "Message to Congress," April 16, 1862: ibid., 192. For Wright's role see Bogue, *Earnest Men*, 153.

50 Abraham Lincoln, "Message to Congress," March 6, 1862: Basler, *CW*, V, 144–45; "Appeal to Border State Representatives to Favor Compensated Emancipation," July 12, 1862: ibid., 317–19 and 319n; Lincoln to the Senate and House of Representatives, July 14, 1862: ibid., 324–25.

51 Abraham Lincoln, "Annual Message to Congress," December 1, 1862: Basler, *CW*, V, 529–37.

52 The Missouri bills are discussed in Leonard P. Curry, *Blueprint for Modern America: Nonmilitary Legislation of the First Civil War Congress* (Nashville, 1968), 52–54, and Bogue, *Earnest Men*, 184–88. Abraham Lincoln to Samuel R. Curtis, January 10, 1863: Basler, *CW*, VI, 52; Lincoln to the Senate and House of Representatives, February 5, 1865: VIII, 260–61 and note.

53 Donald cites Lincoln's bill for compensated emancipation as "notably exceptional" (see "Whig in the White House," 52). In a sense, that is true, but if we view Lincoln's relations with the congressmen in broader context a different picture of Lincoln's congressional relations emerges.

54 Charles A. Dana, *Recollections of the Civil War: With the Leaders at Washington and in the Field in the Sixties* (New York, 1898), 175–78; Abraham Lincoln, "Annual Message to Congress," December 6, 1864: Basler, *CW*, VIII, 149. In their biography of Lincoln, Nicolay and Hay reprinted the former's memorandum describing a conference between Lincoln and Ashley in which the president informed the Ohioan that he would be unable to convince Senator Sumner to desist in his efforts to win passage of a measure destroying the through-passenger monopoly enjoyed in New Jersey by the Camden and Amboy Railroad, action that would favorably influence the votes of the New Jersey Democrats. That conversation establishes Lincoln's interest in Ashley's activity and strategies, but in this instance Lincoln apparently believed that he could not be of assistance (Nicolay and Hay, *Abraham Lincoln*, X, 84–85). Albert G. Riddle, *Recollections of War Times: Reminiscences of Men and Events in Washington, 1860–1865* (New York, 1895), 324–25, contradicts Nicolay's memorandum to some degree but supports the thesis that there was White House involvement in the mobilization effort. I have discussed some of the historiography of this issue elsewhere and shown that two New Jersey Democrats, including a spokesman of the Camden and Amboy Railroad, did abstain (Bogue, *Earnest Men*, 253 n. 62).

55 Abraham Lincoln to William T. Sherman, July 18, 1864: Basler, *CW*, VII, 449–50.

56 Abraham Lincoln, "Proclamation of Amnesty and Reconstruction," December 8, 1863: Basler, *CW*, VII, 56.

57 Abraham Lincoln to Edwin M. Stanton, December 18, 21, 1863: Basler, *CW*, VII, 78–79, 84; Dennett, *Diaries and Letters of John Hay*, 139–40.

58 Edward Haight to Abraham Lincoln, August 24, 1862: RTLC.

59 Abraham Lincoln to Hiram Walbridge, December 28, 1862: Basler, *CW*, VI, 21–22; Lincoln to John D. Defrees, February 8, 1864: VII, 172; William P. Cutler, Diary, December 16, 1862, Marietta College Library; *Springfield Republican*, January 21, 1863; 38 Cong., 2 Sess., *CG*, *App.*, 103.

60 Donald, "Whig in the White House," 52. U.S. Congress, Senate Library, *Presidential Vetoes, 1789–1976* (Washington, 1978), provides identification of the vetoes. A comparative listing is found in Louis Fisher, *The Politics of Shared Power: Congress and the Executive* (Washington, 1981), 26.

61 Donald, "Whig in the White House," 52; Lincoln, "Proclamation Concerning Reconstruction": Basler, *CW*, VII, 433–34.

62 Abraham Lincoln to Solomon Foot, July 15, 1862: Basler, *CW*, V, 325; Lincoln to Galusha A. Grow, July 15, 1862: ibid., 326; Foot to Lincoln, July 15, 1862: RTLC.

63 Abraham Lincoln to Solomon Foot, July 15, 1862: Basler, *CW*, V, 326; Lincoln, "To the Senate and House of Representatives," July 17, 1862: ibid., 328–31.

64 Abraham Lincoln, "To Members of the Cabinet," December 23, 1862: Basler, *CW*, VI, 17; Lincoln, "Opinion on the Admission of West Virginia Into the Union," December 31, 1862: ibid., 26–28.

65 Abraham Lincoln to the Senate and House of Representatives, May 26, 1862: Basler, *CW*, V, 240–43.
66 Abraham Lincoln to the Senate and House of Representatives, February 8, 1865: Basler, *CW*, VIII, 270.
67 Abraham Lincoln to Ward H. Lamon, ca. June 28, 1864: Basler, *CW*, VII, 414–15.
68 Abraham Lincoln to James W. Grimes, October 29, 1863: Basler, *CW*, VI, 546–47. This is the fullest of a number of communications to key members of Congress.
69 Abraham Lincoln, "Inaugural Address," March 4, 1861: Basler, *CW*, IV, 262–71; Lincoln, "Message to Congress in Special Session," July 4, 1861: ibid., 421–41 (see particularly 438–40); Lincoln, "Annual Message to Congress," December 3, 1861: V, 35–53 (see particularly 51–53).
70 Dennett, *Diaries and Letters of John Hay*, 239.

Chapter 3. An "inquiring disposition"

1 Marshall E. Dimock, *Congressional Investigating Committees* (Baltimore, 1929), 109; *Boston Evening Journal*, April 24, 1862; *New York Herald*, April 9, 1863. For later perspectives see Alan Barth, *Government by Investigation* (New York, 1955); James Hamilton, *The Power to Probe: A Study of Congressional Investigations* (New York, 1976); Arthur M. Schlesinger, Jr., and Roger Bruns (eds.), *Congress Investigates: A Documentary History, 1792–1974*, 5 vols. (New York, 1975).
2 Dimock, *Investigating Committees*, 87.
3 Ibid., 17–21.
4 Roger H. Davidson, "The Political Dimensions of Congressional Investigations," *Capitol Studies* 5 (Fall 1977), 41–63. See particularly pp. 49–62.
5 For the use of "Devil's Day" as a synonym for resolution day see *New York Herald*, June 17, 1862.
6 For a listing of committees, both standing and special, see Walter Stubbs (comp.), *Congressional Committees, 1789–1892: A Checklist* (Westport, Conn., 1985). *New York Herald*, December 16, 1863. 37 Cong., 2 Sess., House Journal, 97.
7 The minutes of the Judiciary Committee of the Thirty-seventh House are contained in two lined copybooks, bound in gray cloth, of which the first is numbered "25" on the spine (36A–D13.12 and 37A–E9.6). I shall call them Judiciary Committee Minute Book 1 and 2, abbreviated to HRJCMB 1 and 2. They are held in the Legislative Records Division of the National Archives. For May, see HRJCMB 1, pp. 129, 133.
8 HRJCMB 1, p. 135.
9 The first reference to "telegraphic censorship of the press" in the Judiciary Committee minutes appears in HRJCMB 1, p. 153; see passim. Final consideration of the subject in the committee is noted in HRJCMB 2, p. 15. See 37 Cong., 2 Sess., House Judiciary Committee, "Hearings, Telegraphic Censorship of the Press," 37A–E9.8, Legislative Records Division, National Archives. (The same volume contains testimony con-

cerning Benjamin Wood.) See also 37 Cong., 2 Sess., House Report no. 64: *Telegraph Censorship.*

10 37 Cong., 2 Sess., *CG,* 879–81. See also National Archives HR37A–G7.16 for a collection of petitions requesting the expulsion of Clement L. Vallandigham.

11 The witnesses' fee schedules for the investigations of telegraphic censorship and of Benjamin Wood appear in HRJCMB 2, pp. 13, 58. For committee action relative to Wood see ibid., 91, 93, 107. The original testimony is found in the volume catalogued as 37A–E9.8.

12 37 Cong., 2 Sess., *CG,* 2954, 3023, 3058, 3101; HRJCMB 2, p. 75.

13 HRJCMB 2, pp. 103, 105, 109, 117.

14 37 Cong., 2 Sess., House Report no. 64, pp. 13, 5, 12, 14.

15 Ibid., 6, 4.

16 *New York Herald,* March 22, 23, 1862. Samuel Wilkeson, Testimony, "Hearings, Telegraphic Censorship," 33–47.

17 Wilkeson, Testimony, 31–32, 38. For a note on Wikoff see Don C. Seitz, *The James Gordon Bennetts, Father and Son: Proprietors of the New York Herald* (Indianapolis, 1928), 187–88. Oliver Caarlson, *The Man Who Made News: James Gordon Bennett* (New York, 1942), 335–38; W. A. Swanberg, *Sickles, the Incredible* (New York, 1956), 135–38; Ben Perley Poore, *Perley's Reminiscences of Sixty Years in the National Metropolis* (Philadelphia, 1886), II, 142–43.

18 *New York Herald,* February 13, 14, 15, 17, 18, March 1, 3, 1862. The *Herald* ridiculed the committee, referring to it as "Beau Hickman's Kitchen Committee," and concluded that "to indulge a petty malice against a lady whose position and sex alike should shield her from insult, Hickman's Committee wastes the public money, disgraces the nation and holds up the government to the bitter but deserved satire and contempt of the civilized world" (February 18, 1862). The *Springfield Republican,* March 4, 1862, reported that the Judiciary Committee room had been burglarized, ostensibly in search of the telegraphic censorship testimony, but that the intruder had failed in his attempt.

19 *New York Herald,* March 3, 1862; Daniel E. Sickles, Testimony, and S. P. Hanscom, Testimony, 27ff., particularly 36, 39, 42, in 37A–E9.8.

20 *New York Evening Post,* February 14, 1862; HRJCMB 1, p. 189; Tyler Dennett (ed.), *Lincoln and the Civil War in the Diaries and Letters of John Hay* (New York, 1939), 234. A fourth-term veteran in the House, Hickman is noted in 85 Cong., 2 Sess., *Biographical Directory of the American Congress, 1774–1961* (Washington, 1961), 1050, as having declined to stand for reelection in 1862. See also Wilmer W. MacElree, *Side Lights on the Bench and Bar of Chester County* (Westchester, Pa., 1918), 292–301, and J. Smith Futhey and Gilbert Cope, *History of Chester County, Pennsylvania, with Genealogical and Biographical Sketches* (Philadelphia, 1881), 600–2. This sketch includes a version of Hickman's resolution that instructed the president to seize the property of the rebels including their slaves. The membership of the Judiciary Committee included three radicals and three moderates from the Republican party, and three Democrats. Agreement

on a confiscation measure that satisfied the radical members was apparently impossible, and Hickman presented this joint resolution as a minority proposal from the committee. See 37 Cong., 2 Sess., *House Journal*, 463, *CG*, 1801.

21 A. T. Allen, Boston, to Hon. W. H. Seward, May 1862, in 37 Cong., 2 Sess., House Judiciary Committee, "Benjamin Wood Hearing," 37A–E9.8, Legislative Records Division, National Archives.

22 37 Cong., 2 Sess., *CG*, 2666.

23 The *New York Tribune*, June 27, 1862, reported that "Ben Wood's case before the Judiciary Committee is said to look very dark" and that the evidence against him was stronger than that on which Senator Jesse Bright had been expelled. But two weeks later that organ was hedging by noting, "There are differences of opinion in the Committee, and it is not impossible that a majority may decide that the evidence, however strong morally, is not legally sufficient to warrant expulsion" (July 10, 1862). See also *Chicago Tribune*, June 17, 1862, and *New York Evening Post*, July 12, 1862.

24 37 Cong., 1 Sess., *CG*, 26. For other discussions of the Potter committee see Harold M. Hyman's two books *Era of the Oath: Northern Loyalty Tests During the Civil War and Reconstruction* (Philadelphia, 1954), 1–12, and *To Try Men's Souls: Loyalty Tests in American History* (Berkeley and Los Angeles, 1959), 155–64.

25 37 Cong., 2 Sess., House Report no. 16: *Loyalty of Clerks and Other Persons Employed by Government*. See also 37 Cong., 2 Sess., House Misc. Doc. no. 39: *George B. Simpson*. A summary of committee activity and methods appears in 37 Cong., 2 Sess., House Report no. 64, 1–4.

26 *New York Herald*, August 12, 1861.

27 *New York Herald*, August 16, 28, 1861, May 25, 1862; *Springfield Republican*, December 13, 1861, January 23, 1862; 37 Cong., 2 Sess., *CG*, 180.

28 William O. Stoddard, Jr. (ed.), *Lincoln's Third Secretary: The Memoirs of William O. Stoddard* (New York, 1955), 83–84; *Columbus* (Ohio) *State Journal*, July 11, 1861; *Springfield Republican*, August 3, December 10, 1861; *Chicago Tribune*, December 21, 1861; *New York Tribune*, January 28, 1862; *New York Evening Post*, July 9, 1862.

29 *Cleveland Plain Dealer*, November 29, 1861; 37 Cong., 2 Sess., *CG*, 159; John F. Potter to Frances E. L. Potter, September 7, 13, 15, 1861: John F. Potter Papers, Wisconsin State Historical Society (addressee not named); Basler, *CW*, V, 25, and VI, 50–51; Simon Cameron to John F. Potter, September 20, 1861: Potter Papers; "Copy of Testimony Against J. W. Irwin," ibid.; Galusha A. Grow to [Gustavus V.] Fox, October 17, 1861: ibid.

30 37 Cong., 2 Sess., *CG*, 178–80. Olin and Wickliffe's remarks appear on p. 179.

31 Ibid., 180; House Report no. 16, 3.

32 37 Cong., 2 Sess., *CG*, 2262, 2327; *Springfield Republican*, December 13, 1861.

33 Montgomery Blair to John F. Potter, February 4, 1862, published in *Washington Evening Star*, February 5, 1862. Potter's response in the *Washington*

Republican was quoted in the *New York Evening Post,* March 3, 1862. *New York Herald,* May 25, 1862.

34 *New York Evening Post,* July 7, 9, 1862.

35 Hyman, *Era of the Oath,* 6–8; *New York Tribune,* January 28, 1862.

36 *New York Evening Post,* January 30, 1862.

37 37 Cong., 2 Sess., House Report no. 64, 16–20; *Philadelphia Press,* January 28, February 13, 1862; John F. Potter to Edward Potter, November 24, 1862, and J. M. Burgess to Potter, November 12, 1862: Potter Papers.

38 37 Cong., 1 Sess., *CG,* 23.

39 37 Cong., 2 Sess., House Report no. 2: *Government Contracts* [Part I] (serial 1142) and [Part II] (serial 1143); 37 Cong., 3 Sess., House Report no. 49: *Government Contracts;* no. 50: *Government Contracts: Views of the Minority.*

40 Each of the published reports includes a journal listing the date and place of the various meetings. The biographer of Henry L. Dawes has published a short account of the Van Wyck committee; See Fred Nicklason, "The Civil War Contracts Committee," *Civil War History* 17 (September 1971), 232–44. Understandably, Nicklason emphasizes Dawes's role in committee activity. I have also examined the relevant Dawes correspondence in the Henry L. Dawes Papers, Library of Congress.

41 37 Cong., 2 Sess., House Report no. 2 [Part I], 83, 69.

42 Ibid. [Part II], 1.

43 37 Cong., 2 Sess., *CG,* 710; R. Gordon Wasson, *The Hall Carbine Affair: A Study in Contemporary Folklore* (New York, 1948).

44 The texts of all these resolutions appear conveniently together in 37 Cong., 2 Sess., *CG,* 1835. Diven's resolution: ibid., 169.

45 Ibid., 710, 712, 714.

46 Ibid., 715–16.

47 Ibid., 1380–83, 1744–47, 1748, 1749–53.

48 Ibid., 1835–42, 1846–53, 1862–71.

49 Ibid., 1865–66.

50 Ibid., 1866.

51 Ibid., 1886–88.

52 37 Cong., 3 Sess., House Report no. 49, 4; 37 Cong., 3 Sess., House Report no. 50, 2, 3.

53 37 Cong., 3 Sess., House Report no. 50, 47; Wasson, *Hall Carbine Affair,* 51–54.

54 37 Cong., 2 Sess., House Exec. Doc. no. 151: *Interest of Members of Congress in Government Contracts,* and 37 Cong., 3 Sess., House Report no. 64: *Employés Interested in Banks or Government Contracts;* 38 Cong., 2 Sess., House Exec. Doc. no. 79: *Kidnapping Colored Men;* 38 Cong., 2 Sess., House Report no. 8: *Marine Engines;* 38 Cong., 2 Sess., House Report no. 24: *Trade with Rebellious States;* 38 Cong., 1 Sess., House Report no. 140: *Treasury Department;* 38 Cong., 1 Sess., House Report no. 111: *New York Custom-house;* 38 Cong., 2 Sess., House Report no. 25: *New York Custom-house.*

55 37 Cong., 2 Sess., House Report no. 96: *Illinois and Michigan Canal Enlargement;* 37 Cong., 2 Sess., House Report no. 53: *Printing Patent Office*

Report for 1860; 37 Cong., 2 Sess., *CG,* 1022, 2763; 37 Cong., 1 Sess., *CG,* 230–31; 37 Cong., 3 Sess., House Report no. 63: *Railroad from Washington City to New York.*

56 Dennett, *Diaries and Letters of John Hay,* 180. Ashley's career is described in Robert F. Horowitz, *The Great Impeacher: A Political Biography of James M. Ashley* (New York, 1979).

57 37 Cong., 3 Sess., House Report no. 47: *Hon. J. M. Ashley,* 1, 15–20, 23–26.

58 Ibid., 31.

59 J. M. Ashley to My Dear Case, February 2, March 12, 1861: ibid., 15, 16.

60 J. M. Ashley to My Dear Case, March 16, 18, 1861: ibid., 16–17.

61 J. M. Ashley to My Dear Case, March 9, 1861: ibid., 17–18; F. M. Case to Ashley, March 20, 21, 1861: ibid., 19–20.

62 Statements from Case and Pierce: ibid., 7–15.

63 Ibid., 30, 31. Various letters in response to inquiries from Chairman Blake are found in Legislative Records Division, National Archives and Records Service, but they add little to the facts of the case as summarized in the committee report.

64 Ibid., 36–38.

65 For general background see Elbert B. Smith, *Francis Preston Blair* (New York, 1980), and William E. Smith, *The Francis Preston Blair Family in Politics,* 2 vols. (New York, 1933).

66 For Blair's opponent Knox, see 38 Cong., 1 Sess., House Misc. Doc. no. 15: *Samuel Knox vs. Francis P. Blair, Jr.* Herman Belz, "The Etheridge Conspiracy of 1863: A Projected Conservative Coup," *Journal of Southern History* 36 (November 1970), 549–67.

67 38 Cong., 1 Sess., *CG,* 426–27. Blair's speech of February 27 is in 38 Cong., 1 Sess., *CG, App.,* 46–51.

68 38 Cong., 1 Sess., *CG, App.,* 51; 38 Cong., 1 Sess., *CG,* 1990–91. The House and Senate authorized an investigation of illegal trade during the second session of the Thirty-eighth Congress by the House and Senate Commerce committees acting jointly. See 38 Cong., 2 Sess., *House Journal,* 123–24, 144, 197.

69 38 Cong., 1 Sess., *CG,* 1017.

70 38 Cong., 1 Sess., *CG,* 1252–53.

71 38 Cong., 1 Sess., *CG,* 1827–28.

72 Blair's remarks appear in 38 Cong., 1 Sess., *CG,* 1828–32. See p. 1829.

73 Ibid.

74 Ibid.; *New York Herald,* April 25, 1864.

75 *New York Tribune,* April 25, 1864; *New York Herald,* April 25, 1864; 38 Cong., 1 Sess., *CG,* 1960–64.

76 *New York Tribune,* December 4, 1863; *Springfield Republican,* April 29, 1864; 38 Cong., 1 Sess., *CG,* 1859. The conflicting signals emanating from the committee can be traced in the press: *New York Tribune,* March 4, 1864 ("damaging, and . . . conclusive argument was made to-day against Frank Blair's right to his seat"); ibid., March 10, 1864 ("There are rumors . . . that Mr. Blair will hang on by a majority of one"); *Chicago Tribune,* March

13, 1864 ("The career of Mr. Frank Blair is likely to be soon run"); *New York Tribune*, March 16, 1864 ("There is no doubt that Blair will be ousted"); *Boston Evening Journal*, April 11, 1864 ("The majority of the Committee . . . have resolved to report in favor of Mr. Blair's right to a seat"); ibid., May 5, 1864 ("The . . . Committee . . . have decided to report that Gen. Blair is not entitled to a seat"); *Springfield Republican*, May 7, 1864 ("Frank Blair not entitled to seat . . . agreed to by bare majority of . . . Committee. All opposition members . . . and Green Clay Smith signed the minority report. . . . At one time the committee was inclined to declare the seat vacant").

77   Abraham Lincoln to House of Representatives, April 28, 1864. 38 Cong., 1 Sess., House Exec. Doc. no. 77: *Francis P. Blair, Jr.*; Lincoln to Montgomery Blair, November 2, 1863: 38 Cong., 1 Sess., House Exec. Doc. no. 80: *Francis P. Blair, Jr.*; 38 Cong., 1 Sess., *CG*, 1939–40.

78   38 Cong., 1 Sess., *CG*, 2861, 2908, 3242, 3355, 3389.

79   38 Cong., 1 Sess., Senate Report no. 84: *Hon. Frank P. Blair, Jr.*, p. 3.

80   This information was provided by the leading specialist on early law in California, Gordon M. Bakken, in a personal communication, June 3, 1987.

81   William W. Pearson, "The Committee on the Conduct of the Civil War," *American Historical Review* 23 (April 1918), 576; T. Harry Williams, *Lincoln und the Radicals* (Madison, 1941), 18, 384; Hans L. Trefousse, "The Joint Committee on the Conduct of the War: A Reassessment," *Civil War History* 10 (March 1964), 18–19; Elizabeth Joan Doyle, "The Conduct of the War, 1861," in Schlesinger and Bruns, *Congress Investigates*, II, 1232. For a discussion of Joint Rule 22 see Allan G. Bogue, *The Earnest Men: Republicans of the Civil War Senate* (Ithaca, 1981), 72–74.

82   Howard K. Beale (ed.), *The Diary of Gideon Welles: Secretary of the Navy Under Lincoln and Johnson* (New York, 1960), II, 23; Basler, *CW*, VII, 302–3, 328–29, 345–46; James G. Randall, *Lincoln the President*, vol. 2: *Springfield to Gettysburg* (New York, 1945), 186–87.

83   William Parker Cutler, Diary, Cutler Collection, Dawes Memorial Library, Marietta College, Marietta, Ohio. The original published version contains various omissions and editorial revisions. For a corrected text see Allan G. Bogue, "William Parker Cutler's Congressional Diary of 1862–63," *Civil War History* 33 (December 1987), 315–30.

84   For the "Simmons Act" see 37 Cong., 2 Sess., *CG, App.*, Laws, 408, Chap. CLXXX. The amplifying amendment appears in 37 Cong., 3 Sess., *CG, App.*, 199, Chap. LXI. Fraudulent contracting and the contracting system are dealt with in 37 Cong., 2 Sess., *CG, App.*, Laws, 358, Chap. XCIII, and 422–23, J.R. 53; 37 Cong., 3 Sess., *CG, App.*, Laws, 199, Chap. LXVII. The amendment to the act of 1857 relating to witnesses appears in 37 Cong., 2 Sess., *CG, App.*, Laws, 334, Chap. XI.

85   38 Cong., 1 Sess., *CG.*, 150.

86   Nicklason, "Civil War Contracts Committee," 241, citing "Van" in *Springfield Republican*, February 8, 1862.

Chapter 4. "God alone can guide us"

1 Kenneth R. Bowling, "Politics in the First Congress, 1789–1791" (Ph.D. dissertation, University of Wisconsin, 1968); Ralph V. Harlow, *The History of Legislative Methods in the Period Before 1825* (New Haven, 1917); Joseph A. Imler, "The First One Hundred Days of the New Deal: The View from Capitol Hill" (Ph.D. dissertation, University of Indiana, 1975); James T. Patterson, *Congressional Conservatism and the New Deal* (Lexington, Ky., 1968); Frank B. Freidel, *Franklin D. Roosevelt*, vol. 4: *Launching the New Deal* (Boston, 1973); Arthur M. Schlesinger, Jr., *The Age of Roosevelt*, vol. 2: *The Coming of the New Deal* (Boston, 1957).

2 The historical bibliography of politics during the Civil War is staggering. See for example Allan Nevins, James I. Robertson, Jr., and Bell I. Wiley, *Civil War Books: A Critical Bibliography* (Baton Rouge, 1969), II. And there has been much addition to the secondary literature since then. The most important titles for my purposes are listed in the citations below.

3 These matters are investigated more thoroughly in Chapter 2.

4 The computations relating to bills and joint resolutions are based on the series in Bureau of the Census, *Historical Statistics of the United States* (Washington, 1975), II, 1081–82. The data relative to House resolutions were tabulated from U.S. Congress, House of Representatives, 32nd–38th congresses, *House Journal*.

5 See 37 Cong., 1 Sess., *House Journal*, 46, for the text of Holman's resolution. Concerning the quorum see Allan G. Bogue, *The Earnest Men: Republicans of the Civil War Congress* (Ithaca, 1981), 69–70. The "iron-clad oath" is treated in Harold M. Hyman, *Era of the Oath: Northern Loyalty Tests During the Civil War and Reconstruction* (Philadelphia, 1954). The laws relative to contracting and representation of constituents are found in 37 Cong., 2 Sess., *CG, App.*, 408, Chap. CLXXX, and 38 Cong., 1 Sess., *CG, App.*, 177, Chap. XIX. The measures bearing on the qualifications and rights of members and states were: 37 Cong., 3 Sess., *CG, App.*, 232, Chap. CVIII, and 38 Cong., 2 Sess., *CG, App.*, 159. J.R. 12. Senate bill 107, debated at length during the second session of the Thirty-eighth Congress, would have seated the delegation from Louisiana but was lost at the end of the session through a radical filibuster. The new committees were Appropriations, Weights and Measures, Banks and Banking, and the Pacific Railroad. Discussion of Representative Pendleton's bill, H.R. 214, with the bill text, appears in 38 Cong., 2 Sess., *CG, App.*, 103–8.

6 James T. DuBois and Gertrude A. Mathews, *Galusha A. Grow: Father of the Homestead Law* (Boston, 1917); *New York Herald*, June 27, 1861. For Francis P. Blair, Jr., see Chapter 3, n. 65. See also *New York Herald*, June 30, 1861. The *Springfield Republican*, July 6, 1861, carried another comparison of Grow and Blair.

7 Colonel Emerson Etheridge, clerk of the House, made the comparison between Grow and Muhlenberg in responding to a serenade tendered to the Speaker and himself and reported in *New York Herald*, July 6, 1861.

See also *Springfield Republican*, July 9, 1861, and *New York Herald*, July 12, 1861. The *Herald* reporter claimed that only Henry Clay had been so honored.

8 *Springfield Republican*, February 21, 1862.

9 *Chicago Tribune*, February 25, 1863. See also January 29, 1862.

10 Ibid., February 25, 1863.

11 DuBois and Mathews, *Galusha A. Grow*, 246–65, 274–80.

12 *New York Herald*, July 4, 1861.

13 O. J. Hollister, *Life of Schuyler Colfax* (New York, 1886); Willard H. Smith, *Schuyler Colfax: The Changing Fortunes of a Political Idol* (Indianapolis, 1952). Accounts relevant to Colfax's election as Speaker and his personality are found in *New York Herald*, December 9, 21, 1863, May 8, July 1, 1864, January 25, 1865; *Chicago Tribune*, December 9, 10, 1863, January 11, 1864; *New York Tribune*, December 8, 1863, May 9, 1864; *Springfield Republican*, November 28, December 2, 5, 1863, January 23, 1864; *Boston Evening Journal*, December 2, 1863. The reporters' encomium is found in *New York Herald*, March 6, 1865. The receptions are described by Colfax's mother in Hollister, *Life of Colfax*, 213–14.

14 Henry J. Raymond's letter is quoted in Hollister, *Life of Colfax*, 218. W. H. Smith, *Schuyler Colfax*, 187–88; *New York Herald*, December 10, 15, 1863; *Chicago Tribune*, December 11, 15, 1863; *Springfield Republican*, December 14, 16, 1863; *Boston Evening Journal*, December 10, 1863.

15 W. H. Smith, *Schuyler Colfax*, 116–17, 133–34, 187, 195–97; Hollister, *Life of Colfax*, 214; Tyler Dennett (ed.), *Lincoln and the Civil War in the Diaries and Letters of John Hay* (New York, 1939), 114, 123–24, 131; John G. Nicolay and John Hay, *Abraham Lincoln: A History* (New York, 1890), X, 315; Howard K. Beale (ed.), *The Diary of Gideon Welles: Secretary of the Navy Under Lincoln and Johnson* (New York, 1960), I, 481. Beale notes that part of this quotation was inserted subsequent to Welles's first notation. For press comment on the Colfax letter see *New York Tribune*, January 21, 1864, and *Springfield Republican*, January 21, 1864.

16 Davis led attacks against both Secretaries Seward and Welles in 1864 as well as attacking General Banks's administration of affairs in Louisiana (Nicolay and Hay, *Abraham Lincoln*, VII, 407–10; IX, 112–15; see also Dennett, *Diaries and Letters of John Hay*, 234–35). Bernard C. Steiner, *Life of Henry Winter Davis* (Baltimore, 1916). For press comment see *Springfield Republican*, January 27, May 31, December 19, 1864, January 17, 1865; *New York Herald*, February 18, December 19, 1864, January 16, 31, February 4, 1865; *Chicago Tribune*, March 2, 1864. For the figurehead metaphor see Randall B. Ripley, *Party Leaders in the House of Representatives* (Washington: Brookings Institution, 1967), 16.

17 The initial composition of the committees appears in 37 Cong., 1 Sess., *CG*, 21–22, and 38 Cong., 1 Sess., *CG*, 18.

18 *New York Herald*, December 7, 13, 1861.

19 *New York Herald*, July 6, 1861; DeAlva S. Alexander, *History and Procedures of the House of Representatives* (Boston, 1916), 108, 110.

20 *Springfield Republican,* December 21, 1861; *Boston Evening Journal,* April 30, May 1, 1862; *New York Herald,* February 25, 1865; Thomas F. Woodley, *Thaddeus Stevens* (Harrisburg, 1934), 300.

21 Woodley, *Thaddeus Stevens,* 302–6.

22 *Springfield Republican,* March 25, June 24, July 8, 19, 1864; *Boston Evening Journal,* April 26, 29, May 1, 5, 1862; *Chicago Tribune,* April 26, 1862; *New York Herald,* January 21, 1863.

23 Woodley, *Thaddeus Stevens,* 349–402.

24 Richard N. Current, *Old Thad Stevens: A Story of Ambition* (Madison, 1942), 190; Woodley, *Thaddeus Stevens,* 405.

25 Harlow, *Legislative Methods,* 184–93; Noble E. Cunningham, Jr., *The Process of Government Under Jefferson* (Princeton, 1978), 278–82.

26 Caucusing and the party candidates for Speaker are discussed in *Springfield Republican,* July 3, 4, 1861; *Chicago Tribune,* July 4, 10, 1861; *New York Tribune,* July 3, 4, 6, 1861.

27 *Boston Evening Journal,* December 3, 7, 1861. The *Journal* of December 7 carried the report of the *New York Times* about the concerns of the Republican leaders and noted the objectives of the caucus scheduled for that day. See also *Springfield Republican,* December 7, 1861.

28 For proceedings of the December 7 caucus see *Springfield Republican,* December 9, 1861; *Boston Evening Journal,* December 9, 1861; *New York Herald,* December 9, 1861. Accounts of the meeting of Monday, December 9, appear in these papers and in the *New York Tribune* on December 10, 1861, with another story in the *Springfield Republican* on December 11. The quoted passages appear in the accounts of the *New York Tribune* and the *New York Herald.*

29 *New York Tribune,* December 12, 1861; *New York Herald,* December 12, 13, 15, 1861; *Boston Evening Journal,* December 12, 13, 1861; *Springfield Republican,* December 13, 1861; *Chicago Tribune,* December 13, 1861.

30 *New York Tribune,* February 11, 1862.

31 *Boston Evening Journal,* April 23, 24, 1862; *Springfield Republican,* April 24, 1862; *New York Tribune,* April 23, 24, 1862. Quotes relating to the House caucus are drawn from the *New York Tribune* of April 24. The same account was reprinted in the *Chicago Tribune* of April 28. See also *Springfield Republican,* June 20, 1862.

32 *New York Tribune,* July 8, 10, 11, 1862; *Springfield Republican,* July 10, 11, 1862.

33 *New York Tribune,* July 11, 14, 1862; *Boston Evening Journal,* July 14, 1862; *Springfield Republican,* July 14, 21, 1862. Bingham's draft statement appeared in the *Philadelphia Press,* July 25, 1862, over the signatures of nine senators and twenty-four representatives.

34 *Chicago Tribune,* July 17, 1862.

35 Theodore C. Pease and James G. Randall (eds.), *The Diary of Orville Hickman Browning* (Springfield, Ill., 1925–33), I, 596–605.

36 Beale, *Diary of Gideon Welles,* I, 194–205; Howard K. Beale (ed.), *The Diary of Edward Bates, 1859–1866* (Washington, 1933), 268–71; Francis Fessenden, *Life and Public Services of William Pitt Fessenden: United States Senator*

from Maine 1854–1864; Secretary of the Treasury 1864–1865; United States Senator from Maine 1865–1896, I (Boston, 1907), 229–53. The quotation appears on p. 253.

37 See particularly Pease and Randall, *Diary of Orville Hickman Browning,* I, 597–603. Collamer's comment is found on p. 603.

38 *New York Herald,* January 17, 18, 19, 23, 1863; *New York Tribune,* January 20, 21, 1863; *Chicago Tribune,* January 19, 1863.

39 Julia P. Cutler, *Life and Times of Ephraim Cutler* (Cincinnati, 1890), 296–304. This document is unreliable in its published form, the editor having made stylistic changes, deleted passages, and suppressed some names. I have used both the published version and the original in the possession of the library at Marietta College, Ohio, in constructing the narrative of the next few paragraphs.

40 This point is made specifically under the heading "From Washington" in a dispatch of January 18 carried in the *Chicago Tribune,* January 19, 1863.

41 *New York Tribune,* January 26, 1863.

42 Herman Belz, "The Etheridge Conspiracy of 1863: A Projected Conservative Coup," *Journal of Southern History* 36 (November 1970), 549–67. For an account of the organizational caucus see *New York Herald,* December 7, 1863.

43 *Chicago Tribune,* December 21, 22, 24, 1863.

44 *New York Tribune,* February 4, 8, 1864; *New York Herald,* February 2, 4, 8, 1864; *Boston Evening Journal,* February 4, 1864; *Boston Semi-Weekly Journal,* February 5, 1864; *Chicago Tribune,* February 4, 1864; *Springfield Republican,* February 4, 1864.

45 The accounts vary somewhat in the details of the arrangements authorized. See *New York Herald,* February 9, 1864; *Chicago Tribune,* February 9, 1864; *New York Tribune,* February 9, 1864; *Boston Evening Journal,* February 10, 1864; *Springfield Republican,* February 10, 1864.

46 *Boston Evening Journal,* March 25, 1864.

47 Howard K. Beale, *The Critical Year: A Study of Andrew Johnson and Reconstruction* (New York, 1930); James G. Randall, *The Civil War and Reconstruction* (Boston, 1937), and "The Civil War Restudied," *Journal of Southern History* 6 (November 1940), 439–57; T. Harry Williams, *Lincoln and the Radicals* (Madison, 1941).

48 Williams, *Lincoln and the Radicals,* 18.

49 David Donald, "The Radicals and Lincoln," *Lincoln Reconsidered: Essays on the Civil War Era* (New York, 1956), 103–27, and "Devils Facing Zionwards," in Grady McWhiney (ed.), *Grant, Lee, Lincoln, and the Radicals* (Evanston, 1964), 72–91; Hans L. Trefousse, *The Radical Republicans: Lincoln's Vanguard for Racial Justice* (New York, 1968).

50 Donald, "The Radicals and Lincoln," 126; James M. McPherson, *Ordeal by Fire: The Civil War and Reconstruction* (New York, 1982), 269.

51 Of scholars using conventional methods, Herman Belz examined the congressional efforts to enunciate a reconstruction policy during this Congress in *Reconstructing the Union: Theory and Policy During the Civil*

War (Ithaca, 1969) and broadened his inquiries somewhat in *Emancipation and Equal Rights: Politics and Constitutionalism in the Civil War Era* (New York, 1978), and Leonard P. Curry surveyed the legislative process more generally in *Blueprint for Modern America: Nonmilitary Legislation of the First Civil War Congress* (Nashville, 1968).

52 Duncan MacRae, Jr., *Issues and Parties in Legislative Voting: Methods of Statistical Analysis* (New York, 1970), 299–309, provides a comprehensive bibliography of early work that notes the contributions of historians as well as social scientists in general.

53 Glenn M. Linden, "Congressmen, 'Radicalism,' and Economic Issues 1861–1873" (Ph.D. dissertation, University of Washington, 1963). Linden published his findings in several articles; here, I have followed his argument from " 'Radicals' and Economic Policies: The House of Representatives, 1861–1873," *Civil War History* 13 (March 1967), 51–65.

54 Aydelotte began to experiment with scaling in the mid 1950s; his first relevant publication was "Voting Patterns in the British House of Commons in the 1840's," *Comparative Studies in Society and History* 5 (January 1963), 134–63. Joel H. Silbey began the first major application of the Guttman scaling technique to American political history in 1957–58 in a doctoral study published in revised form as *The Shrine of Party* (Pittsburgh, 1967). My application of Guttman scaling to Civil War issues dates from the publication of Allan G. Bogue, "Bloc and Party in the United States Senate, 1861–1863," *Civil War History* 13 (September 1967), 221–41.

55 *Springfield Republican*, March 27, May 12, 14, 15, 1862.

56 The *New York Tribune-Almanac's* identification of affiliation among House members at the beginning of the long legislative sessions of the Thirty-seventh and Thirty-eighth congresses provides us with the basic political arithmetic of these bodies, although the *Almanac's* totals are best viewed as predictions of tendencies, since changing political convictions, constituency, and party considerations worked to modify policy positions, and illness, death, military service, committee business, election contests, vacancies, and various other contingencies affected party voting totals as a session went on. With that understood, the reported affiliations were:

	Republicans	Democrats	Unionists
37 Congress, 2 session			
Northern states	105	38	4
Border states	1	4	24
Total	106	42	28
38 Congress, 1 session			
Northern states	86	70	0
Border states	16	5	9
Total	102	75	9

The *Almanac* lumped "Unconditional Unionists" and Republicans together in the Thirty-eighth Congress. Certainly the UU.s are best considered as being pro-administration and appear generally to have supported the Republicans. The sixteen border state men in that column were obviously vital to the Republican majority. But in both congresses party strategy should have dictated that the most moderate third of the Republican scalogram array be held in the Republican camp.

57 David Donald, *The Politics of Reconstruction, 1863–1867* (Baton Rouge, 1965), 26–52 and, in the second edition (Cambridge, Mass., 1983), viii; Michael Les Benedict, *A Compromise of Principle: Congressional Republicans and Reconstruction, 1863–1869* (New York, 1974), 56. Professor David Brady kindly provided me with his analysis of marginal seats during the Civil War and the electoral data that I used in the correlation computation.

Chapter 5. Conclusion

1 Howard K. Beale (ed.), *The Diary of Edward Bates, 1859–1866* (Washington, 1933), 382–83, 272.

Sources cited

Unpublished materials

Cutler, William Parker. Diary. Marietta College Library, Marietta, Ohio.
Dawes, Henry L. Papers. Library of Congress.
Lincoln, Robert Todd. Collection. Manuscript Division, Library of Congress. Also microfilm edition.
Potter, John F. Papers. Wisconsin State Historical Society, Madison.

Government records and publications

Petitions requesting expulsion of Clement L. Vallandigham. HR37A–G7.16. National Archives.
U.S. Congress. 28–39 Congress. *Congressional Globe.* Washington: Congressional Globe Office, 1844–67.
 32–38 Congress. *House Journal.* Washington: various publishers, 1852–65.
 37 Congress. House Judiciary Committee. Minute Book. 2 vols. (36A–D13.12 and 37A–E9.6). Legislative Records Division, National Archives.
 37 Congress 2 Session. House Executive Document no. 151. *Interest of Members of Congress in Government Contracts.* Washington: Government Printing Office, 1864.
 37 Congress 2 Session. House Judiciary Committee. "Hearings, Telegraphic Censorship of the Press" and "Benjamin Wood Hearing" (37A–E9.8). Legislative Records Division, National Archives.
 37 Congress 2 Session. House Miscellaneous Document no. 39. *George B. Simpson.* Washington: Government Printing Office, 1862.
 37 Congress 2 Session. House Report no. 2. *Government Contracts.* Washington: Government Printing Office, 1862.
 37 Congress 2 Session. House Report no. 16. *Loyalty of Clerks and Other Persons Employed by Government.* Washington: Government Printing Office, 1862.
 37 Congress 2 Session. House Report no. 53. *Printing Patent Office Report for 1860.* Washington: Government Printing Office, 1862.
 37 Congress 2 Session. House Report no. 64. *Telegraph Censorship.* Washington: Government Printing Office, 1862.

174

37 Congress 2 Session. House Report no. 96. *Illinois and Michigan Canal Enlargement.* Washington: Government Printing Office, 1862.

37 Congress 3 Session. House Report no. 47. *Hon. J. M. Ashley.* Washington: Government Printing Office, 1863.

37 Congress 3 Session. House Report no. 49. *Government Contracts.* Washington: Government Printing Office, 1863.

37 Congress 3 Session. House Report no. 50. *Government Contracts: Views of the Minority.* Washington: Government Printing Office, 1863.

37 Congress 3 Session. House Report no. 63. *Railroad from Washington City to New York.* Washington: Government Printing Office, 1863.

37 Congress 3 Session. House Report no. 64. *Employés Interested in Banks or Government Contracts.* Washington: Government Printing Office, 1863.

38 Congress 1 Session. House Executive Document no. 77. *Francis P. Blair, Jr.* Washington: Government Printing Office, 1864.

38 Congress 1 Session. House Executive Document no. 80. *Francis P. Blair, Jr.* Washington: Government Printing Office, 1864.

38 Congress 1 Session. House Miscellaneous Document no. 15. *Samuel Knox vs. Francis P. Blair, Jr.* Washington: Government Printing Office, 1864.

38 Congress 1 Session. House Report no. 111. *New York Custom-house.* Washington: Government Printing Office, 1864.

38 Congress 1 Session. House Report no. 140. *Treasury Department.* Washington: Government Printing Office, 1864.

38 Congress 1 Session. Senate Report no. 84. *Hon. Frank P. Blair, Jr.* Washington: Government Printing Office, 1864.

38 Congress 2 Session. House Executive Document no. 79. *Kidnapping Colored Men.* Washington: Government Printing Office, 1865.

38 Congress 2 Session. House Report no. 8. *Marine Engines.* Washington: Government Printing Office, 1864.

38 Congress 2 Session. House Report no. 24. *Trade with Rebellious States.* Washington: Government Printing Office, 1865.

38 Congress 2 Session. House Report no. 25. *New York Custom-house.* Washington: Government Printing Office, 1865.

85 Congress 2 Session. House Document no. 442. *Biographical Directory of the American Congress, 1774–1961.* Washington: Government Printing Office, 1961.

Senate Library. *Presidential Vetoes, 1789–1976.* Washington: Government Printing Office, 1978.

U.S. Department of Commerce. Bureau of the Census. *Historical Statistics of the United States,* vol. 2. Washington: Government Printing Office, 1975.

Newspaper publications

Boston Evening Journal
Boston Semi-Weekly Journal

Chicago Tribune
Cleveland Plain Dealer
Columbus (Ohio) *State Journal*
New York Evening Post
New York Herald
New York Times
New York Tribune
New York Tribune-Almanac
Philadelphia Press
Springfield (Mass.) *Republican*
Washington Evening Star
Washington Republican

Primary published works and memoirs

Basler, Roy P., ed. *The Collected Works of Abraham Lincoln*. 9 vols. and supplement. New Brunswick, N.J.: Rutgers University Press, 1953–55.

Beale, Howard K., ed. *The Diary of Edward Bates, 1859–1866*. Washington: Government Printing Office, 1933.

The Diary of Gideon Welles: Secretary of the Navy Under Lincoln and Johnson. 3 vols. New York: Norton, 1960.

Colton, Calvin, ed. *The Works of Henry Clay: Comprising His Life, Correspondence, and Speeches*. 10 vols. New York: Putnam, 1904.

Cutler, Julia P. *Life and Times of Ephraim Cutler*. Cincinnati: R. Clark, 1890.

Dana, Charles A. *Recollections of the Civil War: With the Leaders at Washington and in the Field in the Sixties*. New York: D. Appleton, 1898.

Dennett, Tyler, ed. *Lincoln and the Civil War in the Diaries and Letters of John Hay*. New York: Dodd, Mead, 1939.

The Federalist: A Commentary on the Constitution of the United States. New York: Modern Library, 1937.

Grinnell, Josiah B. *Men and Events of Forty Years: Autobiographical Reminiscences of an Active Career from 1850 to 1890*. Boston: D. Lothrop, 1891.

MacElree, Wilmer W. *Side Lights on the Bench and Bar of Chester County*. Westchester, Pa., 1918.

Pease, Theodore C., and Randall, James G., eds. *The Diary of Orville Hickman Browning*. 2 vols. Springfield: Illinois State Historical Library, 1925–33.

Poore, Ben Perley. *Perley's Reminiscences of Sixty Years in the National Metropolis*. 2 vols. Philadelphia: Hubbard, 1886.

Reynolds, John. *My Own Times: Embracing Also the History of My Life*. Chicago: Chicago Historical Society, 1879.

Richardson, James D., ed. *A Compilation of the Messages and Papers of the Presidents, 1789–1897*. 10 vols. Washington: Government Printing Office, 1897.

Riddle, Albert G. *Recollections of War Times: Reminiscences of Men and Events in Washington, 1860–1865*. New York: Putnam, 1895.

Stoddard, William O., Jr., ed. *Lincoln's Third Secretary: The Memoirs of William O. Stoddard*. New York: Exposition Press, 1955.

Welles, Gideon. *Lincoln and Seward: Remarks Upon the Memorial Address of Chas. Francis Adams on the Late Wm H. Seward*. New York: Sheldon, 1874.

Secondary materials

Alexander, DeAlva S. *History and Procedures of the House of Representatives*. Boston: Houghton Mifflin, 1916.

Aydelotte, William O. "Voting Patterns in the British House of Commons in the 1840's," *Comparative Studies in Society and History* 5 (January 1963): 134–63.

Ayers, Edwin L. *Vengeance and Justice: Crime and Punishment in the Nineteenth Century American South*. New York: Oxford University Press, 1984.

Barth, Alan. *Government by Investigation*. New York: Viking, 1955.

Barzun, Jacques. *Lincoln's Philosophic Vision*. Twenty-first Annual Robert Fortenbaugh Memorial Lecture. Gettysburg, Pa.: Gettysburg College, 1982.

Beale, Howard K. *The Critical Year: A Study of Andrew Johnson and Reconstruction*. New York: Harcourt Brace, 1930.

Belz, Herman. *Emancipation and Equal Rights: Politics and Constitutionalism in the Civil War Era*. New York: Norton, 1978.

Reconstructing the Union: Theory and Policy During the Civil War. Ithaca, N.Y.: Cornell University Press, 1969.

"The Etheridge Conspiracy of 1863: A Projected Conservative Coup," *Journal of Southern History* 36 (November 1970): 549–67.

Benedict, Michael Les. *A Compromise of Principle: Congressional Republicans and Reconstruction, 1863–1869*. New York: Norton, 1974.

Benét, Stephen Vincent. *John Brown's Body*. New York: Rinehart, 1928.

Bogue, Allan G. *The Earnest Men: Republicans of the Civil War Senate*. Ithaca, N.Y.: Cornell University Press, 1981.

"Bloc and Party in the United States Senate, 1861–1863," *Civil War History* 13 (September 1967): 221–41.

"William Parker Cutler's Congressional Diary of 1862–63," *Civil War History* 33 (December 1987): 315–30.

Bogue, Allan G., Clubb, Jerome M., McKibbin, Carroll R., and Traugott, Santa A. "Members of the House of Representatives and the Processes of Modernization, 1789–1960," *Journal of American History* 63 (September 1976): 275–302.

Bowling, Kenneth R. "Politics in the First Congress, 1789–1791." Ph.D. dissertation. University of Wisconsin, 1968.

Brown, Thomas. *Politics and Statesmanship: Essays on the American Whig Party*. New York: Columbia University Press, 1985.

Caarlson, Oliver. *The Man Who Made News: James Gordon Bennett*. New York: Duell, Sloan and Pearce, 1942.

Carman, Harry J., and Luthin, Reinhard H. *Lincoln and the Patronage.* New York: Columbia University Press, 1943.

Cleaves, Freeman. *Old Tippecanoe: William Henry Harrison and His Time.* New York: Scribner, 1939.

Colton, Calvin. *The Life and Times of Henry Clay.* 2 vols. New York: A. S. Barnes, 1846.

Cunningham, Noble E., Jr. *The Process of Government Under Jefferson.* Princeton, N.J.: Princeton University Press, 1978.

Current, Richard N. *The Lincoln Nobody Knows.* New York: McGraw-Hill, 1955.

  Old Thad Stevens: A Story of Ambition. Madison: University of Wisconsin Press, 1942.

Curry, Leonard P. *Blueprint for Modern America: Nonmilitary Legislation of the First Civil War Congress.* Nashville: Vanderbilt University Press, 1968.

Davidson, Roger H. "The Political Dimensions of Congressional Investigations," *Capitol Studies* 5 (Fall 1977): 41–63.

Davis, Cullom, Strozier, Charles B., Veach, Rebecca M., and Ward, Geoffrey C., eds. *The Public and the Private Lincoln: Contemporary Perspectives.* Carbondale: Southern Illinois University Press, 1979.

Degler, Carl. "The Two Cultures and the Civil War," in Stanley Coben and Lorman Ratner, eds., *The Development of an American Culture.* Englewood Cliffs, N.J.: Prentice-Hall, 1970.

Dimock, Marshall E. *Congressional Investigating Committees.* Baltimore: Johns Hopkins University Press, 1929.

Donald, David. *Charles Sumner and the Coming of the Civil War.* New York: Knopf, 1960.

  Lincoln Reconsidered: Essays on the Civil War Era. New York: Knopf, 1956.

  The Politics of Reconstruction, 1863–1867. Baton Rouge: Louisiana State University Press, 1965. Second edition, Cambridge: Harvard University Press, 1983.

  "Abraham Lincoln: Whig in the White House," in Norman A. Graebner, *The Enduring Lincoln,* pp. 47–66. Urbana: University of Illinois Press, 1959.

  "Devils Facing Zionwards," in Grady McWhiney, ed., *Grant, Lee, Lincoln, and the Radicals,* pp. 72–91. Evanston, Ill.: Northwestern University Press, 1964.

Doyle, Elizabeth Joan. "The Conduct of the War, 1861," in Arthur M. Schlesinger, Jr., and Roger Bruns, eds., *Congress Investigates: A Documentary History, 1792–1974,* vol. 2, pp. 1197–1357. New York: Chelsea House, 1975.

DuBois, James T., and Mathews, Gertrude A. *Galusha A. Grow: Father of the Homestead Law.* Boston: Houghton Mifflin, 1917.

Eulau, Heinz, and Sprague, John D. *Lawyers in Politics: A Study in Professional Convergence.* Indianapolis: Bobbs-Merrill, 1964.

Fessenden, Francis. *Life and Public Services of William Pitt Fessenden: United States Senator from Maine 1854–1864; Secretary of the Treasury 1864–1865;*

United States Senator from Maine 1865–1896, vol. 1. Boston: Houghton
  Mifflin, 1907.
Fisher, Louis. *The Politics of Shared Power: Congress and the Executive.*
  Washington: Congressional Quarterly Press, 1981.
Freidel, Frank B. *Franklin D. Roosevelt*, vol. 4: *Launching the New Deal.*
  Boston: Little, Brown, 1973.
Futhey, J. Smith, and Cope, Gilbert. *History of Chester County, Pennsylvania,
  with Genealogical and Biographical Sketches.* Philadelphia: L. H. Everts,
  1881.
Graebner, Norman A. *The Enduring Lincoln.* Urbana: University of Illinois
  Press, 1959.
Greenberg, Kenneth S. *Masters and Statesmen: The Political Culture of
  American Slavery.* Baltimore: Johns Hopkins University Press, 1985.
Hall, Kermit. *The Politics of Justice: Lower Federal Judicial Selection and the
  Second Party System, 1829–61.* Lincoln: University of Nebraska Press,
  1979.
Hamilton, Holman. *Zachary Taylor: Soldier in the White House.* Indianapolis:
  Bobbs-Merrill, 1951.
Hamilton, James. *The Power to Probe: A Study of Congressional Investigations.*
  New York: Random House, 1976.
Harlow, Ralph V. *The History of Legislative Methods in the Period Before 1825.*
  New Haven, Conn.: Yale University Press, 1917.
Hollister, O. J. *Life of Schuyler Colfax.* New York: Funk and Wagnalls, 1886.
Horowitz, Robert F. *The Great Impeacher: A Political Biography of James M.
  Ashley.* New York: Brooklyn College Press, 1979.
Howe, Daniel W. *The Political Culture of the American Whigs.* Chicago:
  University of Chicago Press, 1979.
Hurst, James Willard. *The Growth of American Law: The Law Makers.* Boston:
  Little, Brown, 1950.
Hyman, Harold M. *Era of the Oath: Northern Loyalty Tests During the Civil
  War and Reconstruction.* Philadelphia: University of Pennsylvania Press,
  1954.
  To Try Men's Souls: Loyalty Tests in American History. Berkeley and Los
  Angeles: University of California Press, 1959.
Imler, Joseph A. "The First One Hundred Days of the New Deal: The
  View from Capitol Hill." Ph.D. dissertation. Indiana University, 1975.
Kernell, Samuel. "Toward Understanding 19th Century Congressional
  Careers: Ambition, Competition and Rotation," *American Journal of
  Political Science* 21 (November 1977): 669–93.
Kraut, Alan M., ed. *Crusaders and Compromisers: Essays on the Relationship of
  the Antislavery Struggle to the Antebellum Party System.* Westport, Conn.:
  Greenwood, 1983.
Linden, Glenn M. "Congressmen, 'Radicalism,' and Economic Issues 1861–
  1873." Ph.D. dissertation. University of Washington, 1963.
  " 'Radicals' and Economic Policies: The House of Representatives, 1861–
  1873," *Civil War History* 13 (March 1967): 51–65.

Lipset, Seymour M. *The First New Nation: The United States in Historical and Comparative Perspective.* New York: Basic, 1963.

McCormick, Richard L., ed. *Political Parties and the Modern State.* New Brunswick, N.J.: Rutgers University Press, 1984.

McCormick, Richard P. *The Second American Party System: Party Formation in the Jacksonian Era.* Chapel Hill: University of North Carolina Press, 1966.

McPherson, James M. *Ordeal by Fire: The Civil War and Reconstruction.* New York: Knopf, 1982.

MacRae, Duncan, Jr. *Issues and Parties in Legislative Voting: Methods of Statistical Analysis.* New York: Harper and Row, 1970.

Maizlish, Stephen E., and Kushma, John J., eds. *Essays on American Antebellum Politics, 1840–1860.* Arlington: Texas A & M University Press, 1982.

May, Robert E. *John A. Quitman: Old South Crusader.* Baton Rouge: Louisiana State University Press, 1985.

Mayhew, David R. *Congress: The Electoral Connection.* New Haven, Conn.: Yale University Press, 1974.

Neely, Mark E., Jr. *The Abraham Lincoln Encyclopedia.* New York: McGraw-Hill, 1982.

Nevins, Allan, Robertson, James I., Jr., and Wiley, Bell I. *Civil War Books: A Critical Bibliography,* vol. 2. Baton Rouge: Louisiana State University Press, 1969.

Nichols, Roy F. *The Disruption of the American Democracy.* New York: Macmillan, 1948.

Nicklason, Fred. "The Civil War Contracts Committee," *Civil War History* 17 (September 1971): 232–44.

Nicolay, John G., and Hay, John. *Abraham Lincoln: A History.* 10 vols. New York: Century, 1890.

Norton, Anne. *Alternative Americas: A Reading of Antebellum Political Culture.* Chicago: University of Chicago Press, 1986.

Oates, Stephen. *With Malice Toward None: The Life of Abraham Lincoln.* New York: Harper and Row, 1977.

Osterweis, Rollin G. *Romanticism and Nationalism in the Old South.* New Haven, Conn.: Yale University Press, 1949.

Patterson, James T. *Congressional Conservatism and the New Deal.* Lexington: University of Kentucky Press, 1968.

Pearson, William W. "The Committee on the Conduct of the Civil War," *American Historical Review* 23 (April 1918): 550–76.

Randall, James G. *The Civil War and Reconstruction.* Lexington, Mass.: Heath, 1937.

   Lincoln: The Liberal Statesman. New York: Dodd, Mead, 1957.

   Lincoln the President. 4 vols. New York: Dodd, Mead, 1945–55. Vol. 4 completed by Richard N. Current.

   "The Blundering Generation," *Mississippi Valley Historical Review* 27 (June 1940): 3–28.

"The Civil War Restudied," *Journal of Southern History* 6 (November 1940): 439–57.

Riddle, Donald W. *Congressman Abraham Lincoln.* Urbana: University of Illinois Press, 1957.

Rossiter, Clinton. *The American Presidency.* New York: Harcourt Brace, 1956.

Schlesinger, Arthur M., Jr. *The Age of Roosevelt,* vol. 2: *The Coming of the New Deal.* Boston: Houghton Mifflin, 1957.

Schlesinger, Arthur M., Jr., and Bruns, Roger, eds. *Congress Investigates: A Documentary History, 1792–1974.* 5 vols. New York: Chelsea House, 1975.

Seitz, Don C. *The James Gordon Bennetts, Father and Son: Proprietors of the New York Herald.* Indianapolis: Bobbs-Merrill, 1928.

Silbey, Joel H. *The Partisan Imperative: The Dynamics of American Politics Before the Civil War.* New York: Oxford University Press, 1985.

The Shrine of Party. Pittsburgh: University of Pittsburgh Press, 1967.

Smith, Elbert B. *Francis Preston Blair.* New York: Free Press, 1980.

Smith, Willard H. *Schuyler Colfax: The Changing Fortunes of a Political Idol.* Indianapolis: Indiana Historical Bureau, 1952.

Smith, William E. *The Francis Preston Blair Family in Politics.* 2 vols. New York: DaCapo, 1933.

Steiner, Bernard C. *Life of Henry Winter Davis.* Baltimore: John Murphy, 1916.

Stubbs, Walter, comp. *Congressional Committees, 1789–1892: A Checklist.* Westport, Conn.: Greenwood, 1985.

Swanberg, W. A. *Sickles, the Incredible.* New York: Scribner, 1956.

Taylor, William R. *Cavalier and Yankee: The Old South and American National Character.* New York: Braziller, 1961.

Thomas, John L., ed. *Abraham Lincoln and the American Political Tradition.* Amherst: University of Massachusetts Press, 1986.

Trefousse, Hans L. *The Radical Republicans: Lincoln's Vanguard for Racial Justice.* New York: Knopf, 1968.

"The Joint Committee on the Conduct of the War: A Reassessment," *Civil War History* 10 (March 1964): 5–19.

Tulis, Jeffrey. "On Presidential Character," in Joseph M. Bessette and Jeffrey Tulis, *The Presidency in the Constitutional Order,* pp. 283–313. Baton Rouge: Louisiana State University Press [ca. 1981].

Wasson, R. Gordon. *The Hall Carbine Affair: A Study in Contemporary Folklore.* New York: Pandick, 1948.

Wilentz, Sean. "On Class and Politics in Jacksonian America," in Stanley I. Kutler and Stanley N. Katz, eds., *The Promise of American History: Progress and Prospects, Reviews in American History* 10 (December 1982): 45–63.

Williams, Jack K. *Dueling in the Old South: Vignettes of Social History.* College Station: Texas A & M University Press, 1980.

Williams, T. Harry. *Lincoln and the Radicals.* Madison: University of Wisconsin Press, 1941.

Woodley, Thomas F. *Thaddeus Stevens*. Harrisburg: Telegraph, 1934.
Wyatt-Brown, Bertram. *Southern Honor: Ethics and Behavior in the Old South.* New York: Oxford University Press, 1982.
Yates, Douglas. "The Roots of American Leadership: Political Style and Policy Consequences," in Walter D. Burnham and Martha W. Weinberg, eds., *American Politics and Public Policy*, pp. 140–68. Cambridge: MIT Press, 1978.

Index